# MMPI-168 CODEBOOK

# Developments in Clinical Psychology

Series Editors

**James H. Johnson**
Illinois Institute of Technology

**Glenn R. Caddy**
Nova University

# MMPI-168 CODEBOOK

Including Conversion Tables
for the New NCS Scoring Keys and the
Psychological Corp. Scoring Keys

## Ken R. Vincent

Iliana M. Castillo
Robert I. Hauser
Javier A. Zapata
H. James Stuart
Cal K. Cohn
Gregory J. O'Shanick

**The Hauser Clinic & Associates
Houston, Texas**

Ablex Publishing Corporation
Norwood, New Jersey 07648

**Library of Congress Cataloging in Publication Data**
Main entry under title:

MMPI-168 codebook.

Bibliography: p.
1. Minnesota multiphasic personality inventory.
I. Vincent, Ken R.  II. Title: M.M.P.I-168 codebook.
RC473.M5M6      1984      155.2'83      84-2936
ISBN 0-89391-189-5

Ablex Publishing Corporation
355 Chestnut Street
Norwood, New Jersey 07648

# Contents

*To Delma Smith*

# Preface

Since its development in 1974 the MMPI-168 has been the subject of approximately 100 investigations, giving it the distinction of being the third most researched clinical assessment device. However, most of the research has focused on comparing the MMPI-168 to the standard MMPI form. The external validity studies that have been carried out, however, have shown the MMPI-168 to be equal to, or, in one case, superior to the standard MMPI form. *The MMPI-168 Codebook* is an actuarially derived system in the tradition of Marks, Seeman and Haller (1974), Gilberstadt and Duker (1965), and Drake and Oetting (1959).

Because it is an actuarially derived empirical system, the *MMPI-168 Codebook* takes the MMPI-168 out of the realm of a screening device and places it in the category of a major assessment instrument which, like the Million Multi-Axial Clinical Inventory, is brief in its number of items.

This brevity will be of particular use to clinicians who face individuals who cannot or will not take the standard MMPI because of poor motiviation, illiteracy, or physical handicaps. With these individuals, the MMPI-168, like its mother the standard MMPI, can be administerd orally or via a tape recorder; however, the MMPI-168 shortens the time of administration to less than one third. Consequently, virtually all individuals, except those who are moderately to severely retarded can now be administered an objective clinical assessment device. The MMPI-168 continues Meehl's classic mandate for good cookbooks.

Chapter 1 presents an overview of the development of the MMPI-168 and a brief synposis of the research to date. Chapter 2 describes the methodology used in the construction of the MMPI-168 Codebook. Chapter 3 compares the results of the present study with those of the past. This is especially concerned with differences between the MMPI-168 code types and interpretations traditionally attributed to high point codes on the standard MMPI. Chapter 4 is a straightforward account of the administration and scoring of the MMPI-168 and the use of the Raw Score Conversion Tables for both adults and adolescents. Chapter 5 is the heart of the book and is a sequential presentation of all the MMPI-168 code types derived from the present sample, including the hypothetical average patient from a sample, as well as the validity scales, False-Normals, all 1 high-point codes, as well as all 2 and 3 high-point codes where there were sufficient numbers for analyses. Appendix A is the Raw Score Conversion Table for the MMPI-168 for Adults. Appendix B is the Raw Score Conversion Table for the MMPI-168 for Adolescents ages 14 through 17, without K corrections. Appendix C is a listing of the responses by code types to the *Social Readjustment Rating Scale* items. Appendix D is a listing of the responses by code type to the *Vincent Biographical Inventory* items.

# Acknowledgements

The authors wish to express their appreciation and thanks to Ms. Delma Smith for typing the endless number of drafts of the manuscript. Additionally, we wish to thank Dr. John Overall for his permission to use material on the MMPI-168 and, additionally, his support for the project. They further wish to thank the *Journal of Clinical Psychology,* the *Journal of Psychosomatic Research,* and Dr. Thomas H. Holmes for their additional permissions. Finally, they wish to thank those who have gone before in the development of actuarial systems; we are especially indebted to the works of Marks, Seeman, and Haller, for the methodology used in this book has as its primary inspiration their earlier work on the standard MMPI.

# CHAPTER 1

# Overview of the Development of the MMPI-168

Attempts to develop a viable short form of the MMPI began almost at the inception of the standard form (Ferguson, 1946). The last ten years have been marked by the development of five MMPI short forms, Minimult (Kincannon, 1968), the Midimult (Dean, 1972), the Maximult (Sepra & Robertson, 1974), the FAM (Faschingbauer, 1973), and the MMPI-168 (Overall & Gomez-Mont, 1974). The latter two have definitely shown to be the most versatile and valid.

The MMPI-168 is the instrument of choice for clinical use because it has the advantage of using the Standard booklets, scoring sheets, and templates. Since its inception in 1974 approximately 100 investigations have been conducted on the MMPI-168, all of which show high correspondence with the standard form. The MMPI-168 is unique in short forms in that it has demonstrated validity independent of the standard instrument (Newmark & Finch, 1976; Newmark, Newmark, and Cook, 1975; Newmark, Ziff, Finch, and Kendall, 1978; Newmark & Thibodeau, 1979). However, the bulk of the research has focused on comparison of the MMPI-168 to the standard form. The best single source relating to the development of Short Forms of MMPI's generally and the early work on the MMPI-168 specifically is Short Forms of the MMPI (Newmark & Faschingauer, 1978). The MMPI-168 has been used in a variety of settings, including private clinic patients and vocational rehabilitation clients (Vincent, 1978), hospitalized adolescent psychiatric patients (Newmark & Thibodeau, 1979) geriatric patients (Rusk, Hyerstay, Cassland and Freeman, 1979), physical medicine patients (Griffin & Danahy, 1982), surgery patients (Svanum, Lance, Lauer, Wampler & Madura, 1981) and most commonly psychiatric outpatients and inpatients. Using Butcher and Owens' (1978) classification table regarding research on clinical assessment devices from 1972–1977, the MMPI-168 has the distinction of being the third most researched clinical assessment device, the first being the standard MMPI and the second being the 16-PF.

The criticism of utilizing the MMPI-168 usually follows the logic that though the MMPI-168 has a high correspondence with the standard MMPI (correlations ranging generally from .77 to .97 (Graham, 1977), clinicians use configural interpretation and high-point code types as the basis for interpretations, and the actual

1

correspondence of two-point code types has generally been reported in a range of 64–75% (Graham, 1977). Vincent (1978), using broad-band diagnoses of neurotic, psychotic, characterlogical, and indeterminate profiles on three separate population samples, obtained an overall hit rate of 95%; however, this was for broad-band as opposed to specific diagnostic categories.

Overall, Higgins, and DeSchweinitz (1976) concluded that external criterion is the essential prerequisite for evaluating the 168 and any other abbreviated form of the MMPI, and in this vein, several validity studies have been carried out. Using judges to classify MMPI and MMPI-168 profiles diagnostic categories, Newmark and Finch (1976) and Newmark et al. (1975) obtained high agreement between the two. Newmark et al. (1978) demonstrated that the MMPI differed little in its relationship to external validation criteria; namely, the brief psychiatric rating scale. In using the brief psychiatric rating scale, Newmark and Tibideaux (1979) found that the standard MMPI-Brief Psychiatric Rating Scale correlations were significantly different on only one of 24 comparisons with the MMPI-168-Brief Psychiatric Rating Scale correlations. Also, in the same study Newmark and Tibideaux (1979) found no significant difference in the ratings of reports based on the standard MMPI versus the MMPI-168, using Lachar's (1974) interpretation system to develop the reports on both. The reports from standard MMPI and the MMPI-168 were then rated by psychiatric teams consisting of a psychiatrist, psychiatric resident, psychologist, and psychiatric nurse.

Other criticisms of the MMPI-168 usually follow the argument that the MMPI does not take clinical time to administer, since it is in a paper-and-pencil format, and can be administered and scored by clerks; however, the authors suspect that proponents of this argument have had very little actual clinical practice experience, which would reveal a significant number of individuals who cannot or will not take the MMPI standard form because of poor motivation, illiteracy, or physical handicaps. When these individuals are encountered, the clinician often has no alternative but to read the MMPI orally or do without it. While an oral administration is valid (Dahlstrom, Welch, & Dahlstrom, 1972) the reading of the MMPI is an ardous task. Also, many of the same subjects who cannot take the MMPI in the standard form cannot keep up with an oral administration via a tape recorder, and sometimes it is not feasible to move the tape recorder to the place where the patient or client is located. This points to a definite need for the MMPI-168. These patients are roughly the same patients who cannot take the MMPI by a computer. When faced with the possibility of sacrificing the useful information of an objective clinical assessment device by not using the MMPI or the MMPI-168, the MMPI-168 is definitely the instrument of choice. However, those who make the argument that additional validation is needed are quite right, and this book is an attempt to satisfy that need, continuing Meehl's (1954) classic mandate for good cookbooks.

CHAPTER 2

# Method

The psychological test files of the Hauser Clinic, a private psychiatric clinic, were sampled. Four hundred consecutive cases, 18 years old or older, from 1981 through mid-1982 were used. All cases were used where the folder contained an MMPI or a MMPI-168 and, in addition, contained a *Social Readjustment Rating Scale, Loevinger Washington University Sentence Completion Blank,* and *Vincent Biographical Inventory.* Most of the subjects also had been given a *Wechsler Adult Intelligence Scale.*

Two hundred and sixty-one of the cases had been given the standard MMPI and, where this was the case, the MMPI-168 was extracted from the standard Form R. The remaining 139 cases had been given the MMPI-168, and virtually all these were given using an oral administration. It should be noted that several research studies have shown no significant difference between the oral administration and the standard administration of the MMPI (Dahlstrom et al., 1972).

The Mythical Average Patient code type was constructed in order to be able to compare code types to a base rate and thereby avoid "P.T. Barnum statements" which merely describe the total sample group and not how each code type is unique. This Mythical Average Patient code type also gives a good description of the patient sample and can be found in Chapter 5.

All patient records were reviewed by their treating psychiatrists and a DSM-III discharge diagnosis was prepared on each. It should be noted that one reason there is little information on private clinic patients (as opposed to institutional patients) is that discharge summaries in private clinics often have "insurance diagnoses" as opposed to formal ones. The treating psychiatrist also noted discharge medication. This contrasts with medication that might have been attempted and discontinued during the course of treatment. Medication presented in this book is broken down by the authors into the broad classifications of neuroleptics, antidepressants (including tricyclics, tetracyclics, tranzadone, and MAO inhibitors), lithium and antianxiety medication. The patients who had received ECT were also identified.

While the total diagnostic classifications of each code type are presented with each code type and then put into a more abbreviated narrative form in the worded description of the code type, information on the *Vincent Biographical Inventory* (Vincent, 1982) and the *Social Readjustment Rating Scale* (Holmes & Rahe, 1967) were compared and contrasted with the base data from the Mythical Average Patient code type in order to eliminate statements which merely describe the total sample. Where an item for a given code type differed by more than 20%, either above or below, the mean of that item on the Mythical Average Patient code type, is enumerated in the descriptive statement section for that particular MMPI-168 code type. Occasionally, low frequency information (such as sexual abuse, which is highly relevant clinically) is included, even though it did not meet the above criterion. Also, the global ego development ratings using Loevinger's system of rating ego development (Loevinger et al., 1970) are listed for each code type.

This method is similar to that used by Marks, Seeman and Haller (1974), Gilberstadt and Duker (1965), Drake and Oetting (1959), and Marks, Seeman, and Haller (1974). The resulting codebook is an actuarial description based on objective data as opposed to what Marks, Seeman, and Haller (1974) call "the distilled experience of one clinician," referring to the systems of the Roche Psychiatric Institute program (Fowler, 1969), the Mayo Clinic program (Pearson & Swenson, 1967), the Behaviordyne Psychodiagnostic Laboratory Service (Finney, 1966), and the Caldwell Report (Caldwell, 1974). Also, Lachar (1974b) relates that his system is a hybrid, in that part of it is empirical and part is based on and reflects his clinical experience. Thus, our MMPI-168 codebook, because it is actuarially derived, is in a very real way superior to many codebooks on the market and computer programs for interpreting the standard MMPI.

Adolescents were not used in making this codebook and no cases in our sample were of patients under 18. However, extrapolating to adolescents from the present study is apt to be a viable procedure, as the literature on this subject, both on the MMPI-168 (Newmark & Thibedeaux, 1979) as well as the standard MMPI (Lachar, 1974a; Lacher, Klinge, & Grissell, 1976) has shown that using adolescent scores without K correction and then interpreting them, using in the above studies the standard Lachar format, were rated accurate and viable for clinicians. For this purpose, Appendix B of this book contains raw score conversion tables for the MMPI-168 for adolescents ages 14 through 17 (without K correction). Further investigation is obviously needed on using the *MMPI-168 Codebook* with adolescents.

The present codebook incorporates validity scales which are invalid as code types in and of themselves. This has been suggested in previous literature. The codebook includes invalid L, F, and K profiles as well as False Normals, Mythical Average Patient, high-point code types 1 through 9 (those selected were where the high-point code was at least five T-score points greater than the next code and was above a T-score of 70). Most two-point code types are included in the book; however, not all had sufficient numbers to justify their inclusion. Two-point code types were included where the two highest codes were within 10 T-score points of one another and were above 70 T. Several three-point code types are included in the book and these included were the second and third code type were within 10 T-score points of one another and all three points were above a T-score of 70.

In compiling the book, only valid profiles were used in determining code types other than L, F, and K invalid profile types. Profiles were considered invalid when L or K was greater than a T-score of 70 or where F was greater than a raw score of 15 (this is equivalent to being greater than a raw score of 26 on the standard MMPI). Code types are listed only where there were a minimum of six cases used. This is consistent with previous research; Gilberstadt and Duker (1965) used this as their cut-off point, as did King and Kelley (1977). The False Normal profile type is based on individuals making a valid profile, but had no clinical scale greater than a T-score of 70.

It should be noted that all two and three-point code types are interchangeable; that is to say that the 28 code type includes all 82 code types. In classifying code types in using this book where several codes are all within one T-score point of one another, the user is advised to either read from left to right and let the first two or three codes determine the classification of the code type; or use what may be a somewhat more superior method: look up each of the several possibilities or combinations of code types in the codebook and compare the mean graphs listed for the code types with the profile in question. It should be noted that if two codes are quite high and the third code is significantly (greater than 10 T-score points) below the second code (listed in descending order) the two-point code type should be used rather than the three-point code type.

Fifty code types are presented in this book. When one considers the L, F, K, and False Normal profile types, as well as all pure high-point codes (those where only one clinical scale was above a T-score of 70), and all two high-point combinations, the cookbook classifies 90% of the patients from the sample from which it was extracted, and this is excluding some that might be picked up on three-point code types.

The following is a breakout of the 400 cases by general category: Invalid code types (L, F, and K), N = 25; False Normal code types (no clinical scale greater than a T-score of 70), N = 45; pure high-point codes (only clinical scale above a T-score of 70), N = 29; two-point code types (highest two clinical scales above a T-score of 70), N = 263.

The bulk of the two-point code types not listed in this study are combinations of 0 and 5 which are often not reported in codebooks on the standard MMPI. It should be noted that only nine (2% on the total sample) had 0 as their highest code or highest two-point code type. This may be due to the fact that previous research (Moreland, 1982) has shown that the 168 conversion does not do justice to 0. Fortunately, 0 has never been considered a major clinical scale and, as with previous codebooks on the MMPI, the reader is enjoined to disregard 0 and the analysis of the code type. In the case of 5, the reader may wish to incorporate 5 data (high in the case of male, low in the case of female) in their analysis of the total profile, but generally should rely primarily on the high-point one, two or three codes irrespective of 5, and then consider the elevated 5 or a depressed 5 in relation to this.

The frequency of code types on the standard MMPI varies from population to population (Lachar, 1974b; Marks, Seeman, & Haller, 1974; Duckworth, 1979;

Swenson et al., 1973). The following MMPI-168 code types, which in this present sample were insufficient for making a profile description, are listed, as well as the number of cases of the sample of 400 which made the infrequent code type: 0 code (N = 1); 14 code ( N = 4); 15 code (N = 0); 16 code (N = 3); 17 code (N = 4); 19 code (N = 3); 10 code (N = 0); 25 code (N = 1); 29 code (N = 4); 20 code (N = 2); 34 code (N = 1); 35 code (N = 0); 39 code (N = 0); 30 code (N = 0); 45 code (N = 3); 40 code (N = 1); 56 code (N = 0); 57 code (N = 2); 58 code (N = 3); 59 code (N = 2); 50 code (N = 0); 67 code (N = 2); 60 code (N = 1); 79 code (N = 1); 70 code (N = 1); 80 code (N = 3); and 90 code (N = 0). It should be noted that the 34 code and the 45 code are infrequent codes in the MMPI-168 codebook sample, but are usually frequent codes for the standard MMPI.

The following is a list of the MMPI-168 code types on which there are profile descriptions and the number of cases for the total sample of 400 which made the code type: Mythical Average Patient code type (N = 50); L greater than a T-score of 70 code type (N = 7); F greater than a raw score of 15 code type (N = 8); K greater than a T score of 70 code type (N = 10); False Normal code type (N = 45); 1 code type (N = 11); 2 code type (N = 15); 3 code type (N = 10); 4 code type (N = 16); 5 code type (male) (N = 7); low 5 code type (female) (N = 44); 6 code type (N = 16); 7 code type (N = 17); 8 code type (N = 58); 9 code type (N = 21); 12 code type (N = 7); 13 code type (N = 13); 18 code type (N = 7); 23 code type (N = 14); 24 code type (N = 7); 26 code type (N = 7); 27 code type (N = 14); 28 code type (N = 29); 36 code type (N = 6); 37 code type (N = 11); 38 code type (N = 7); 46 code type (N = 17); 47 code type (N = 14); 48 code type (N = 14); 49 code type (N = 7); 68 code type (N = 17); 69 code type (N = 8); 78 code type (N = 32); 89 code type (N = 22); 123 code type (N = 7); 128 code type (N = 7); 237 code type (N = 12); 238 code type (N = 7); 246 code type (N = 7); 248 code type (N = 10); 268 code type (N = 6); 278 code type (N = 25); 289 code type (N = 7); 468 code type (N = 7); 469 code type (N = 8); 478 code type (N = 15); 489 code type (N = 6); 678 code type (N = 9); 689 code type (N = 8); and 789 code type (N = 6).

The next chapter outlines significant highlights of the research and compares and contrasts the findings of this sample on the MMPI-168 with actuarial studies performed on the standard MMPI.

CHAPTER 3

# Highlights of the Results

The 50 actuarially derived code types identified and enumerated in this book are, on the whole, similar to previous narratives on the standard MMPI that were based on actuarial descriptions or clinical lore. There are, however, three major areas of variance. One is the fact that the MMPI-168, though correlating highly with the full form, is somewhat different, especially when the minute differences of configural analyses and high-point codes are the basis for interpreting the test. Second, this codebook is unique in that it is based on private patients, whereas most previous samples have been on institutionalized patients or occasionally on college students. The third major source of variance is that the DSM-III was used as the diagnostic criterion in this codebook and the DSM-III is a major departure from its predecessors.

*That the MMPI-168 differs from the original form is a major focus of writing this book.* When one compares the 400 cases on the MMPI-168 with the 261 cases in which the 168 was extracted from a full MMPI, a few differences emerge in what is essentially the same sample. The sample of full MMPI's was analyzed using the identical procedure as the codebook in developing diagnostic classification statements for the article: MMPI Code Types and DSM-III Diagnoses (Vincent et al., 1984). On the full MMPI, 24 code types were identified and the three most frequent high-point code types were, respectively, 28, 23, and 27. On the MMPI-168 sample from the same private clinic the three most frequent high-point code types were 78, 28, and 89, respectively. Only the 28 code type overlapped. Using the 28 code as a point of comparison, we find that on the standard MMPI, 70% of the patients with the 28 code type received a primary diagnoses of affective disorder versus only 35% of the MMPI-168 code type having as their primary diagnosis affective disorder. On the MMPI-168, however, the second major diagnostic category was adjustment disorder with depressed mood. The primary underlying personality category for both the MMPI and the MMPI-168 on this code type was, however, the personality disorder cluster of anxious and fearful personality disorders (avoidant, compulsive, passive-agressive, or dependent).

The fact that the MMPI-168 codebook is based on a private sample is significant, and this could probably be highlighted best by looking at a code type that appears not only in this sample but also three codebook samples on the standard MMPI which were done on different populations. The 68 code will be used for purposes of comparison. On our MMPI-168 private clinic sample, 4.3% of the total sample received this as their high-point code, making it the fourth most frequent high-point code. Lachar (1974) found the 68 code to be the most frequent code type in his state hospital sample. Marks, Seeman, and Haller (1974) found this to be the twelfth most frequent code in a teaching hospital population, comprising 6.3% off their total sample. Unlike our MMPI-168 sample and Lachar (1974b), however, Marks, Seeman, and Haller's (1974) configural rules included more than the simple high-point codes). Gilberstadt and Duker (1965) found the 68 code to be the 12th most frequent code in their Veterans Administration all-male sample, composing 10% of their total sample. Like Marks et al., (1974), however, their configural rules were more elaborate than the high-point codes used by Lachar (1974b) and our present sample based on the MMPI-168.

Analyzing the 68 code further takes us into the third major source of variance and that is differences in the classification manuals used in various codebooks. The MMPI-168 codebook uses the DSM-III. The DSM-III is a major change from its predecessors and, though the extrapolation between DSM-I and DSM-II is rather simple, the extrapolation back and forth between these older classification systems and DSM-III is major and at times all but impossible.

Consider the 68 code. Traditionally, this has been considered to be most representative of paranoid schizophrenia and, in fact, Gilberstadt and Duker (1965) found this as their modal diagnosis. They list no differential in their codebook. Lachar (1974b) found that 87% of the patients of this code type in his state hospital population were psychotic, with 70% of these evidencing schizophrenia and 17% evidencing other types of psychoses. Marks, Seeman, and Haller in their teaching hospital sample found 68% of the population to be psychotic, with 55% of these evidencing schizophrenia and 14% of them evidencing depression (involutional) psychoses. Our present MMPI-168 sample, converting backward into DSM-I or DSM-II terminology, would have classified 48% of the sample as psychotic; however, in DSM-III terminology this breaks into quite a different pattern, showing that on our private patients 18% of the sample were seen as evidencing a major affective disorder, 6% a paranoid disorder, 12% paranoid schizophrenia, and 12% were seen as having a schizotypal personality. It should be noted that the schizotypal personality, together with the borderline personality disorder enumerated in DSM-III, would in DSM-II have been classified as schizophrenia, latent type, and in DSM-I would have been classified as schizophrenic reaction, chronic undifferentiated type. Still, our sample is lower than the other samples with regard to psychoses. While this can be due in part to the fact that the MMPI-168 is not standard MMPI, it is also quite likely because ours is a private population and a much newer sample. The newness is underscored by the fact that 18% of our 68 code type private patients had as their primary disorder substance abuse-a new horror when compared to the preceding classic studies on the MMPI, which range from one to almost four decades older as far as data-gathering is concerned (Zuckerman, Sola, Masterson, & Angelone, 1975; Duckworth, 1979). The fact that the sample is private, however, probably is in this case the most significant factor when you consider that half our patients were in earlier terminology, classified as psychotic, compared to 87% of Lachar's in the state hospital sample. In between the two extremes is Marks, Seeman, and Haller's teaching hospital population, with two thirds of their population evidencing the 68 code type, and seen as psychotic. Anyone who, like the senior author, has worked in all three populations, instantly can sense that the base rate of the samples is apt to be a significant factor.

To better understand the base rate on figures that are available, let us now compare the MMPI teaching hospital sample of Marks et al. (1974) with our private patient MMPI-168 sample. The False Normal profile and also on the Mythical Average Patient profiles should give a good idea of base rates. Converted backward into DSM-II, in order to classify psychotic disorders, we find not too many differences between the individuals making the false normal or, in Marks, Seeman, and Haller's terminology, the K$^+$ profile. Half of Marks, Seeman, and Haller's false normals were seen as psychotic, with 19% evidencing an affective psychosis, with 33% evidencing schizophrenia. On the present MMPI-168 sample, 47% of ours would be classified as psychotic in DSM-II terminology, with 27% evidencing an affective disorder, 13% evidencing schizophrenia (including schizoaffective disorders) and 7% evidencing schizophrenia, latent type (schizotypal or borderline personality in DSM-III).

Analyzing the Mythical Average Patient of the MMPI-168, campared to Marks, Seeman, and Haller's average patient, we find on the same analysis that 50% of Marks, Seeman and Haller's patients were seen as psychotic, with 19% evidencing an affective disturbance and 31% evidencing schizophrenia. On our 168 private patient sample, 46% of our Mythical Average Patient sample was seen as psychotic, as classified by DSM-II, with 26% evidencing an affective disorder, 6% seen as schizoaffective, and 14% as evidencing latent schizophrenia (borderline and schizotypal personality in DSM-III terms).

It can be seen that on base rates, the teaching hospital sample, which is more apt to resemble our private sample than Lachar's state hospital sample, shows very few differences on the false normal profiles; and the same is true for the average patient with regards to psychotic classifications. The similarity is further underscored in overall treatment with psychoactive medication in that in the Marks et al. sample, 35% of their patients were receiving psychoactive medication and 9% received ECT. Among our private clinic patients 36% were discharged on psychoactive medication and 8% received ECT.

In summary, there are three main sources of variance that caused the MMPI-168 code types to be somewhat different from previous codebooks on the standard MMPI; the two tests are different, though highly comparable, and the population is private rather than public, though on the base rate and false normal codes there was little difference between the teaching hospital patients of Marks, Seeman, and Haller and the private patients in the present study. We did find a major difference that affects not only the MMPI-168 codebook but also analysis of the MMPI using earlier codebooks whether or not one is extrapolating to the MMPI-168; namely, the DSM-III classification system. In the senior author's experience in compiling the MMPI-168 Codebook, as well as his previous experience on the field trials of DSM-III and in the previously mentioned MMPI code types and DSM-III diagnosis article (Vincent et al., 1982) the major variance between DSM-III classification and previous classifications is in the schizophrenia area. In fact, one reason for the development of the DSM-III was to get the American classification system in line with international classification, since Americans had always tended to classify more patients as schizophrenic than the psychologists and psychiatrists of other nations (Vincent et al., 1982). What has happened to schizophrenia is that some patients previously classified as having schizophrenia are not listed under affective disorders (major affective disorders), psychotic disorders now elsewhere classified (schizophreniform disorder, schizoaffective disorder, atypical psychosis), and in the personality categories of schizotypal and borderline.

Our analysis of the MMPI-168 has incorporated into the Loevinger method of rating ego development via sentence completion (Loevinger et al., 1970) and the global ego development ratings resulting from this method are listed for each code type. Briefly stated, the conformity level of ego development is the modal level for normal adults and was modal for our population. Generally speaking, individuals who had 4 as a high point in their code type are apt to be below the general conformity level of ego development and at a more hedonistic level. This is consistent with previous work with the standard MMPI (Vincent & Vincent, 1979), though not all researchers have reached the same conclusion (Gold, 1980). Also, in general the number of people above the conformity level of ego development are under-represented in our present sample. Whether this is because, as Maslow (1970) postulated, people who are generally more intact as far as their overall level of personality development is concerned, are not as apt to succomb to psychopathological illnesses or whether it is due to some other reason is beyond the scope of this study.

This study also incorporated, as did Marks, Seeman, and Haller's (1974) study, a tabulation of drug usage on patients and the number of patients who received ECT. Since Marks et al. a variety of new drugs have been introduced on the market; however, some of these, such as trazodone and tetracyclics, are even so new as to preclude an adequate representation in our sample. For this reason the drugs are broken down merely into the major categories of neuroleptic, antidepressants, lithium, and anxiety medication. Also, the usage of electroshock therapy (ECT) is noted, where appropriate.

Additionally, age, education, intellect as measured by the WAIS (Wechsler, 1955), and ratio of males to females in code types are noted. Furthermore, the narrative report is substantially based on the variance of any particular code type from the Mythical Average Patient code type on two objective instruments; namely, the *Social Readjustment Rating Scale* and the *Vincent Biographical Inventory*.

## CODE TYPE SUMMARIES

What follows now is a brief summary of highlights on each individual code type.

*Mythical Average Patient Code Type.* As mentioned earlier, this code type in many ways is similar to that of Marks, Seeman, and Haller's (1974) average patient, in psychotic diagnoses as well as utilization of psychiatric drugs and ECT. The age of both samples was also not significantly different, with the Marks et al. sample having a mean age of 40 versus the MMPI-168 private patient sample having a mean age of 38. Marks et al.'s sample included 59% outpatients and 41% inpatients as compared to 68% inpatients and 32% outpatients for our MMPI-168 sample.

*L greater than T-score 70.* It has been noted frequently in previous research on the MMPI that the validity scales are, in fact, also personality scales and are included as such in our codebook. As might be expected from previous research on this code, this was a rather conforming group of people and, when married, tended to be married to their first spouse; but interestingly, half of this group lived alone. They were apt to present somatic concerns as a reason for seeking help. Nearly half these patients were seen as evidencing affective disorders of a bipolar nature.

*F greater than a Raw Score of 15.* In his research with the standard MMPI, John E. Overall (personal conversation) noted that this profile type tends to be a good predictor of borderline personality disorders. In our sample, the majority had their personality disorders deferred often because of being obscured by psychosis, but the remainder were seen as borderline, histrionic, or schizotypal individuals, definitely an unstable group. One fourth of the sample was psychotic and one fourth received a diagnosis of organic brain syndrome. Half received a secondary diagnosis of substance abuse.

*K greater than T-score 70.* These patients tended to be a fairly stable group and to be married and have families. They tended to be somatic complainers and listed this as their reason for seeking psychiatric assistance. They were primarily seen as adjustment disorders or suffering from some sort of psychosomatic condition.

*False Normal code type.* As has been mentioned previously, these patients were quite similar to the patients of Marks, et al.'s (1974) false normal patients in a teaching hospital (see above).

*1 Code.* As with previous studies, most of these patients were seen as somatizers and one fourth were seen as having major depressions.

*2 Code.* This code type had some surprises on the MMPI-168, since only half these patients were diagnosed as having a primary disorder with some sort of affective component. In general, this low incidence may be explained either by the fact that a large percentage of this sample left against medical advice or by the fact that these patients had a high incidence of marital separations and marital conflicts; it would appear that in its pure form a high-point code 2 on the MMPI-168 is identifying not pure depression but rather a reactive depression often mixed with anxiety.

*3 Code.* Though the majority of patients of this code type were seen as evidencing some sort of psychosomatic disorder, an even greater number (80%) were viewed as having an affective disorder. The underlying personality of these patients, as has been noted on previous MMPI research (Leavitt & Garron, 1982), was not hysterical but rather their personalities tended to cluster in the areas of anxious or fearful personality disorders (avoidant, dependent, compulsive, passive-agressive).

*4 Code.* These patients generally were substance abusers and three fourths of them had this as their primary, secondary, or tertiary diagnosis. Interestingly, in this private sample using the MMPI-168, a large amount of affective disorders were noted and half the patients of this profile type were discharged on medication, mainly antidepressants or neuroleptics. The underlying personalities of these patients were, as with studies with this code on the standard MMPI, in the area of dramatic, emotional, or erratic personality disorders (histrionic, antisocial, or borderline), though an additional one third were seen as having passive-agressive personalities.

*5 Code (male).* One third of the patients of this all-male profile code type reported being homosexual and living with homosexual lovers. This verifies, to some extent, the original reason for placing a masculinity-femininity scale on the MMPI. As with previous studies, a high 5 code is not definitely indicative of homosexual behavior in a male but does tend to depict an individual who is more sensitive, as evidenced in our study by the fact that these patients were significantly higher in their overall level of ego-conscience development. Their underlying personalities tended to be passive-agressive or dependent, and almost half these patients were not seen as having any significant personality disorders. Their primary diagnoses were usually in the area of adjustment disorders.

*Low 5 Code (female).* The picture here is one of a depressed woman who has an anxious or fearful personality disorder (avoidant, dependent, or passive-aggressive); however, one third of these patients were seen as having a histrionic personality disorder. These women tended to be fairly conforming and only half worked outside the home.

*6 Code.* Though slightly lower in frequency than previous studies, half of these patients were seen as having some sort of psychosis with a paranoid flavor. The nonpsychotic patients of this code type tended to fall in areas of mixed organic brain syndrome or adjustment disorders.

*7 Code.* These patients were primarily seen as adjustment disorders, though a significant minority were seen as major depressions and a few were seen as evidencing anxiety disorders. This smorgasbord of diagnostic categories was, however, significantly high in medication usage, with two thirds of the patients of this profile type being discharged on psychoactive medication, though no specific category was predominant. The underlying personality of these patients was also uneventful and what one would expect from studies on the standard MMPI; namely, that these patients clustered in the area of anxious or fearful personality disorders (avoidant, dependent, compulsive, or passive-agressive).

*8 Code.* One half of these patients were seen as having some sort of diagnosis that would have traditionally placed them in the psychotic category, including paranoid schizophrenia, schizoaffective, major affective, bipolar, and major depression. Another third represented the new wave of patients who make a high-point code 8; namely, substance abusers. Half these patients were discharged on medication, which was most frequently antidepressants, followed by patients receiving neuroleptics.

*9 Code.* Only a fifth of these patients were seen as having an affective disorder. This differs from the traditional interpretation of the high point code type as being indicative of mania, with the differential being hypomania. In our sample, most of these patients were seen as adjustment disorders or substance abusers, and their underlying personalities were histrionic or antisocial. This is a major difference between our MMPI-168 code type findings on private patients and that of what the high-point code 9 traditionally represents. However, our findings on the MMPI-168 do resemble those found by King and Kelley (1977) in a university mental health center population.

*12 Code.* Traditionally, this has been basically seen as a neurotic, somatizing code and while our MMPI-168 sample had somatic complaints as the primary presenting problem and a significant number were seen as evidencing psychological factors affecting physical conditions, half of these patients received a primary diagnosis of a major affective disorder. Three fourths were discharged on medication and half the total sample were discharged on a therapeutic dosage of antidepressants, further reinforcing the idea that a good deal of their somatization may be secondary to depression.

*13 Code.* This code type has classically been seen as being associated with neurotic somatizers, though in recent years some of this has been called into question. The Mayo Clinic (Schwartz, Osborne, & Krupp, 1972) found that on the standard form of the MMPI the 13 code was more apt to be associated with psychosomatic conditions in younger patients and in female patients. In our study on the MMPI-168, when age was taken into account, virtually all the patients under 40 had psychosomatic disorders as their primary, secondary, or tertiary diagnosis; but this was the case in only one third of the patients over age 40. Also, this would appear to be another code on the MMPI-168 in which somatization is secondary to depression since two thirds of our patients were diagnosed as having affective disorders and one third was seen as having a major affective disorder. Three fourths of the total sample received some sort of psychosomatic diagnosis as their primary, secondary, or tertiary diagnoses. Virtually all these patients were discharged on psychoactive medication, with the majority being on antidepressants.

*18 Code.* On the standard MMPI the 18 code is an infrequent one, and these patients are usually seen as borderline schizophrenics with somatic problems which, in DSM-III terminology, would convert to borderline or schizotypal personality disorders with somatization. On our MMPI-168 sample, these patients were seen primarily as substance abusers, though almost one half received some sort of psychosomatic disorder as their primary, secondary, or tertiary diagnosis. The underlying personality profile of this type was somewhat similar to what one would think, from extrapolation from the standard MMPI form with a DSM-III conversion—a borderline personality disorder—though a few patients of this personality type were seen as having histrionic personality disorders. In general, the modal profile was that of a somatizing drug abuser who was a borderline.

*23 Code.* On the standard MMPI this has classically been seen as a code type that is evenly divided between neurotic and psychotic diagnoses. On our MMPI-168 sample, these patients were about evenly divided between major affective disorders (bipolar disorder or major depression) and adjustment disorders with depressed mood. As on the standard MMPI, the somatic factors were secondary, and one third of these patients  received as a secondary diagnosis some sort of psychosomatic disorder. Half the patients were discharged on medication and one in seven received ECT. Their underlying personality was seen primarily as passive-agressive or histrionic, though a few were seen as dependent and compulsive.

*24 Code.* In classic MMPI literature this patient has been traditionally interpreted as a character disorder which has been caught and whose depression and distress are caused by this external pressure. On our MMPI-168 sample, this was partially the case in that these patients tended to have a lower level of ego-conscience development than the average patient and were quite likely to be substance abusers. However, almost half these patients were seen as evidencing a major depression and slightly over half were discharged on antidepressant medication. Those not seen as evidencing a major depression were primarily seen as evidencing an adjustment disorder, which fits the more classic pattern. The personality disorder of these patients tended to be seen as either passive-agressive or dependent.

*26 Code.* In standard MMPI literature, this is usually seen as an infrequent code and has variously been interpreted as either evidenced by individuals on the brink of psychosis or who have frustrated angry feelings toward significant others. In our MMPI-168 sample, our patients tended to resemble the previous findings on the standard form, in that half the patients were seen as evidencing what in DSM-II terminology would be classified as psychotic disorders (major depressive disorders, paranoid schizophrenia, or schizoaffective disorders). The remainder were seen as adjustment disorders and the underlying personalities of these patients were seen as avoidant, paranoid, or schizotypal.

*27 Code.* As with the standard MMPI findings of previous studies, our MMPI-168  sample on this profile type revealed primarily individuals who were polite, conforming, anxious, worrisome, and depressed. The modal diagnostic category for these patients was an affective disorder, especially major affective disorder : major depression, and the majority of these patients were discharged on psychoactive medication and most often this was an antidepressant medication.

*28 Code.* Like their counterpoints on the standard MMPI, our MMPI-168 sample of this code type consisted of a significant number of individuals with affective disorders, especially major depression or bipolar disorders, though schizoaffective disorders were also reported. Slightly more of our sample was seen as less severely depressed and evidencing either dysthymic disorders of adjustment disorders with depressed mood. A significant number of these patients were also seen as substance abusers. The majority were discharged on medication and a third of the patients of the total sample were on antidepressants at the time of discharge. Their underlying personalities were primarily seen as avoidant, compulsive, passive-aggressive, or dependent, though a significant amount were seen as histrionic or borderline.

*34 Code.* The significance of the 34 code on the MMPI-168 is that it was extremely infrequent and made by only one individual of the total sample. On the standard format this is usually seen as a reasonably frequent code type.

*36 Code.* This is an infrequent code type on the standard MMPI and, though not terribly frequent in our sample, was common enough to be represented by slightly over 2% of the sample. In our MMPI-168 sample, this was an all-female code type and generally these women were seen as conformists who were unhappily married but toughing it out. They were typically seen as adjustment disorders, though a third were seen as evidencing a major depression. These patients tended to be seen as having either histrionic or borderline personalities.

*37 Code.* On the standard MMPI these patients are typically somewhat infrequent and generally seen as somatizers. In our MMPI-168 sample, these patients tended to fall into three categories: one third were seen as evidencing some sort of psychosomatic disorder; one third were seen as major depressions; and a third were seen as adjustment disorders. Their underlying personalities were primarily in the anxious and fearful category; namely, passive-aggressive or avoidant.

*38 Code.* On the standard MMPI this profile type is usually seen as half neurotic and half psychotic, with a substantial portion of the psychotics and neurotics both being in the depressed category. On our MMPI-168 sample the same was true, with 70% of the patients being seen as evidencing an affective disorder of either a major depression or dysthmic disorder. One third received a secondary or tertiary diagnosis of a psychosomatic condition. The underlying personalities generally tended to be in the anxious or fearful category (avoidant, dependent, compulsive, or passive-aggressive). A little over half the patients of this profile type were discharged on antidepressant medication.

*45 Code.* This male code type on the standard MMPI has been reported in several studies; however, less than 1% of the MMPI-168 sample made this code type, which was insufficient for developing a profile of the code.

*46 Code.* On the standard MMPI this has been associated with psychotic or severely characterlogical individuals, with the men tending to be more psychotic and the women more apt to be characterlogical. On our MMPI-168 sample, slightly less than half these patients were seen as substance abusers. Quite a few were seen as adjustment disorders with mixed emotional features. Their underlying personality tended to cluster in the area of dramtic, emotional, or erratic personality disorders (histrionic, borderline, or antisocial) with a significant number being seen as paranoid or passive-aggressive (these latter categories were more in line with the standard interpretation of the full MMPI).

*47 Code.* The traditional MMPI interpretation of this code type is an unsocialized individual who acts out episodically and then feels guilty. Our MMPI-168 sample was not very far from this traditional interpretation in that as the modal patient of this profile type was seen as a substance abuser manifesting an adjustment disorder, who is apt to have a histrionic, borderline, antisocial, or passive-aggressive personality.

*48 Code.* As with the standard MMPI, our MMPI-168 sample of this code type was among one of the most miserable and unhappy code types, with a high incidence of acting out. The modal patient was a substance abuser or an adjustment disorder whose personality was borderline, histrionic, or antisocial.

*49 Code.* On the standard MMPI, this is traditionally seen as exemplifying the classic psychopath, with the differential being from a major affective disorder, bipolar disorder, or manic. Our sample did tend to be slightly below average in their overall level of ego-emotional development, but on the whole were not as immature as to be psychopathic. The minority were seen as histrionic personalities, with the differential being dependent or passive-aggressive. One fourth were seen, however, as substance abusers and one fourth were seen as having an affective disorder (major depression or dysthymic disorder).

*68 Code.* This is classically seen in MMPI literature as being indicative of paranoid schizophrenia, but in our sample, as was discussed above, these patients presented a mixed assortment of diagnostic classification, including one-third psychotic disorders (paranoid schizophrenia, acute paranoid disorder, and a major affective disorder: bipolar disorder), one eighth were seen as evidencing organic impairment, and one fifth were seen as substance abusers. A schizotypal personality was also a classification, and as was noted above, would have been included in the schizophrenic category in the earlier diagnostic classification systems.

*69 Code.* This code type on the standard MMPI is generally seen as one primarily indicative of psychosis; namely, schizophrenia or a major affective syndrome. On our MMPI-168 sample, this was a heterogenous code type, as was the 68 code mentioned above. One fourth of these patients were seen as substance abusers and only one fourth were seen as psychotic (bipolar disorder, manic, or schizoaffective disorder). One eighth were retarded and one eighth were reported as evidencing organic impairment. The remainder of this code type were primarily seen as adjustment disorders. Most of these patients had their personality disorder diagnosis deferred because it was obscured by their primary classification, with the remainder being seen as schizotypal or passive-aggressive.

*78 Code.* On the standard MMPI, patients of this profile type are about evenly divided between neurotic and psychotic diagnoses. On our MMPI-168 code sample, these patients tended to fall into three main categories: major affective disorder (bipolar disorder or major depression), adjustment disorders with mixed emotional features and, interestingly, substance abusers. Regarding their underlying personality, half these patients received a diagnosis of avoidant, dependent, compulsive, or passive-aggressive personalities and the bulk of the remainder were seen as borderline or histrionic.

*89 Code.* On the standard MMPI, this has primarily been viewed as a psychotic code type and our MMPI-168 sample was no exception, with the modal diagnosis of this profile type being seen as either major affective disorder (bipolar disorder or major depression) or schizoaffective disorder. The second most frequent classification of these patients was less severe and was adjustment disorder; one third of our patients were seen as substance abusers. This latter classification was not surprising, in that more recent studies on the MMPI (Zukerman et al, 1975; Duckworth, 1979) have shown this to be a common code type for drug abusers. This classification had been seen as almost exclusively psychotic on all studies of the MMPI before drug abuse came into vogue.

*123 Code.* On the MMPI-168 the general picture presented by patients of this profile type was generally the same as previously described in the studies on the standard MMPI; namely, these patients tend to be individuals evidencing moderate or greater depression who were also somatizers and who have a chronically anxious personality stance.

*128 Code.* This profile type on the standard MMPI is often associated with an overly psychotic or pre-psychotic individual evidencing somatic concerns. On our MMPI-168 sample, these patients were primarily seen as individuals evidencing an affective disorder (major depression and, to a lesser extent, dysthymic disorder). The major differential was adjustment disorder with depressed mood. A significant number of patients of this profile type also received as their primary, secondary, or tertiary diagnosis some sort of psychosomatic disorder. Their personalities were generally seen as passive-aggressive or avoidant, though paranoid, schizotypal, and borderline personality disorders were also represented by this code. This latter cluster of personality disorders would be quite similar to the earlier diagnostic categories of pre-psychotic mentioned in previous studies of this code type with the standard MMPI.

*237 Code.* This code type holds few surprises, as the majority of these patients were seen as evidencing an affective disorder (major depression or dysthymic), with the major differential being adjustment disorders with depressed mood. Slightly less than half received psychological factors affecting physical condition as a primary or secondary diagnosis. Their underlying personalities tended to be in the anxious or fearful personality category; namely, dependent, compulsive, or passive-aggressive.

*238 Code.* On the standard MMPI this is an infrequent code but has been described as primary associated with psychotic depressions and on our MMPI-168 sample, the majority were seen as evidencing major affective disorders (bipolar or major depression). Their underlying personality disorders were seen as primarily anxious or fearful disorders (avoidant, dependent, or passive-aggressive), though a significant minority were seen as borderline personality disorders.

*246 Code.* This code type holds few surprises, and almost half the patients of this profile type on the MMPI-168 received a primary diagnosis of adjustment disorder, with one third being seen as evidencing major depressions. The underlying personality was primarily passive-aggressive (as would have been predicted from previous studies on the MMPI), but paranoid, schizoid, antisocial, and borderline classifications were also evidenced in this code type.

*248 Code.* Lachar (1974) noted that this code type on the standard MMPI was seen differently in different settings. On our MMPI-168 private clinic patients, this was a heterogenous code type, in that one third were seen as evidencing an affective disorder (major depression or dysthymic) disorder, one third were seen as adjustment disorders, and one third were seen as substance abusers. The personality disorders of these patients were primarily seen as histrionic or borderline.

*268 Code.* This is an infrequent code type on the standard MMPI. On our MMPI-168 sample, half these patients were seen as having adjustment disorders with depressed mood, and the next major cluster was major affective disorders. The bimodal classification of these patients' personality disorders was somewhat unusual and almost at either extreme of the spectrum in that the two major categories were histrionic and avoidant personality disorders.

*278 Code.* There were few differences between our MMPI-168 code type 278 and previous studies on the standard MMPI regarding this code type. Two thirds of these patients were seen as evidencing what in DSM-II terminology would be classified as psychotic disorders; namely, major depression, bipolar disorder, or schizoaffective disorder. In general, this profile type is a remarkably consistent profile, with these patients being seen as moderately to severely depressed individuals who are chronically anxious and worried.

*289 Code.* This is an infrequent code type on the standard MMPI. On our MMPI-168 sample half of these patients were seen as psychotic and evidencing a schizoaffective disorder or major depression. Almost one third were seen as having organic impairment as a primary diagnosis, and one fourth received a substance abuse disorder as their primary or secondary diagnostic category. Over one half the patients of this profile type had their personality disorder deferred because it was obscured by their  primary disorder, with the remainder seen primarily as avoidant, dependent or passive-aggressive personalities.

*468 Code.* Our MMPI-168 sample of this code tended to be, in one sense, somewhat more mature than previous studies of this code type on the standard MMPI in that their overall level of emotional development was generally at the conformity level. Nevertheless, almost half these patients did receive a substance abuse diagnosis as their primary, secondary, or tertiary classification. Their primary diagnostic category, however, was adjustment disorder with depressed mood or mixed emotional features. One third were seen as having a major affective disorder (bipolar disorder). Their personality classifications were homogenous in that all of their personality disorders primarily contained an element of wariness, but ran the gamut of personality disorder clusters, which included paranoid, schizotypal, borderline, and avoidant.

*469 Code.* On the standard MMPI this profile type has often been associated with violence and a generally aggressive character disorder. This was not the case on our MMPI-168 sample. These patients were typically adjustment disorders, though a third were seen as having alcohol abuse problems. Their underlying personality was bimodally distributed, and they were typically seen as either paranoid or in the anxious or fearful category (passive-aggressive or, in some cases, surprisingly dependent).

*478 Code.* This is an infrequent code type on the standard MMPI, but one usually associated with immature character disorders. On our MMPI-168 sample this was also modal, in that these patients tended to have a below-average level of ego-conscience development, and their primary personality disorder category was that of dramatic, emotional, or erratic personality disorders; namely, histrionic, antisocial, or borderline. The modal picture was one of an immature personality disorder who was also evidencing an adjustment disorder and/or substance abuse disorder, though a fourth of these patients were seen as psychotic and evidencing schizoaffective disorders or major depressions.

*489 Code.* On the standard MMPI these patients are usually seen as aggressive, immature, poorly socialized character disorders, and apt to be substance abusers, though a few are seen as psychotic. On our MMPI-168 sample the same was true. These patients tended to have histrionic or antisocial personalities and evidenced adjustment disorders and/or substance abuse disorders, but one third were seen as psychotic, evidencing either a major affective disorder or schizoaffective disorder.

*678 Code.* This is a very infrequent code type on the standard MMPI. On our MMPI-168 sample the patients were bimodally distributed, with half these patients receiving a major affective disorder classification (major depression) and the other half were seen as adjustment disorders with depressed mood or mixed emotional features. The underlying personality was heterogenous, though a majority were seen as either histrionic or passive-aggressive; however, schizotypal, paranoid, and avoidant personality disorders were also reported.

*689 Code.* This is a fairly infrequent code type on the standard MMPI, but one that would be definitely classified as psychotic. It was heterogenous in our MMPI-168 sample in that the patients tended to cluster into three main groups: organic mental disorders, substance abusers, and adjustment disorders. The underlying personality was often deferred in these patients but, when reported, spanned all three major clusters and included schizotypal, histrionic, and passive-aggressive.

*789 Code.* This is an infrequent MMPI code type in the standard MMPI. On our MMPI-168 sample these patients were primarily seen as substance abusers, with the major differential being adjustment disorders. The underlying personalities were bimodal in distribution, with one cluster being in the area of dramatic, emotional, or erratic personality disorders (antisocial, borderline) and the other cluster being in the category of anxious and fearful personality disorders (avoidant or passive-aggressive).

## COMPARISON BETWEEN THE MMPI AND THE MMPI-168

In summary, there are some significant differences in the code types enumerated in our sample, using the MMPI-168 as compared to the standard MMPI. These differences are represented by three major sources of variance: first, the MMPI-168 is a somewhat different test from its mother, the standard MMPI; however, the majority of code types discussed here are close enough to previous descriptions on the standard MMPI to reinforce a reasonable degree of confidence in mere extrapolation, which has been the only alternative for users prior the the development of this codebook. The second major source of variance is the fact that, unlike the majority of previous studies, our sample was on private psychiatric patients. As this was noted above, our sample was somewhat different but generally similar to Marks et al.'s (1974) teaching hospital patients and some similarities were noted to King and Kelley's (1977) college student sample. There did appear to be some dissimilarity between our patients and Lachar's (1974b) state hospital patients. The third major source of variance is the fact that our MMPI-168 codebook uses the DSM-III as a classification guide and that the DSM-III is a major departure from DSM-I and DSM-II. Another way to put this is, "Where has all the schizophrenia gone?" This is not surprising, in that DSM-III was an attempt to get the American classification system in line with the international classification system (Vincent, et al., 1982). In doing so, disorders previously classified as schizophrenia, (e.g., latent schizophrenia) have been down-graded into the personality disorder category and have become the borderline personality disorder and schizotypal personality disorder. Also, because of the changes in classification, some previous schizophrenic disorders now appear as psychotic disorders not elsewhere classified or are in the affective disorder category (APA, 1980).

When the MMPI-168 is a test of choice (which in our opinion is any time the standard MMPI cannot be given), the *MMPI-168 Codebook* offers the clinician actuarial information using DSM-III diagnostic classifications. The user should note that our sample was on private patients, and individuals working with the backward mentally ill should use caution in applying this book. Hopefully, further studies will be forthcoming on the MMPI-168 using these and other patient samples.

CHAPTER 4

# How to Score and Use the MMPI-168

Since its development in 1974 (Overall & Gomez-Mont, 1974), several variations on scoring the MMPI-168 have emerged. In the original article, Overall and Gomez (1974) listed regression equations for estimating the MMPI Clinical Scale scores using the scores derived from the first 168 items. Overall, Higgins, and DeSchweinitz (1976) published a Raw Score Conversion Table for the MMPI-168, whereby the raw scores derived from using the standard templates on the MMPI for the 168 could be converted into equivalent raw scale scores for the full MMPI. This is probably the most used scoring system. More recently, Ward, Wright, and Taulbee (1979) modified the scoring procedure to add a few items to Pa and Sc that are scored at the end of the book in the full MMPI and therefore are not picked up by the standard MMPI scoring keys of The Psychological Corporation. The scoring keys now published by National Computer Systems (NCS) incorporate these items. This book was based on The Psychological Corporation scoring keys and the Raw Score Conversion table of Overall et al. (1976). However, conversion tables based on Ward et al. (1979) are provided and should be used when the NCS scoring keys are used.

## ADMINISTERING THE MMPI

The MMPI-168 can be administered in three different ways. First, the 168 questions of the MMPI can be administered either using the booklet form or the standard Form R. When the standard Form R is used, this ends the administration at the bottom of the seventh page on Form R. Alternatively, the first 168 items of the standard MMPI can be administered using a tape recorder. Finally, the MMPI-168 can be read orally to the patients.

No additional research was done on administering the MMPI-168 orally or by tape since the oral administration of the standard MMPI has been well researched, and anyone who doubts this should read the first chapter, Administering the Test, in *An MMPI Handbook, Vol. 1* (Dahlstrom, Welsh & Dahlstrom, 1972).

Obviously, if reading the long form is valid, reading the first 168 items in their exact sequence will be valid also.

The oral administration of the MMPI-168 is probably what will be most helpful to the clinician in using the MMPI-168 for it enables one to test people who, because of intellectual, educational, emotional, motivational, or physical handicaps, cannot or will not take standardized tests of psychopathology on their own.

After the test has been administered, the scoring templates for the standard MMPI are used to derive the MMPI-168 raw scores for the standard validity and clinical scales. Here again, either the booklet form or Form R form may be used. If the scoring templates are the ones published by The Psychological Corporation, use the Raw Score Conversion Table, Appendix A. If NCS scoring templates are used, use Appendix A-1. These raw scales can then be plotted immediately above where L, F, K, Hs, D, Hy, Pd, Mf, Pa, Pt, Sc, Ma, and Si are written on the standard profile sheet. Then, using the Raw Score Conversion Table for the MMPI-168 (Appendix A and Appendix A-1), the converted scores are plotted directly where the raw scores would be on the standard MMPI. Using the standard K corrections for the standard MMPI, the K correction is added where it would normally be, and then the raw score with K is summed and plotted directly on the graph.

For adolescents, conversion tables are provided in Appendix B and Appendix B-1, Raw Score Conversion Tables for the MMPI-168 for Adolescents Ages 14 through 17 (without K correction). These were produced by Iliana Castillo (Vincent, 1980c) using the raw score conversion table for the MMPI-168 and referring to the adolescent norms provided in the *MMPI Handbook, Vol. 1* (Dahstrom, Welsh, & Dahstrom, 1972). The resulting tables enable raw score conversions to be plotted on the standard MMPI profile sheet, since adolescent conversions are referenced in terms of T-scores. If the scoring templates used are the ones published by The Psychological Corporation, use the Raw Score Conversion Tables in Appendix B. If NCS scoring templates are used, use Appendix B-1. Please note that using the above information with adolescents should be tentative, because this book was based on adults. However, Lachar's previous investigation, using adolescent norms with his code book for the standard MMPI, resulted in a favorable outcome (Lachar, 1974b, and Lachar, et al., 1976). Also, more recently, Newmark and Thibodeau (1979) obtained positive results with the MMPI-168, using adolescent scores without K corrections to generate interpretive statements based on Lachar's 1974 codebook.

Once the profile has been plotted, we are now ready to interpret the MMPI-168. Several points in this process are worth noting. In reading code types, unless stated in the manual, the high-point code types refer to those codes which are "primed," i.e., a T-score of above 70. In a very real sense, the validity scales are also clinical scales. Invalid profiles should be analyzed in light of the actuarial information presented in this book relating to them as diagnostic and personality entities in and of themselves. L is considered to invalidate the profile when it is elevated above a T-score of 70 and the same is true of K. F is considered to invalidate the profile when the MMPI-168 actual raw score is above 15 or the converted raw score (i.e., converted to what it would be  to what would be in the standard MMPI) is above

26. After this, all high point codes are listed. Following this, most two-point codes are listed, as well as some three-point codes.

When an infrequent code type is obtained and there is no profile type in the codebook, several methods are available to the reader: (1) look at all code types that approximate the profile in question and choose the one that more closely resembles it; (2) combine the high point codes into a narrative; or (3) use when available a MMPI high-point code type and extrapolate it to the MMPI-168. It should be noted that in the case of ties, the profile is read from left to right. For example, if 1, 3, and 4 are all above a T-score of 70, 1 is at 80 and 3 and 4 are at 75, the profile would be interpreted as a 13 profile type, or the reader may look at all the possible variations of the "tie" code type and try to match as closely as possible the overall configuration. All two and three-point codes are interchangeable. Please note that in the case of three-point code types, the second and third code types should be within 10 points of one another. For example, a profile that consists of scales 1 at 90, 3 at 85, and 8 at 72 is to be interpreted as a 13 profile, not as a 138 profile.

# CHAPTER 5

# MMPI-168 Code Types

*Mythical Average Patient:* The mythical average patient was constructed from samples of 50 of the 400 cases (one of every eight were drawn). Two thirds were inpatients, one third were outpatients. Ninety-two percent were Caucasian, 8% were Black. The mean level of education was 12.9 years. Twenty percent were single, 52% were married, 12% were separated, 10% were divorced, and 6% were widowed.

The average patient was just about as apt to be male as female, and the average age was an individual in the late 30's. Mythical Average Patient had average intellect and was generally a conformist regarding overall level of ego development. The modal diagnosis in Axis I of the Mythical Average Patient was an affective disorder, and most likely a major affective disorder, the primary differential being adjustment disorder, most often with depressed mood. Thirty percent of these patients received substance abuse as their primary, secondary, or tertiary diagnosis; 20% included somatoform disorders or psychological factors affecting physical condition as their primary, secondary, or tertiary diagnosis. On Axis II the primary personality disorder cluster was anxious and fearful personality disorders, with 34% of the patients of this profile type being seen as avoidant, dependent, or passive-aggressive personalities. The differential was evenly divided between odd or eccentric personality disorders (paranoid, schizoid, or schizotypal) and dramatic, emotional, or erratic personality disorders (histrionic, antisocial, or borderline). Upon discharge, 8% of the Mythical Average Patients had been treated with ECT and 14% were discharged with multiple medications; 6% of the patients were receiving antianxiety minor tranquilizers; 2% were receiving antidepressants in the form of MAO inhibitors; 4% in the form of tetracyclic antidepressants; 16% in the form of tricyclic antidepressants; 4% were on lithium; and 18% were receiving neuroleptic medication. All in all, approximately half (44%) were discharged with medication (36%) or had received ECT (8%) as part of their treatment.

One of the most frequently reported life event on the Social Readjustment Rating Scale was sleep disturbance (68%), followed closely by a major change in eating habits (62%). Half the patients reported a major change in their financial state and a change in residence in the year preceding their hospital admission. Other categories receiving a greater than 25% reporting rate were: trouble with

# MYTHICAL AVERAGE PATIENT

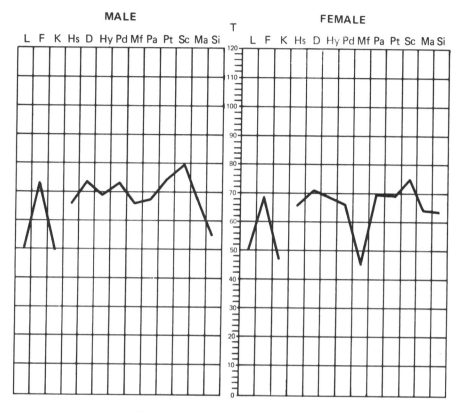

N = 50
Sex: Male 52%          Female 47%
Age: Average = 37.9    Range: 18-85
WAIS IQ:   VS  103     Range: 62-124
           PS  105     Range: 72-138
           FS  104     Range: 65-129

Modal ego level: Conformity 79%
Other ego levels:
    Self-protective/Conformist: 19%
    Self-protective: 2%

the boss (32%), death of a close friend (28%), revision of personal habits (34%), outstanding personal achievement (30%), major change in health or behavior of a family member (26%), sexual difficulties (40%), major change in working hours or conditions (32%), major change in work responsibilities (32%), major personal injury or illness (38%), major change in social activities (40%). Of major life events, those receiving 50 life-change units or more, which were reported with low frequencies among our mythical "average patient", were: marriage, (10%); detention in jail, (10%); death of a spouse, (0); death of a close family member, (24%); marital separation from mate, (14%); divorce (0%); and major business readjustment, (8%).

One fourth of these "average patients" reported marital unhappiness and 8% reported spouse abuse; 6% were having affairs at the time of seeking treatment; 6% reported their spouses as having affairs. Forty-two percent had been married previously; 14% reported their children had difficulties (learning disabilities, physical handicaps, and emotional or discipline problems); 10% reported they had difficulty caring for their children. The majority of our patient sample was employed (72%), with 22% reporting they were unhappy with their careers. Six percent reported being on disability; 6% reported having a work-related lawsuit pending; and 8% reported having trouble holding a job. Regarding their childhood history, a full 34% said they had few friends as a child, and the same number reported having few friends as a teenager. Twenty-four percent reported having frequent temper tantrums as a child; 24% told of having frequent crying spells as a child. Twenty-eight percent of our patient sample reported being sickly children; 10% reported not dating as teenagers; and 22% were either adopted or raised away from their natural parents. Twenty-four percent related being abused as children, (evenly divided between physical and emotional abuse), but none told of being sexually abused.

Educationally, 12% reported having learning disabilities; 6% told of being hyperactive; 14% revealed having frequent problems with their teachers; 6% reported frequent fights at school; 8% reported having difficulty making friends at school; and 8% reported failing an entire year. Regarding family history and family of origin, half of our sample (48%) had one or both parents deceased. Forty percent reported having either a first- or second-degree relative having a drinking problem; 10% reported a first- or second-degree relative having a drug problem; and 32% reported having a first- or second-degree relative with a history of a mental disorder (nervous breakdown). Regarding legal and addiction problems, 30% revealed having been arrested in the past, but two-thirds of these (20%) stated that their arrests were related to substance abuse (public intoxication, DWI, or marijuana possession). Sixteen percent of our sample reported drinking problems and 28% reported a drug problem or a history of a drug problem. Two percent reported a problem with gambling. A full 40% of our patients reported having a chronic illness, major handicap, or other health problem; 12% were taking medication at the time they sought psychiatric services; 14% had been treated previously in psychotherapy as an outpatient; and 28% had had a previous psychiatric hospitalization.

Regarding their own families, 16% reported living alone; 52% reported living with a spouse and children; 16% reported living with parents and siblings; 2% were living with a boy friend or girl friend; 2% with a homosexual lover; 6% with roommates; and 8% with other relatives. Sixteen percent of our sample had no children; 14% had one child; 34% had two children; 6% had three children; and 10% had more than three children. Regarding their own childhood, 6% reported being only children; 16% reported being the eldest child; and 20% reported being the youngest child.

Regarding their reason for hospitalization, marriage and family crises accounted for 20% of the reasons for seeking assistance, and somatic complaints accounted for 34% of the reasons for seeking psychiatric assistance. Six percent reported alcohol abuse as the primary reason for their hospitalization and 10% reported drug abuse as their primary reason for hospitalization. Two percent were involuntary admissions and 4% came in because of a suicide attempt. Six percent reported pure depression as their reason for hospitalization; 14% reported anxiety as their primary difficulty; 6% reported anger or fear of hurting some as their reason for seeking psychiatric assistance. Two percent reported homosexuality, 2% reported amnesia, and 2% reported boy friend or girl friend problems.

## L GREATER THAN T-SCORE OF 70 CODE

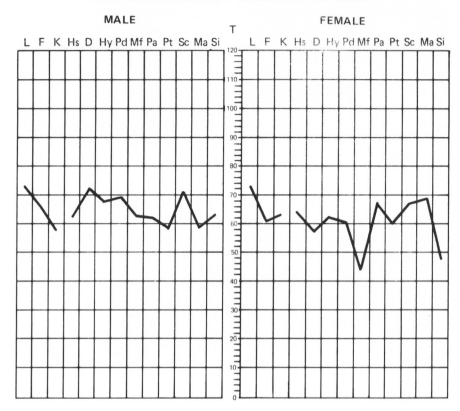

N = 7
Sex: Male 57%            Female 43%
Age: Average = 43.7     Range: 21-81
WAIS IQ:   VS  93        Range: 67-109
           PS  96        Range: 65-111
           FS  94        Range: 66-111
Modal ego level: Conformity 100%

*L greater than a T-score of 70 code:* Patients producing an invalid profile because of an elevated Lie Scale tend to be lower in intelligence than the average patient, and all were at the conformity level of ego development. In general, these patients had encountered significantly lower amounts of psychosocial stress the year prior to seeking psychotherapeutic assistance; had fewer, or at least did not report, arguments with their spouses or other home and marital problems; nor did they report much in the way of job problems. These patients denied marital unhappiness (this may be in keeping with their defensive posture on the MMPI-168), and reported a low incidence of previous marriages. Patients of this profile type tended to be loners, with over half the group living alone. They are also less likely to be discharged with medication. A significant minority of these patients presented with health concerns as their reason for seeking assistance.

Diagnostically, the majority of patients of this profile type were seen as evidencing affective disorders and nearly half were seen as evidencing major affective disorders of a bipolar nature. The underlying personality of patients of this profile type tended to be either schizoid or passive-aggressive, though a significant minority had their personality diagnoses as deferred.

# F GREATER THAN RAW SCORE OF 15 CODE

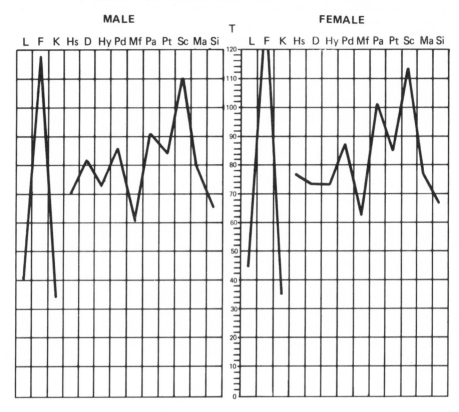

N = 8
Sex: Male 63%            Female 37%
Age: Average = 30.6      Range: 18-80
WAIS IQ:   VS  85        Range: 62-96
           PS  90        Range: 69-111
           FS  88        Range: 65-97

Modal ego level: Conformity 50%
Other ego levels:
  Self-protective/Conformist: 37%
  Self-protective: 13%

*F greater than raw score of 15 code:* Patients of this profile type tended to be of lower intellect than the average patient; in fact, their mean IQ was in the dull-normal range. Also, they were emotionally underdeveloped, with half the patients with this profile type having ego development levels below the average-conformity level. These patients tended to reveal a greater amount of psychosocial stressors than average for the preceding year prior to seeking assistance. They reported significantly more marital separation and change in their social activities. Half the patients of this profile type told of marital unhappiness; one fourth reported having an affair; and 38% reported that their spouses were having affairs. These patients were significantly more likely to have been emotionally labile and volatile in childhood. Half revealed frequent temper tantrums and crying spells, as well as easily becoming upset. They also had a very high incidence of alcoholosm in family members. Half the sample had been arrested; half reported drinking problems; and half had a drug problem. Only one fourth of the patients of this profile type lived with a spouse and/or children, significantly below the average for the average patient sample.

Diagnostically, the modal diagnosis was adjustment disorder with either depressed mood or mixed emotional features. One fourth received diagnoses of organic brain syndrome and one fourth were seen as psychotic and either evidencing an organic or schizophreniform psychosis. One half received a secondary diagnosis of substance abuse. The majority of patients of this profile type had their personality disorders deferred, usually because of them being obscured by psychoses. The remainder were seen as either evidencing borderline, histrionic, or schizotypal personalities.

# K GREATER THAN T-SCORE 70 CODE

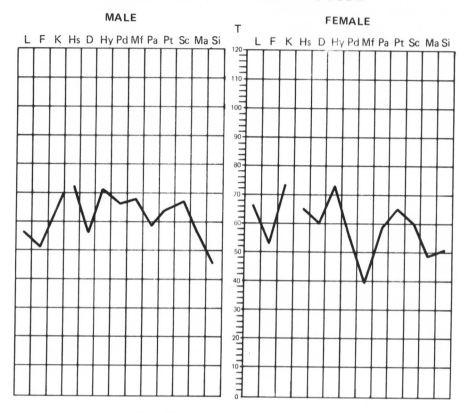

N = 10
Sex: Male 70%              Female 30%
Age: Average = 37.0       Range: 23–69
WAIS IQ:  VS  103         Range: 79–112
          PS  105         Range: 72–123
          FS  104         Range: 75–124

Modal ego level: Conformity 80%
Other ego levels:
    Self-protective/Conformist: 10%
    Self-protective: 10%

*K greater than a T-score of 70 code:* Patients of this profile type were primarily male, and their intellectual ability and ego development was consistent with that of the average patient. These patients tended to report fewer psychosocial stressors occurring within the previous year prior to seeking help in the average patient; also, they were less likely to have had trouble with the boss, a major change in eating habits, a major change in financial state, a change in residence, or a major change in social activities. These patients tended to report fewer relatives with alcoholism. The majority of these patients had a chronic illness, major handicap, or other ongoing health problem. They were a fairly stable group and were more apt than the average patient to be married and have families. Ninety percent of the patients of this profile type reported somatic complaints as the reason for seeking assistance. These patients mentioned health problems of all sorts including: migraine headaches, chronic pain, phobic anxiety, numbness and tingling in extremities, and headaches.

The modal diagnosis for patients of this profile type was an adjustment disorder with depressed mood or anxious mood. Though a third of the patients of this profile type had as either a primary or secondary diagnosis some form of somatization (psychogenic pain or psychological factors affecting a physical condition). A significant minority of these patients were seen as manifesting a major affective disorder: bipolar disorder. The underlying personality of patients of this profile type tended to be either dependent, histrionic, or passive-aggressive.

# FALSE NORMAL CODE

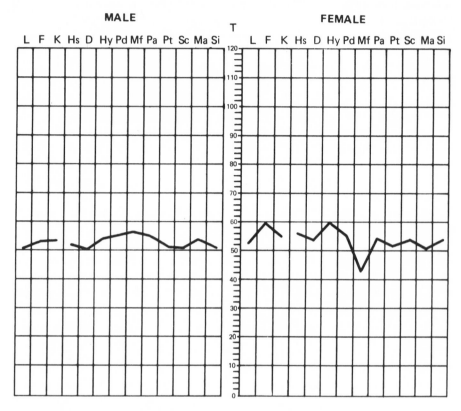

N = 45

Sex: Male 29%          Female 71%

Age: Average = 41.6    Range: 19–82

WAIS IQ:  VS  105      Range: 86–130

          PS  105      Range: 83–132

          FS  103      Range: 86–135

Modal ego level: Conformity 84%

Other ego levels:

   Conformist-Conscientious: 7%

   Self-protective: 9%

*False normal code:* Patients of this profile type, which composed 11% of the total sample, were primarily female. They do not differ from the average patient in major intellect and, generally, their ego development was at the conformity level. These patients tended to have experienced significantly less environmental stress in the year prior to seeking psychotherapeutic assistance. They were especially low in reporting sexual difficulties, death of a close friend, or change in their eating habits. These patients are slightly less likely than the general sample to be employed, though this may be because a high percentage of them were female. They tended not to report having few friends as children or adolescents. Though the incidence of child abuse was not significantly below the general population, sexual abuse was reported by a small percentage of the sample. They were not significantly different from the total sample in being prescribed psychotherapeutic medication by their psychiatrists; slightly one-third were taking medication at the time of discharge.

Diagnostically, about one third of the patients of this profile type fit into the category of affective disorders (primarily major affective disorders) and about one third of the patients of this profile type were seen as evidencing adjustment disorders. When major affective disorders are included, 40% of the sample were seen as evidencing some sort of psychosis including: paranoid schizophrenia, schizo-affective disorders, bipolar disorders, and major depressions. The underlying personality of patients of this profile type tended to cluster in the area of avoidant, dependent, compulsive and (especially) passive-aggressive personalities. A significant minority were seen as histrionic.

# HIGH-POINT 1 CODE

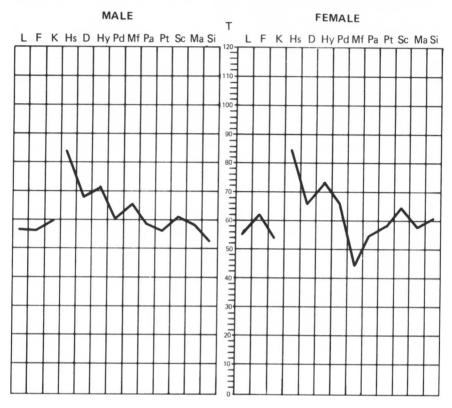

N = 11

Sex: Male 27%          Female 73%

Age: Average = 42.7    Range: 24–73

WAIS IQ:  VS  104      Range: 85–143

         PS  99       Range: 73–123

         FS  102      Range: 80–135

Modal ego level: Conformity 90%

Other ego levels:

   Conformist-Conscientious: 10%

*High point 1 code:* Patients of this profile type were more apt to be women than that of the general sample. Their intellect tended to cluster in the average range, as did the general sample, and they had a significantly higher overall level of ego development, with none in this sample being seen as below the average-conformity level. Like the average patient, this code type reports a high amount of psychosocial stressors in the past year and were more apt to tell of having incurred a major personal injury or illness during the past year than the general sample. Otherwise, the nature of their stresses was not significantly different from the general group. Surprisingly, in their social histories these patients did not reveal being sickly as a child—and this was quite low, since one fourth of the general sample did. Their amount of abuse was the same as the general sample (roughly one fourth), but this included a significant amount of sexual abuse which was not the norm in the general sample. These patients overwhelmingly reported high incidents of having either a chronic illness, major handicap, or other ongoing health problem. One fourth revealed ulcers in their history; other somatic complaints included colitis and back pain. The primary reason for seeking assistance was physical and somatic complaints.

Diagnostically, the majority of patients of this profile type received some sort of psychosomatic classification as their primary or secondary diagnosis, which included: somatization disorder, conversion disorder, and psychological factors affecting physical condition. Significantly, one fourth of the patients of this profile type were seen as evidencing a major depressive disorder. The underlying personality was mainly clustered in the area of anxious and fearful personality disorders (dependent, compulsive, or passive-aggressive).

# HIGH-POINT 2 CODE

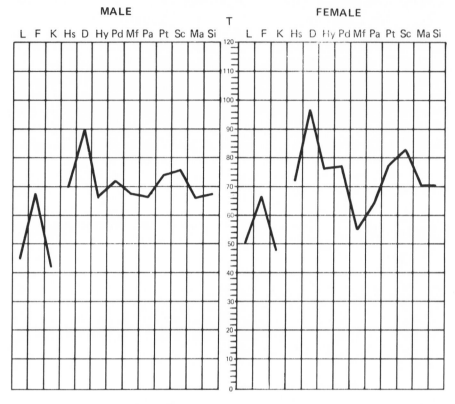

MALE                                              FEMALE

L F K Hs D Hy Pd Mf Pa Pt Sc Ma Si     L F K Hs D Hy Pd Mf Pa Pt Sc Ma Si

N = 15
Sex: Male 60%            Female 40%
Age: Average = 36.1      Range: 21–59
WAIS IQ:  VS  102        Range: 72–118
          PS  104        Range: 88–116
          FS  103        Range: 83–118

Modal ego level: Conformity 73%
Other ego levels:
    Self-protective/Conformist: 20%
    Self-protective: 7%

*High point 2 code:* These patients tended to resemble the general sample in intellect and overall emotional development. Regarding their psychosocial stressors, in addition to a high degree of distress, these patients were somewhat more likely to report occupational problems, having problems with the boss, and change in working hours; they definitely experienced a high incidence of marital separations, marital reconciliations, and major change in number of arguments with their spouses. In fact, this might be called the marital-crisis code type. Interestingly, they were low in reporting sexual difficulties and changes in living conditions. Regarding their past social histories, they did not differ significantly with the average patient sample. Regarding their current history, they evidenced a low incidence of living with their spouse and children—which is not surprising, given the degree of marital crises reported in the recent past. Almost half the patients of this profile type cited depression or suicide as a reason for seeking psychiatric assistance.

One fourth of the patients of this profile left against medical advice. Surprisingly, this code type, when compared to the average patient sample, had a low incidence of being discharged on psychoactive medication, though one in seven of these were antidepressants. This low incidence of medication may be explained by the fact that such a large number left against medical advice. Also, this code type would appear not to be identifying depression but rather a more reactive depression often mixed with anxiety.

Diagnostically, only one half of these patients were diagnosed as having a disorder with some form of affective component. In general, they tended to fall into three succinct groups: those evidencing a major affective disorder (20%); those evidencing an adjustment disorder with depressed mood or mixed emotional features (33%); and those evidencing substance abuse disorders (27%). The underlying personality disorder of this profile type was overwhelmingly within the broad category of anxious and fearful personality disorders (avoidant, passive-aggressive, and dependent personalities).

# HIGH-POINT 3 CODE

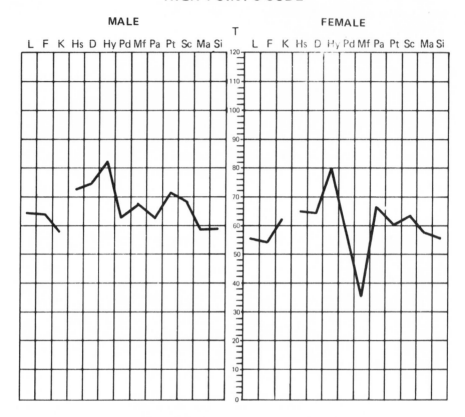

N = 10
Sex: Male 40%                    Female 60%
Age: Average = 42.4             Range: 24-67
WAIS IQ:   VS  106             Range: 92-119
           PS  109             Range: 92-120
           FS  107             Range: 91-121
Modal ego level: Conformity 100%

*High point 3 code:* Patients of this profile type tended to be a bit older than the average patient. By and large they had average intelligence and a conformity level ego development. One third of the patients of this profile type were on tricyclic antidepressants and 20% received electroshock therapy in the course of treatment. Generally, these individuals had incurred less psychosocial stress during the past year than the general patient sample. Nevertheless, they had a high incidence of sleep difficulties but were low in reporting changes in their eating habits, a change in residence, a change to different lines of work, or a change in work responsibilities. These patients were also low in reporting unhappy marriages. It would appear that patients of this profile type are either satisfied with their marriages or at least report it that way. They tended to be a little less likely to be employed than the general sample. These patients had a low incidence of friendlessness in childhood and adolescence and also did not report being emotionally labile. They report a high incidence of drinking problems in their families of origin, and 90% of the patients of this profile type experienced chronic health problems, major handicaps, or chronic illnesses. This was a very stable population and 90% of them were married and had children. They tended to be slightly high in their reports of physical–somatic complaints as the reason for seeking hospitalization.

Diagnostically, 80% of patients of this profile type were seen as having an affective disorders and 60% patients were seen as evidencing psychosomatic disorders (conversion disorder, psychogenic pain, hypochondriasis, or psychological factors affecting physical condition) as primary, secondary, or tertiary diagnoses. Their underlying personalities tended to cluster in the areas of anxious or fearful personality disorders (avoidant, dependent, compulsive, or passive-aggressive).

# HIGH-POINT 4 CODE

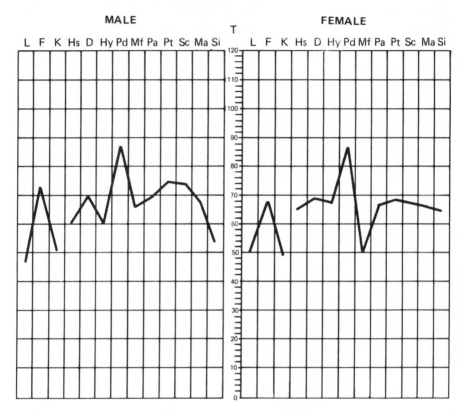

N = 16
Sex: Male 44%              Female 56%
Age: Average = 29.9       Range: 18-50
WAIS IQ:   VS  105        Range 87-123
           PS  106        Range: 91-122
           FS  106        Range: 90-119

Modal ego level: Conformity 63%
Other ego levels:
    Self-protective/Conformist: 31%
    Self-protective: 6%

*High point 4 code:* Patients of this profile type tended to be significantly younger than the general sample and also tended to have a lower level of ego-conscience development. In fact, 37% of the sample was below the general conformity level and none were above. As with the general sample, these patients tended to have average intellect. About one half were on medication, and this was mainly divided between antidepressants (26%) and neuroleptics (18%). These patients revealed having a high percentage of psychosocial stressors for the past year. Two thirds had troubles with their bosses, and 44% reported major changes in working hours or conditions in the year preceding their seeking treatment. Also, one third were seen as evidencing marital separation, and one third were seen as beginning or ceasing formal schooling. The latter is not surprising in view of the fact that this was a younger sample. Half the patients of this profile type reported marital unhappiness, and nearly that many remembered incidents in childhood of temper tantrums, crying spells, and being easily upset. Also revealed in their social histories was a high rate of failing a grade in school. These patients tended not to report having trouble making friends in adolescence. Two thirds of the patients of this profile type reported relatives with drinking problems. One third themselves admitted to a drinking problem; one half the patients of this profile type had been arrested.

Diagnostically, patients of this profile type were seen as substance abusers, with half being diagnosed with this as their primary disorder and a full 75% reporting this as a primary, secondary, or tertiary problem. The second major category of primary problems was affective disorders. The underlying personality of these patients tended to cluster in the area of dramatic, emotional, or erratic personality disorders (histrionic, antisocial, or borderline) though a full one third of these patients were seen as passive-aggressive personalities.

# HIGH POINT 5 CODE (MALE)

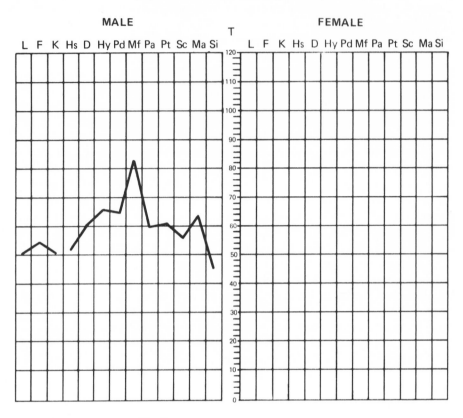

N = 7

Sex: Male 100%          Female 0%

Age: Average = 29.4     Range: 20-37

WAIS IQ:  VS  112       Range: 101-125
          PS  112       Range: 100-120
          FS  112       Range: 102-124

Modal ego level: Conformity  86%

Other ego levels:

　　Conformist-Conscientious: 14%

*High point 5 code-male:* This all-male sample of high point 5 codes tended to be a younger group, who were significantly higher in intellect and had a mean intellectual quotient in the bright-normal range. These patients were significantly higher in their overall level of ego-conscience development, with the majority being at the conformity level and one in seven achieving an emotional development above conformity level. Like the average patient, only slightly more than a third were taking medication at their time of discharge. These patients tended to report fewer changes in eating habits or sexual difficulties the year preceding seeking psychotherapeutic assistance than did the general patient sample. They were also not likely to experience having incurred a major personal injury or illness in the past year. They had a high incidence of gaining a family member and change in work responsibilities. These patients tended not to have been married previously; also, their social histories revealed that they did not have problems making friends as children and adolescents. They tended to be low in reporting chronic illness, major handicaps or other health problems, or in changes in financial state or change to a different line of work. Not one had previous psychiatric hospitalization. As with previous studies, this code type had a high incidence of homosexuality, with a third reporting being homosexual and living with a homosexual lover.

Diagnostically, the majority of patients of this profile type were seen as evidencing adjustment disorders with depressed mood, anxious mood, or mixed emotional features. Their underlying personality was either dependent or passive-aggressive, though almost half the patients of this profile type were not seen as having any significant personality disorder.

# LOW 5 CODE (FEMALE)

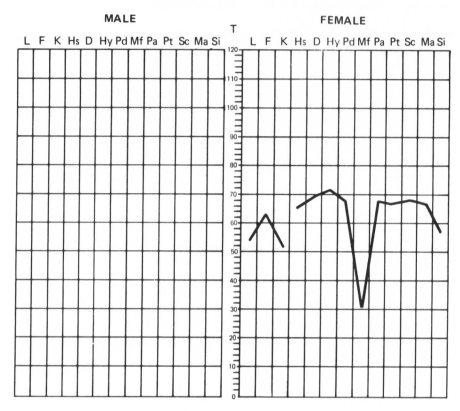

N = 44
Sex: Male 0%              Female 100%
Age: Average = 38.8       Range: 20–78
WAIS IQ:   VS  105        Range: 85–127
           PS  105        Range: 80–138
           FS  105        Range: 82–130

Modal ego level: Conformity 91%
Other ego levels:
    Self-protective/Conformist: 9%

*Low 5 code-female:* This all-female sample resembled the total sample in age, -late 30's- and having a mean IQ in the average range. These patients were almost overwhelmingly conformists in their overall level of ego development. These women had engendered a large amount of psychosocial stressors in the year preceding seeking psychotherapeutic assistance; however, the nature and kind of psychosocial stressors resembled the general patient sample. Their social histories reveal a high incidence of problems with their children: over one third of these women reported children with learning disabilities, emotional problems, physical handicaps, and discipline problems. These women were less likely than the general patient sample to be employed, with only one half working outside the home. They were low in reporting problems making friends as teenagers. One third of these women recalled being abused as children, which was slightly higher than the general sample; and one in eight revealed a history of sexual abuse. These women had a low incidence of arrest records in their social histories and tended not to be drug abusers. Most were married and had children. These women had a high incidence of being treated with a psychoactive medication, with two thirds being discharged on some sort of psychiatric medication. Half (one third of the code type sample) were taking antidepressant medication at the time of discharge.

Diagnostically, this profile type was bimodal and receiving as its primary diagnosis either affective disorders (most frequent major depression or bipolar) or adjustment disorders (with depressed mood or mixed emotional features). Sixteen percent of the total sample received substance abuse as their primary, secondary, or tertiary diagnosis. Twenty-one percent of the total sample received some sort of psychosomatic diagnosis (somatoform disorders or psychological factors affecting phsyical condition) as their primary or secondary diagnosis. The underlying personality of patients of this profile type tended to cluster in the area of anxious and fearful personality disorders (avoidant, dependent, and passive-aggressive). This includes half of the total sample. However, one third of the patients of this profile type were seen as having a histrionic personality disorder.

# HIGH-POINT 6 CODE

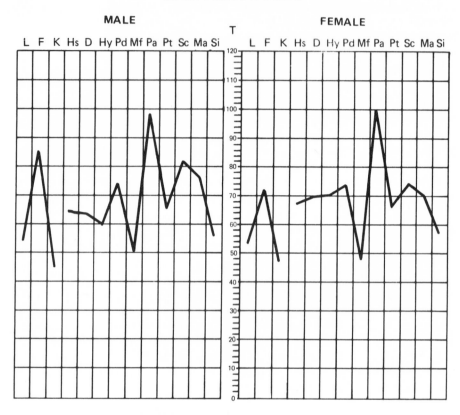

N = 16
Sex: Male 37%              Female 63%
Age: Average = 47.4       Range: 24–85
WAIS IQ:   VS  94          Range: 72–110
           PS  92          Range: 76–110
           FS  94          Range: 75–107

Modal ego level: Conformity 75%
Other ego levels:
    Self-protective/Conformist: 19%
    Self-protective: 6%

*High point 6 code:* Patients of this profile type were, by and large, an older sample than the general sample and significantly lower in intellect; however, they resembled the general overall sample in ego development, with the majority being at the average-conformity level. These patients were more likely than the general patient sample to report gaining a new family member in the year prior to seeking pyschotherapeutic assistance; they were less likely to report having had a death of a close freind, outstanding personal achievement, or a change in residence. As with the patient sample, a virtual smorgasbord of recent psychosocial stressors were presented, including those relating to marriage and family, work, and other interpersonal problems. Regarding their family history, these patients revealed a higher incidence of sexual abuse, though their overall child abuse level was not significantly different from the general population. They also recalled a higher incidence of relatives with psychiatric histories. Otherwise, their social histories were unremarkable. These patients were more apt than the general sample to be on medication and one-third of them were on neuroleptics.

Diagnostically, half the patients of this profile type were seen as psychotic with a paranoid flavor and either manifesting a paranoid disorder: paranoia or acute paranoia, or paranoid schizophrenia, though a significant number of these patients were seen as evidencing a major depression. Nonpsychotic categories tended to fall in the areas of mixed organic brain syndrome or adjustment disorder with depressed mood or mixed emotional features. In the personality category the majority had their diagnoses deferred because of psychosis in Axis I. The remainder were seen as either paranoid or schizotypal, passive-aggressive or histrionic personalities.

# HIGH-POINT 7 CODE

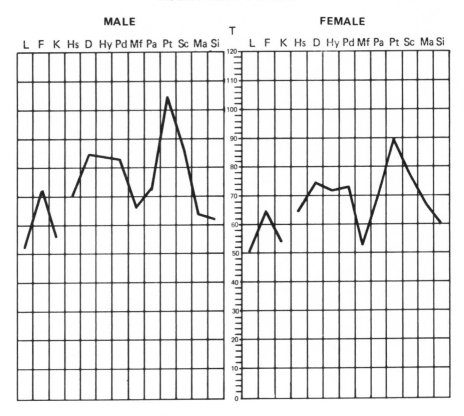

N = 17
Sex: Male 59%          Female 41%
Age: Average = 33.5    Range: 22–54
WAIS IQ:   VS  103     Range: 85–125
           PS  102     Range: 83–120
           FS  102     Range: 87–117
Modal ego level: Conformity 100%

*High point 7 code:* Patients of this profile type resembled the general sample, in that they were about evenly divided between men and women, had average intellect, and had a mean age in the early 30's. All the patients of this profile type were seen as having an ego development at the conformity level. Their medication usage was significantly above average, with roughly two thirds of this profile type on medication. The types of medication spanned all categories: antidepressants, 24%; neuroleptics, 18%; lithium, 27%; and ECT's, 18% of the sample. These patients, like the average sample, had incurred a high amount of psychosocial stressors in the past year; however, they were low in reporting difficulties with the boss. Virtually all the patients of this profile type experienced sleep difficulties. Very few of these patients recalled being sickly as children; also fewer reported chronic illnesses, major handicaps, or other health problems in their histories. These patients tended to live alone more so than the average patient sample.

Diagnostically, almost half the patients of this profile type were seen as evidencing adjustment disorders with depressed mood or mixed emotional features. A significant minority were seen as evidencing major depressions and a few were seen as having anxiety disorders. One third received substance abuse as a primary, secondary, or tertiary diagnosis. The underlying personality of patients of this profile type tended to cluster in the area of anxious or fearful personality disorders (avoidant, dependent, compulsive, or passive-aggressive).

# HIGH POINT 8 CODE

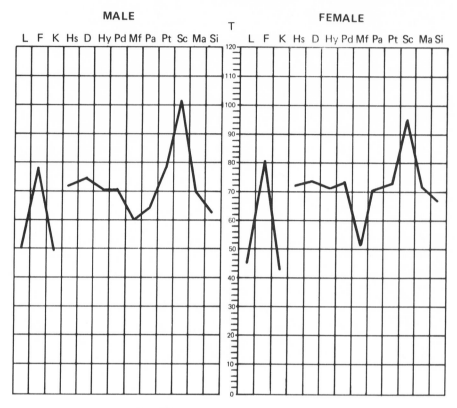

MALE                          T                    FEMALE

N = 58
Sex: Male 47%          Female 53%
Age: Average = 33.6    Range: 18-64
WAIS IQ:   VS  101     Range: 60-127
           PS   95     Range: 57-127
           FS   98     Range: 56-124

Modal ego level: Conformity 69%
Other ego levels:
    Self-protective/Conformist: 28%
    Conformist-Conscientious: 3%

*High point 8 code:* Patients of this profile type were about evenly divided between men and women; also, they tended to have average intelligence and their mean age was in the 30's, as was the general patient sample. Their overall level of ego-conscience development was not significant compared to the general patient sample, with the bulk being at the conformity level. As to medication, half the patients were discharged with psychoactive medication. Antidepressants were the most frequently prescribed (one fourth of the total code type sample) with neuroleptics as the next category. Although these patients engendered a high amount of psychosocial stressors in the past year, the overall nature of the stressor was not significantly different from that of the general patient sample, except for their reporting a major change in the health or behavior of a family member. As with the general patient sample, these patients had engendered high incidents of difficulties of all sorts. Their social histories were also not significantly different from the general patient sample.

Diagnostically, almost half of the patients of this profile type were seen as evidencing some sort of psychosis. Their labels included: paranoid schizophrenia, schizoaffective disorder, major affective disorder (bipolar), and major depression. This sample had a high incidence of substance abuse with almost a third of the patients reporting substance abuse as their primary, secondary, and tertiary diagnostic category. The bulk of the other classifications were adjustment disorders, with one in four receiving this as their primary diagnosis. In terms of their personality, patients of this profile type tended to cluster in two groups: one being the dramatic, emotional, and unstable personality cluster (histrionic and borderline) and the other being the anxious and fearful personality cluster (avoidant, dependent, compulsive, or passive-aggressive).

# HIGH-POINT 9 CODE

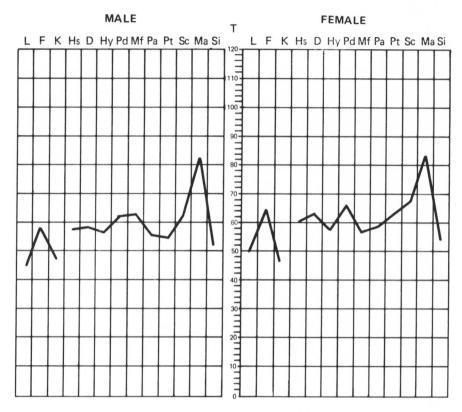

N = 21
Sex: Male 43%              Female 57%
Age: Average = 35.9       Range: 18–71
WAIS IQ:   VS  108        Range: 90–132
           PS  108        Range: 88–145
           FS  109        Range: 90–140

Modal ego level: Conformity 57%
Other ego levels:
   Conformist-Conscientious: 10%
   Self-protective/Conformist: 29%
   Self-protective: 4%

*High point code 9:* Patients of this profile type were about evenly divided between males and females and, as with the general sample, tended to have a mean age in their mid-30's. They were slightly brighter than average, though this was not significant when compared to the general patient sample. These patients tended to be a bit low in their overall level of ego-conscious development as a group, though the majority of these patients were at the conformity level of overall ego development. Over one fourth were seen as in the transition stage between conformity and being self-protective. As with the general patient sample, roughly one third of the patients of this profile type were discharged on psychoactive medication with no one medication category predominating. Patients of this profile type had high incidents of psychosocial stressors in the year preceding psychotherapeutic assistance. The most significant psychosocial stressor in the past year for this group was major change in health or behavior of a family member. Interestingly, this group, in spite of their reputation for overactivity and instability in makeup, had a low incidence of changing residence for the previous year. These patients were also less likely than the general sample to report not being able to make friends as children, as well as being low in reporting chronic illnesses. These patients had a high incidence of school failure.

Diagnostically, one third of the patients of this profile type were seen as adjustment disorders with depressed mood or mixed emotional features; another one third were seen as having substance abuse disorders; and one fifth of them were seen as evidencing a major affective disorder, either a bipolar disorder or an atypical disorder. The underlying personality of patients of this profile type tended to cluster in the area of dramatic, emotional, or erratic personality disorders (histrionic or antisocial personality).

## 12 CODE

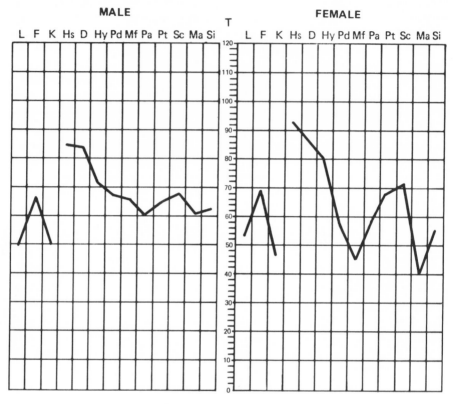

N = 7
Sex: Male 71%              Female 29%
Age: Average = 46.6        Range: 20–65
WAIS IQ:   VS  108         Range: 92–143
           PS  101         Range: 93–120
           FS  105         Range: 93–135

Modal ego level: Conformity 71%
Other ego levels:
    Conformist-Conscientious: 29%

*12 code:* Patients of this profile type were primarily male and of average intelligence. They tended to be a bit older than the general sample and were average or above in their overall level of emotional development, having either an ego level at average-conformity level or higher. As with the general sample, these patients reported a high amount of psychosocial stressors for the past year; they were higher than the general patient sample in reporting the following categories of stressor: a major personal injury or illness in their recent past; revision of personal habits; death of a close friend; change in residence; and taking on a mortgage of over $20,000 in the past year. These patients did not have remarkable family history. The overwhelming majority of patients of this profile type experienced having either a chronic illness, major handicap, or other health problem. These patients had health problems of all sorts, including stomach ulcers and migraine headaches. These patients also cited somatic complaints as their primary presenting problem. Three fourths of the patients of this profile type were discharged on psychoactive medication, with almost half being discharged on antidepressants.

Diagnostically, however, half the patients of this profile type were seen as evidencing a major affective disorder–either a major depression or a bipolar disorder. The remainder were seen as either psychological factors affecting physical condition, adjustment disorders, or panic disorders. The overwhelming majority of patients of this profile type had a personality disorder that fell in the broad cluster of anxious or fearful personality disorders (dependent, compulsive, or passive-aggressive).

# 13 CODE

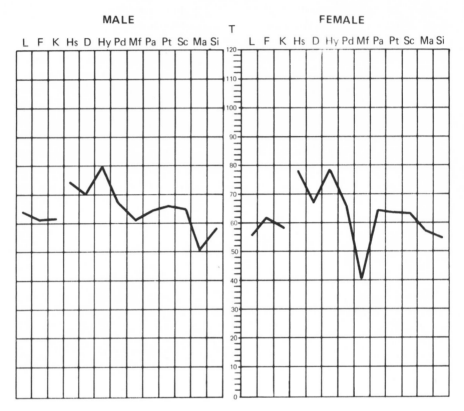

N = 13
Sex: Male 23%          Female 77%
Age: Average = 39.8    Range: 24–67
WAIS IQ:   VS  104     Range: 92–114
           PS  104     Range: 86-121
           FS  104     Range: 90–118

Modal ego level: Conformity 100%

*13 code:* Patients of this profile type tend to be primarily female and of average intelligence. All of the patients of this profile type had as their overall level of ego development the average-conformity level. These patients, as did the general sample, reported a high incidence of psychosocial stressors during the past year, but were only significantly greater in the reporting of major personal injury or illness as a psychosocial stressor. They were less likely to have a revision in personal habits or change in residence. Although their overall level of reporting of being abused in their childhood resembled the general sample, these patients also revealed a significant amount of sexual abuse as children. They were high in their reporting of having had histories of chronic illness, major handicap, or other ongoing health problems; these included ulcers and colitis. The majority of patients of this profile type reported somatic complaints as the reason for seeking assistance. Three fourths of the patients of this profile type had some sort of psychosomatic complaint as their primary, secondary, or tertiary diagnoses. These included somatization disorder, conversion disorder, hypochondriasis, and psychological factors affecting physical condition. When age is taken into account, 100% of the patients of this profile type under age 40 had psychosomatic disorders as their primary, secondary, or tertiary diagnosis; but this was the case in only one third of the patients over age 40. Interestingly, though, one half of the patients of this profile type were also seen as having an affective disorder, with almost one thid reporting a major affective disorder. Not surprisingly, virtually all of the patients of this profile type were discharged on psychoactive medication, with the majority being on antidepressants. In terms of their personality, the major cluster was in the area of anxious and fearful personality disorders (passive-aggressive, dependent, or compulsive personality).

## 18 CODE

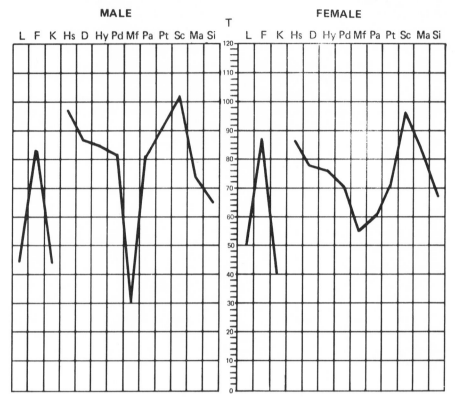

N = 7
Sex: Male 43%              Female 57%
Age: Average = 34.1        Range: 20–47
WAIS IQ:   VS 96           Range: 85–102
           PS 99           Range: 90–107
           FS 97           Range: 86–105

Modal ego level: Conformity 57%
Other ego levels:
    Self-protective: 43%

*18 code type:* Patients of this profile type are seen as of average intelligence, but of below average ego development, with almost half in transition between the self-protective to the conformity level. This is low when compared to the general sample of patients as well as Loevinger's normative population for adults. These patients reported a high amount of psychosocial stressors in their past, and were especially high in the areas of sleep disturbance, sexual difficulty, major personal injury or illness, death of a close family member, and major change in the health or behavior of a family member. The patients revealed a high incidence of crying spells in their childhood as well as temper tantrums. They also had a high incidence of being adopted or being raised away from their natural parents. They also reported a high incidence of learning problems in school. Over half the patients of this profile type had drug problems and arrests; nearly half these patients had family members with histories of drug problems. They also had a high incidence of chronic illness, major handicap, or other health problems. Over half had been previously hospitalized for psychiatric reasons. They were more likely than the general population to live alone, with almost half of them reporting this. These patients have various reasons for their seeking psychiatric assistance, but over one fourth said their reason for seeking psychiatric assistance was a fear of hurting someone else.

Diagnostically, the overwhelming majority of patients of this profile type were seen as substance abusers and received this as a primary or secondary diagnosis. Almost one half received some sort of psychosomatic disorder as their primary, secondary, or tertiary diagnosis; these included somatization disorders and psychogenic pain. The majority of patients of this profile type belong in a cluster of dramatic, emotional, or erratic personality disorders (histrionic or borderline personality disorder). In general, the modal picture that emerges with this profile type is of a somatizing drug abuser who is a borderline.

# 23 CODE

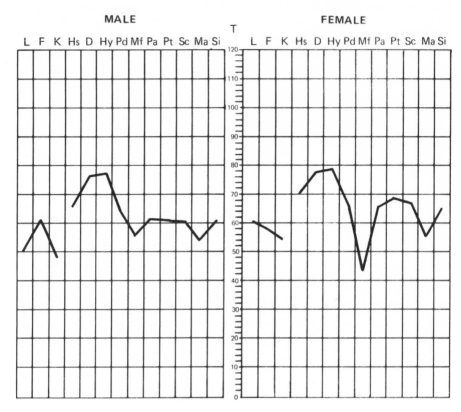

N = 14
Sex: Male 36%            Female 64%
Age: Average = 43.1      Range: 26–76
WAIS IQ:   VS  107       Range: 92–120
           PS  108       Range: 86–138
           FS  107       Range: 90–128

Modal ego level: Conformity 93%
Other ego levels:
    Self-protective/Conformist: 7%

*23 code:* Patients of this profile type are a lot more apt to be female and slightly older than the average patient sample. These patients in general had as their overall level of emotional development at the average-conformity level. As with the general sample, these patients were apt to have incurred a high amount of psychosocial stressors in the past year, but were only significantly higher from the patient sample in that half of them had had a major change in the health or behavior of a family member in the recent past. Almost half the patients of this profile type reported their marriages as unhappy, and this was significantly high when compared to the average patient. Also, in their family histories these patients report a high incidence of family members having a history of a drinking problem. These patients were also high in their reporting of being abused as a child, with over half of them suffering from child abuse. In spite of this, these patients were fairly stable. They were significantly more likely than the average patient to be married and have children in spite of their marital unhappiness. Another way of looking at this is that though these patients are conscientious, conforming, and apt to be stable family people, they are also apt to be unhappy with their family life. The largest cluster of reasons for seeking assistance was marriage and family problems. Slightly less than half the patients of this profile type were discharged on psychoactive medication (most frequently antidepressants) and one in seven received ECT.

Diagnostically, patients of this profile type were about evenly divided between major affective disorders (bipolar of major depression) and adjustment disorders with depressed mood. One third of the patients of this profile type received as a secondary diagnosis some sort of psychosomatic disorder; somatization disorder (conversion disorder, hypochondriasis) or psychological factors affecting physical condition. These patients were seen primarily as passive-aggressive personalities or histrionic personalities, though a few were seen as dependent or compulsive in thier personality stance.

## 24 CODE

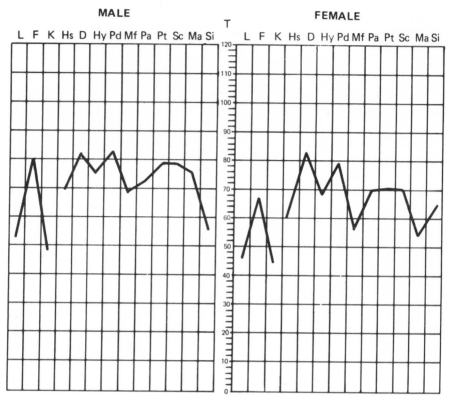

N = 7
Sex: Male 29%              Female 71%
Age: Average = 35.9       Range: 21–70
WAIS IQ:   VS  104        Range: 81–141
           PS  101        Range: 78–119
           FS   79        Range: 79–133

Modal ego level: Conformity 57%
Other ego levels:
    Self-protective/Conformist: 29%
    Conformist-Conscientious: 14%

*24 code:* Patients of this profile type tended to be female and, as a whole, their overall level of ego-conscience development tended to be a bit lower than the average patient. Almost one third were at the self-protective-conformity transition stage of ego development. These patients had a high incidence of psychosocial stressors and were especially likely to experience arguments with their spouses, as well as marital separation, financial difficulties, and in-law troubles. One hundred percent of the patients of this profile type reported sleep disturbances. These patients also tended to report having had few friends as a child, as well as frequent crying spells and becoming easily upset as a child. They were more likely than the average patient to report having been abused in childhood, with over one half being abused as children (this included sexual abuse). Forty two percent of the patients of this profile type reported drug abuse as the reason for seeking assistance.

This tended to be seen as a secondary factor by their psychiatrists, whose diagnosis was bimodal, with almost half being seen as evidencing a major depression, and the remainder being seen as evidencing an adjustment disorder with eith a depressed mood or mixed emotional features. Not surprisingly, slightly over half of the patients of this profile type were discharged on antidepressant medication. These patients had as their personality disorder category the cluster of anxious and fearful disorders (passive-aggressive or dependent personality).

# 26 CODE

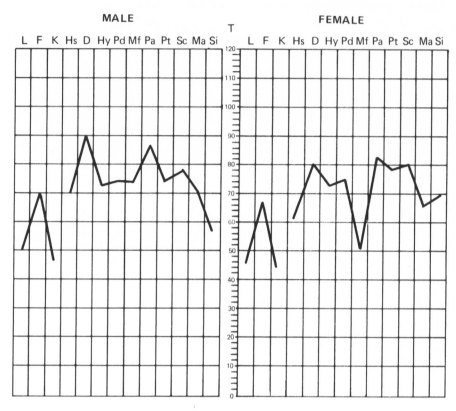

N = 7
Sex: Male 29%          Female 71%
Age: Average = 36.9    Range: 18–59
WAIS IQ:  VS 97        Range: 84–110
          PS 96        Range 88–114
          FS 96        Range: 80–112

Modal ego level: Conformity 86%
Other ego levels:
   Self-protective/Conformist: 14%

*26 code:* Patients of this profile type were slightly more apt to be female than the general sample. Their overall level of ego-conscience development was like the average patient sample, with the majority being seen as having the average-conformity level of ego-emotional development. Not only did these patients report a high incidence of psychosocial stressors in the past year, (the incidence was higher than was reported by the average patient) but also 100% of these patients experienced a major change in eating habits in the past year. Three fourths reported a major change in financial state. Half had trouble with the boss, as well as a major change in behavior of a family member, gaining a new family member, major change in arguments with spouse, and changes in living conditions. Almost half the patients of this profile type report in their social histories, that their marriages were unhappy. They are more apt than the general sample to have been in psychotherapy previously as an outpatient, but they were low in reporting a previous psychiatric hospitalization in their history. These patients were diffuse in their reasons for hospitalization. All the patients of this profile type were discharged on psychoactive medication, with the majority receiving antidepressants.

Diagnostically, the majority of patients of this profile type were seen as psychotic, evidencing a major depressive disorder, paranoid schizophrenia, or a schizoaffective disorder. The remainder were seen as evidencing adjustment disorders with either depressed mood or mixed emotional features. The underlying personality of patients of this profile type were apt to be seen as avoidant, paranoid, or schizotypal.

## 27 CODE

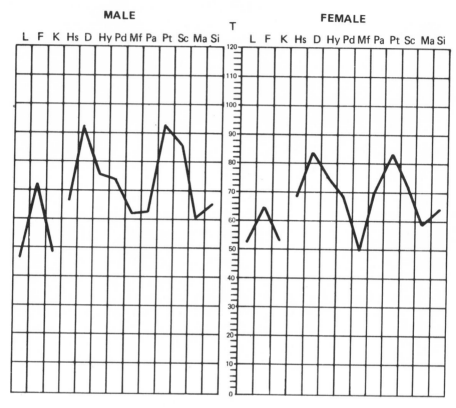

N = 14
Sex: Male 57%              Female 43%
Age: Average = 38.4        Range: 21-67
WAIS IQ:   VS  105         Range: 88-128
           PS  106         Range: 89-131
           FS  106         Range: 88-131
Modal ego level: Conformity 100%

*27 code:* Patients of this profile type were all seen as evidencing an ego level at the average-conformity level. They reported somewhat low incidents of psychosocial stressors in their recent past and were especially low experiencing troubles with their bosses, arguments with their spouses, sexual difficulties, or having had eating problems or having moved in the recent past. Their social histories were rather bland. The most frequent reason for seeking psychiatric assistance was depression. The overwhelming majority of patients of this profile type were discharged on psychoactive medication, with the majority of these patients being on antidepressants.

The modal diagnostic category for patients of this profile type was an affective disorder, especially major affective disorder—and especially major depression. A significant minority were seen as having alcohol abuse problems. Virtually all the patients of this profile type fell into the personality disorder category of anxious or fearful personality disorders, with the primary classification being that of avoidant personality. Also included were compulsive, dependent, and passive-aggressive personalities.

## 28 CODE

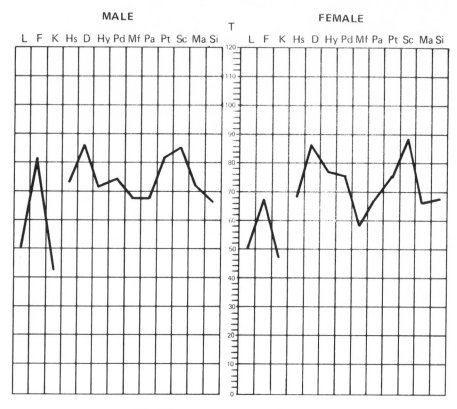

N = 29
Sex: Male 45%                     Female 55%
Age: Average = 35.3              Range: 18–60
WAIS IQ:   VS   102               Range: 72–124
           PS   103               Range: 72–124
           FS   102               Range: 74–122

Modal ego level: Conformity 79%
Other ego levels:
    Self-protective/Conformist: 17%
    Conformist-Conscientious: 4%

*28 code type:* Patients of this profile type tended to resemble the general sample in their age, intellect (average) and overall ego level (that of the average-conformity level). These patients reported a higher overall incidence of psychosocial stressors for the recent past, but this was a diffuse reporting and resembled the general sample; namely, a high incidence of marriage and family, occupational, health, and other interpersonal difficulties. These patients were more apt than the average sample to report having had few friends as a child in their social histories. They also were somewhat higher than the average in having failed an entire school year. The majority of patients of this profile type (58%) were discharged on psychoactive medication, with one third of the total sample being on antidepressant medication.

Patients of this profile type tended to have as their primary disorder an affective disorder (especially major depression, bipolar, and dysthymic). Schizoaffective disorders were also reported. The second major diagnostic category was adjustment disorder with depressed mood. Almost a third of the patients of this profile type received as a primary or secondary classification substance abuse. The underlying personality disorder of patients of this profile type tended to cluster in the area of anxious and fearful disorders (avoidant, compulsive, passive-aggressive, or dependent), though a significant amount of patients of this profile type were seen as evidencing dramatic, emotional or erratic personality disorders (histrionic or borderline).

## 36 CODE

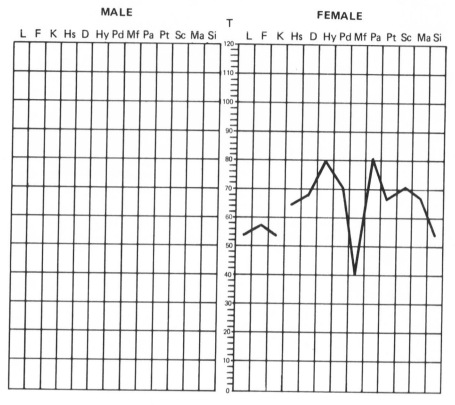

N = 6
Sex: Female 100%
Age: Average = 37.7          Range: 23-54
WAIS IQ:   VS  105           Range: 92-118
           PS  103           Range: 91-110
           FS  104           Range: 91-102
Modal ego level: Conformity 100%

*36 code:* This is an all-female code type and all of these patients were seen as manifesting an ego level at the average-conformity level. These women reported a significantly lower amount of psychosocial stressors in the recent past. They were low in having had changes in their living conditions, low in reporting changes in eating habits, and low in reporting sleeping difficulties. They experienced a high incidence of arguments with spouses; three fourths of them stated in their social histories that their marriages were unhappy. Also, the social histories of these patients revealed that they were sickly as children. In spite of their marital unhappiness, these patients were more likely than the average patient to be living with their spouse and children. Apparently they were unhappy but "toughing it out." Not surprisingly, one third of these patients came in, in the context of a marital crisis.

Diagnostically, the majority of patients of this profile type were seen as evidencing adjustment disorders of either depressed mood or mixed emotional features, with the remainder (one third) seen as evidencing a major depression. These patients tended to cluster in the personality disorder area of dramatic, emotional, or erratic personality disorders (histrionic or borderline).

# 37 CODE

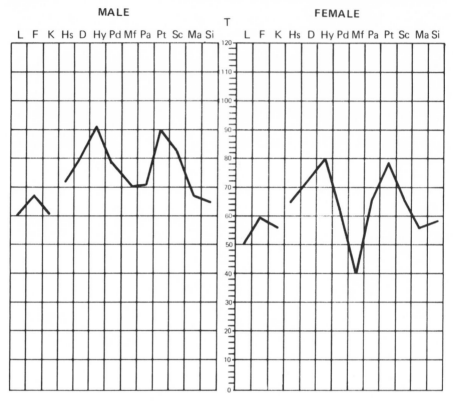

N = 11

Sex: Male 55%              Female 45%

Age: Average = 37.1       Range: 20-54

WAIS IQ:   VS  100        Range: 85-116
           PS  105        Range: 83-120
           FS  102        Range: 87-115

Modal ego level: Conformity 100%

*37 code:* Patients of this profile type were almost exclusively individuals of average intelligence and all had as their overall level of ego development the average-conformity level. These patients were lower than the general patient sample in their reporting of psychosocial stressors for the past year. They were especially low in incurring troubles with their bosses, sleep disturbances, or deaths of family members and close friends. Also, they had low incidents of sexual difficulties or change in work responsibilities. These patients did not relate anything significantly different than the general patient sample in their social histories. The overwhelming majority of patients of this profile type were discharged on psychoactive medication, with almost half the total sample being on antidepressent medication.

Diagnostically, one third of the patients of this profile type received as their primary or secondary diagnoses a psychosomatic classification: psychogenic pain or psychological factors affecting physical condition. About one third were seen as evidencing major depression and one third were seen as evidencing adjustment disorders with depressed mood. The majority of patients of this profile type had as their personality disorder a disorder in the area of the anxious or fearful personality disorder category (passive-aggressive or avoidant personality).

## 38 CODE

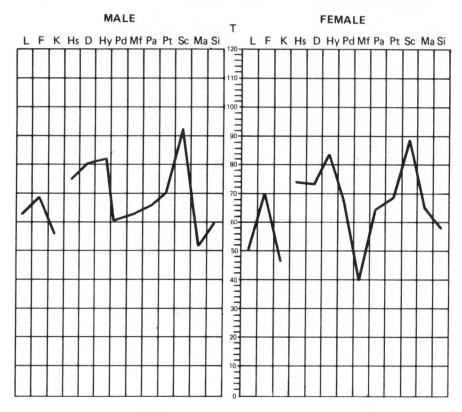

N = 7
Sex: Male 43%              Female 57%
Age: Average = 36.6        Range: 21–57
WAIS IQ:   VS 102          Range: 60–127
           PS 102          Range: 57–120
           FS 100          Range: 56–112

Modal ego level: Conformity 71%
Other ego levels:
    Conformist-Conscientious: 29%

*38 code:* Patients of this profile type had a higher than normal reporting of above-average levels of ego development and none reported below-average levels of ego development. These patients also reported a lower-than-average amount of psychosocial stressors for the previous year. They tended not to change jobs or residences, to have outstanding personal achievements, and did not experience much in the way of eating problems. They were high in having recently gained family members. Their social histories, however, revealed half the patients of this profile type had children with problems (learning disabilities, physical, emotional, handicaps, or discipline problems). These patients also were more apt than the average patient to have been adopted or reared away from their parents and to have had outpatient psychotherapy in the past. None of them had been arrested, and this was low for the general patient sample. Another half the patients of this profile type reported depression as the reason for seeking psychiatric assistance. A little over half the patients of this profile type were discharged on psychoactive medication and all of these were on antidepressant medication. One in seven received ECT.

This was underscored diagnostically, as 70% of this profile type were seen as evidencing an affective disorder (major depresssion or dysthymic disorder) as their primary diagnoses. Almost one third received as a secondary or tertiary diagnosis a psychosomatic classification (somatization disorder or psychological factors affecting physical condition). The primary cluster of personality disorders for patients of this profile type was the anxious or fearful personality disorder category, namely, avoidant, dependent, compulsive, or passive-aggressive.

# 46 CODE

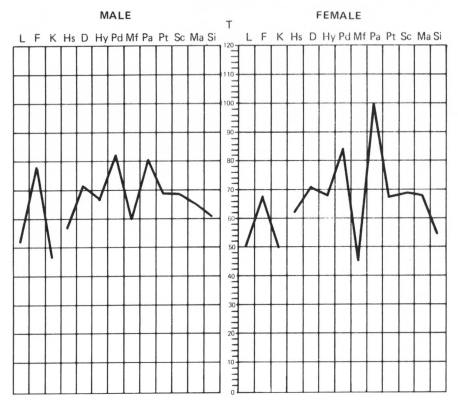

N = 17
Sex: Male 35%          Female 65%
Age: Average = 35.1    Range: 18–57
WAIS IQ:  VS 95        Range: 75–124
          PS 93        Range: 83–132
          FS 94        Range: 80–129

Modal ego level: Conformity 59%
Other ego levels:
  Self-protective/Conformist: 29%
  Self-protective: 12%

*46 code:* Patients of this profile type were slightly more apt to be female and had a lower-than-average IQ when compared to the average patient sample. Patients of this profile type were also likely to be below average in the overall level of ego development. These patients, as did the general sample, reported a high amount of psychosocial stressors in the past year, especially in the areas of change in their working conditions, gaining a new family member, foreclosures and change in number of family get-togethers. They were less likely than the general patient sample to have had a revision of personal habits, outstanding personal achievement, or death of a close friend. Their social histories revealed a somewhat higher amount of being abused as children, including sexual abuse. One third were reared away from their parents, but this code type was below average in reporting having parents who had died. These patients were somewhat high in recalling histories of school problems, including hyperactivity, school failure, and problems with teachers. They also reported a higher-than-average incidence of drug problems, with over half the patient sample reporting this as a difficulty. One fourth of the patients of this profile type had incurred a DWI in their histories. Half of them came in because of marital crises and one fourth of the remainder came in because of depression or suicide attempts. This profile type had a low incidence of being prescribed psychoactive medication, with less than one in five being discharged on psychoactive medication.

Diagnostically, two fifths of the patients of this profile type received substance abuse as their primary, secondary, or tertiary diagnoses. The second highest category was that of adjustment disorders with mixed emotional features. The modal personality cluster for patients of this profile type was dramatic, emotional or erratic personality disorders (histrionic, borderline, or antisocial personalities), with a significant number receiving paranoid or passive-aggressive personality disorder categories.

## 47 CODE

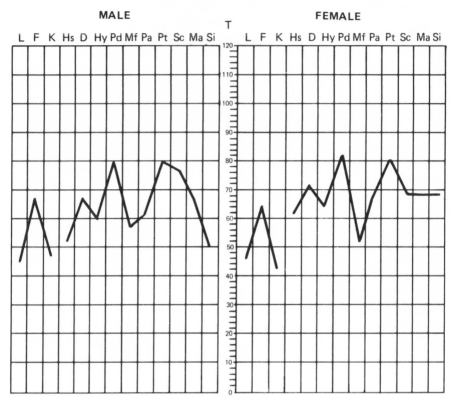

N = 14
Sex: Male 36%              Female 64%
Age: Average = 30.9        Range: 18-51
WAIS IQ:   VS  106         Range: 88-117
           PS  108         Range: 83-131
           FS  107         Range: 85-124

Modal ego level: Conformity 69%
Other ego levels:
    Self-protective/Conformist: 23%
    Self-protective: 8%

*47 code:* Patients of this profile type were slightly more apt to be female and, as a group, were younger than the average sample. Their intellects were in the average range and resembled the average patient sample. They were more apt than the average patient population to be below average in their level of ego development. These patients, like the average sample, reported a high incidence of psychosocial stressors for the past year; they were especially apt to report a major change in number of family get-togethers. One half had had problems with the boss in the past year and one in five had recently married. They reported in their social histories a high incidence of relatives with drinking problems and nearly one third had drinking problems. They were quite apt to recall temper tantrums in childhood; very few had problems making friends as children or teenagers. None of the sample had been reared away from their natural parents. They were low in reporting chronic health problems and handicaps. Few patients of this profile type were discharged on psychoactive medication. They were also more apt than the general sample to live alone.

Diagnostically, over half the patients of this profile type received substance abuse as their primary or secondary diagnoses. The second major category was that of adjustment disorders with either depressed mood or mixed emotional features. The majority of patients of this profile type tended to have personality disorders clustered in the areas of dramatic, emotional, or erratic personality disorders (histrionic, borderline, or antisocial), with the remainder being seen as passive-aggressive.

# 48 CODE

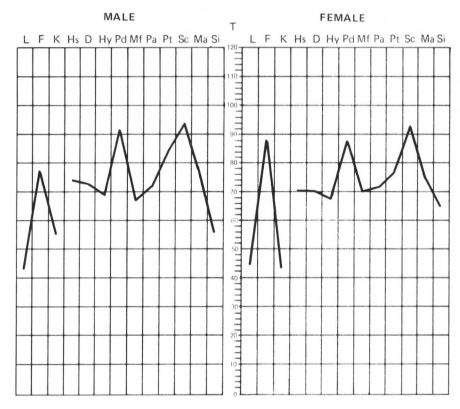

N = 14
Sex: Male 64%              Female 36%
Age: Average = 27.9       Range: 18–38
WAIS IQ:   VS  100         Range: 67–113
           PS  101         Range: 68–117
           FS  101         Range: 65–115

Modal ego level: Conformity 57%
Other ego levels:
    Self-protective/Conformist: 43%

*48 code:* Patients of this profile type were slightly more apt to be male and were significantly younger than the general sample. Also, they were significantly more apt to have ego development below the average-conformity level. These patients, as did the general sample, reported high incidents of psychosocial stressors for the past year and were especially apt to report a major change in the health or behavior of a family member. In their social histories, these patients recalled a high incidence of temper tantrums in their childhood as well as a fair amount of crying spells and easily becoming upset as children. Nearly one third reported difficulty holding a job. In spite of the fact that these patients had, as a group, average intelligence, half of them had failed an entire year of school. They also experienced a high incidence of trouble with the teachers at school. Apparently, their difficulties were more of a behavioral-emotional nature than in the area of learning disabilities. These patients had a high incidence of arrests in their histories, were high in their reporting of drinking problems, and had a fair amount of drug use. These patients were low when compared to the average patient sample in being discharged on psychoactive medication.

Almost half the patients of this profile type were diagnosed as having substance abuse disorders. The remainder were primarily seen as evidencing adjustment disorders with either depressed mood or mixed emotional features. The modal cluster of personality disorders for patients of this profile type was the dramatic, emotional, or erratic personality disorder categories of borderline, histrionic, or antisocial personality disorders.

## 49 CODE

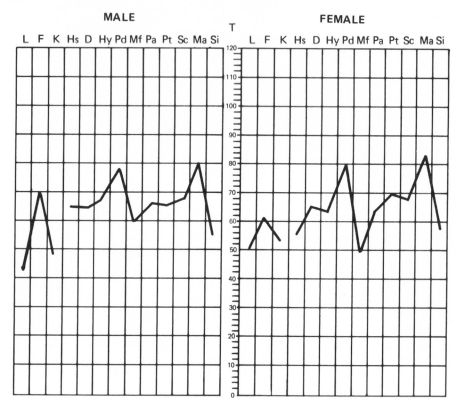

N = 7
Sex: Male 43%          Female 57%
Age: Average = 32.0    Range: 24–57
WAIS IQ:   VS  108     Range: 80–132
           PS  110     Range: 85–145
           FS  110     Range: 81–140

Modal ego level: Conformity 57%
Other ego levels:
   Conformist-Conscientious: 14%
   Self-protective/Conformist: 29%

*49 code:* Patients of this profile type were a bit more apt to be female than the general sample, as well as a bit younger than the general sample. These patients tended to be below-average in their overall ego-emotional level of development. These patients reported a lower amount of psychosocial stressors in the past year than the average patient sample, though it was still fairly high. They cited a high incidence of change in number of arguments with spouses. They were less apt to report difficulties in sleeping and eating, change in residence, change in social activities, or death of a close friend. Almost one third of the patients of this profile type indicated that they were having an affair at the time of evaluation. Their marriages were unhappy and three fourths had had previous marriages. These patients were apt to report a high incidence of family members with drinking problems and drug problems, but were low in reporting a history of a family member having a nervous breakdown and equally low in having parents who deceased.

Diagnostically, almost half the patients of this profile type were seen as evidencing adjustment disorders with depressed mood, anxious mood, or mixed emotional features. Slightly over one fourth of the patients of this profile type were seen as having substance abuse disorders and received this as their primary or secondary diagnosis. The other one fourth received diagnoses of affective disorders (major depression or dysthymic disorder). The majority of patients of this profile type were seen as having a histrionic personality disorder, with the differential being a dependent or passive-aggressive personality.

## 68 CODE

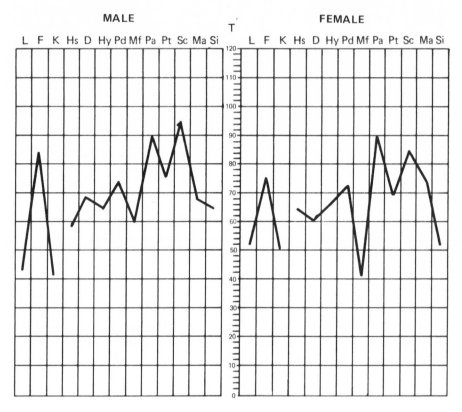

N = 17
Sex: Male 41%          Female 59%
Age: Average = 37.5    Range: 19-78
WAIS IQ:   VS  97      Range: 72-116
           PS  94      Range: 72-112
           FS  96      Range: 75-113

Modal ego level: Conformity 70%
Other ego levels:
    Conformist-Conscientious: 6%
    Self-protective/Conformist: 18%
    Self-protective: 6%

*68 code:* Patients of this profile type were slightly more apt to be female and tended to be a bit lower in intellect than the average patient sample. Their overall level of ego development was generally in line with the average patient sample in that the majority of patients of this profile type evidenced the average-conformity level of ego development. Patients of this profile type, as with the general sample, exhibited a high level of life change in the year preceding their hospitalization or consultation. They were especially high in the areas of in-law troubles and gaining a new family member. These patients tended to be low in having major changes in financial state for the previous year. Developmentally, these patients reported in their social history that they tended to have few friends as a child; they were apt to have had frequent crying spells and were upset easily as children. They were slightly more likely to be either adopted or raised away from their natural parents; they reported a high incidence of being abused as children and had an especially high incidence of being sexually abused as children. One third of them recalled failing a grade in school, and this might possibly be because this sample was a bit lower in intellect than the average sample. Also, a large number of these patients had relatives with a history of mental illness. Half of these patients had been arrested and half had a history of a chronic illness, major handicap, or major health problem. Two thirds of the patients of this profile type were discharged on psychoactive medication. Of these, one third of the total sample were taking neuroleptics and one sixth were on lithium.

Diagnostically, half the patients of this profile type were seen as evidencing adjustment disorders with depressed mood and mixed emotional features or a mixed disturbance of emotions and conduct. Over one third of them were seen as evidencing some sort of psychosis (paranoid schizophrenia, acute paranoid disorder, or a major affective disorder: bipolar disorder). One fifth of the patients of this profile type received substance abuse as a primary or secondary diagnostic category. Of the patients of this profile type, in terms of their personality, 42% had their diagnoses deferred, primarily because it was obscured by psychosis or organic impairment in Axis I. The remainder ran the gamut of personality disorders but were especially seen as evidencing avoidant, schizotypal, or histrionic personality disorder. It is noteworthy that one eighth of the patients of this profile type were seen as evidencing organic impairment.

## 69 CODE

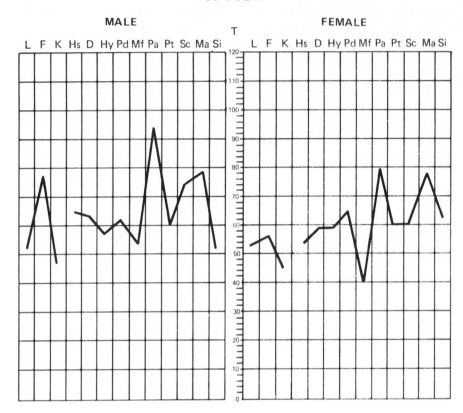

N = 8
Sex: Male 50%            Female 50%
Age: Average = 42.3      Range: 26–85
WAIS IQ:   VS   96       Range: 71–113
           PS  100       Range: 72–117
           FS   97       Range: 71–114

Modal ego level: Conformity 100%

*69 code:* Patients of this profile type tended to resemble the general sample and were seen as having average intelligence; *all* were seen as evidencing the average-conformity level of ego development. These patients reported a lower incidence of psychosocial stressors for the past year than did the general sample, one that would be considered in the moderate range for the general population. They were especially low in changes in their financial state, changes in residence, or having incurred a major personal injury or illness in the year preceding treatment. Developmentally, these patients tended to recall being adequately socialized as teenagers, and none were adopted or raised apart from their families. They also were not abused as children, but one fourth revealed being abused by their spouses.

This profile type was a heterogenous one, with one-fourth evidencing substance abuse disorders, one fourth evidencing adjustment disorders with either depressed mood or mixed emotional features, and one fourth evidencing psychosis (bipolar disorder, manic, or schizoaffective disorder). One in eight reported being retarded and one in eight reported organic impairment. In terms of their personality, these patients were primarily divided into three groups: those whose diagnoses were deferred, those obscured by their primary classification, or those who were schizotypal or passive-aggressive.

## 78 CODE

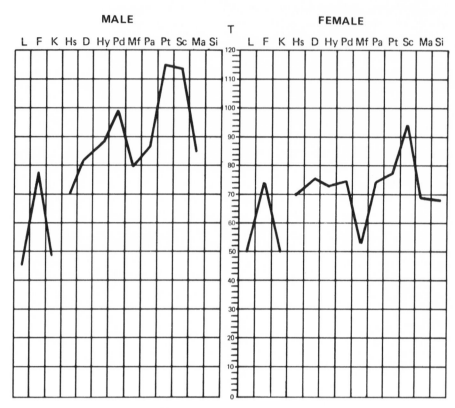

N = 32
Sex: Male 56%          Female 44%
Age: Average = 32.1    Range: 18–64
WAIS IQ:   VS  102     Range: 69–125
           PS   99     Range: 74–125
           FS  101     Range: 73–125

Modal ego level: Conformity 78%
Other ego levels:
    Self-protective/Conformists: 22%

*78 code:* Patients of this profile type were slightly younger than the general population sample, tended to be of average intelligence, and resembled the general sample in their overall level of emotional development; namely, the majority were seen as evidencing a conformist level of ego development. These patients reported a significant amount of psychosocial stressors in the past year, but these were generally consistent in magnitude and nature with the average patient sample. These patients had a higher incidence of change in number of arguments with spouses. Their social histories were likewise unremarkable when compared to the general patient sample, with the exception of having had fewer previous marriages. Half the patients of this profile type were discharged receiving psychoactive medication, but no distinct pattern of medication emerged: one sixth were on antidepressants, one sixth were on neuroleptics, and one in eleven were on lithium at the time of discharge.

Diagnostically, the patients of this profile type tended to fall into three major categories: major affective disorder (bipolar disorder or major depression), adjustment disorder (with either depressed mood or mixed emotional features), or substance abuse. The modal personality disorder category for patients of this profile type was anxious or fearful personality disorders, with half the patients receiving a diagnosis in this category avoidant, dependent, compulsive, or passive aggressive personalities. The bulk of the remainder were seen as borderline or histionic.

# 89 CODE

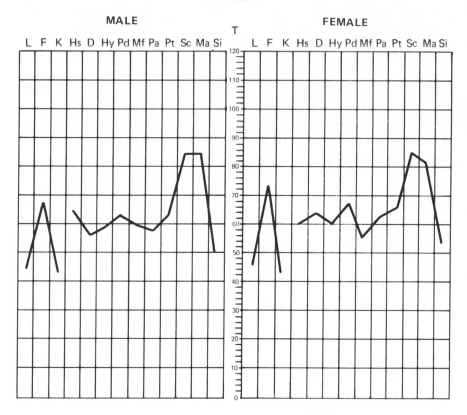

N = 22
Sex: Male 36%            Female 64%
Age: Average = 30.3      Range: 18–50
WAIS IQ:   VS   99        Range: 84–127
           PS  101        Range: 83–131
           FS  100        Range: 83–130

Modal ego level: Self-protective/Conformist 50%
Other ego levels:
   Conformist-Conscientious: 9%
   Conformist: 41%

*89 code:* Patients of this profile type were more apt than the general sample to be female. They were generally of average intelligence, but below-average in overall ego-conscience development. The modal ego level for patients of this profile type was at a transition stage between the self-protective and conformity levels. These patients, like the general sample, had a high incidence of psychosocial stressors during the previous year and were especially high in reporting sexual difficulties and major change in their financial state. Their social histories reflected a high incidence of sexual abuse as children. Also, the majority of patients of this profile type had a relative with a drinking problem. Seventy percent of the patients of this profile type were discharged on psychoactive medication and half of these (one third of the total sample) were taking antidepressant medication.

Diagnostically, the modal diagnosis of patients of this profile type was some sort of psychotic classification, either major affective disorder (bipolar or major depression) or a schizoaffective disorder. This was followed closely by adjustment disorders with depressed mood or mixed emotional features. One third of the sample received a diagnosis of substance abuse as either their primary or secondary classification. In terms of personality, these patients were mainly divided into three groups: one third had their diagnosis deferred; one third were seen as anxious and fearful personality disorders and the bulk of the rest were seen as borderline or histrionic.

## 123 CODE

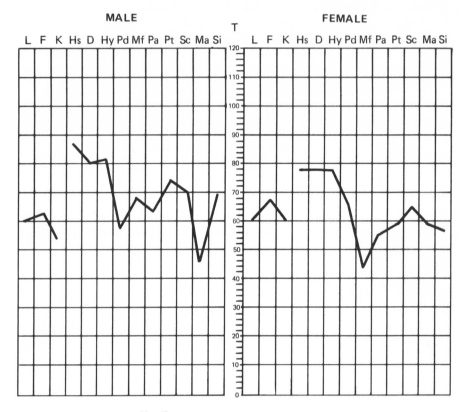

N = 7
Sex: Male 29%          Female 71%
Age: Average =  41.7      Range: 20–76
WAIS IQ:   VS  116      Range: 92–143
           PS  120      Range: 97–138
           FS  117      Range: 93–135

Modal ego level: Conformity 86%
Other ego levels:
    Conformist-Conscientious: 14%

*123 code:* Patients of this profile type were significantly more apt to be female and were a bit older than the general patients sample. Also, they were brighter and had a mean IQ in the bright-normal range. Moreover, they tended to be above average in their overall level of ego-conscience development, with none of them scoring below the modal general conformity level of emotional-ego development. These patients, as did the general sample, incurred a high incidence of psychosocial stressors for the past year preceding seeking psychotherapeutic assistance. They differed from the general sample in being low in reporting problems with their bosses, high in reporting major personal injuries or illnesses, and high in reporting arguments with their spouses. These patients were also high in experiencing difficulties with children, including emotional problems, discipline problems and–quite frankly–problems caring for their children. These patients tended not to have problems making friends as adolescents; they were low also, when compared to the general patient sample, in having deceased parents; none were raised away from their natural parents. None reported occupational problems, legal problems or addiction problems. These patients had a high incidence of chronic illnesses in their histories, including migraines and hypertension. Also, they were more likely than the general sample to be on psychoactive medication; over half were, with over one fourth being on tricyclic antidepressants.

Diagnostically, the majority of patients of this profile type received their primary diagnosis as an affective disorder (bipolar disorder or dysthymic disorder) The second major category was adjustment disorder with depressed mood. Forty-three percent of the patients of this profile type received a somatization disorder as either the secondary or tertiary diagnosis (psychogenic pain or hypochondriasis); 86% of these patients were seen as having psychological factors affecting physical condition. The overwhelming majority of patients of this profile type received a personality disorder diagnosis, clustering in the category of anxious or fearful personality disorders (dependent, compulsive, or passive-aggressive). In general, the picture emerged as that of a moderate-or-greater depressed patient who is a somatizer and who has a chronically anxious personality stance.

## 128 CODE

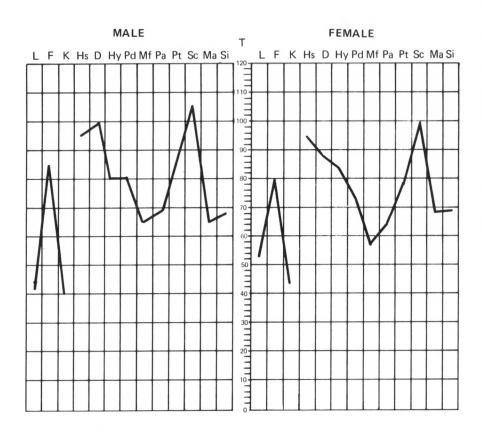

MALE                                          FEMALE

T

L  F  K  Hs  D  Hy Pd Mf Pa  Pt  Sc Ma Si    L  F  K  Hs  D  Hy Pd Mf Pa  Pt  Sc Ma Si

N = 7
Sex: Male 71%              Female 29%
Age: Average = 40.7        Range: 23-65
WAIS IQ:   VS  102         Range: 97-112
           PS  105         Range: 97-120
           FS  103         Range: 95-116

Modal ego level: Conformity 86%
Other ego levels:
    Self-protective/Conformist: 14%

*128 code:* Patients of this profile type were more apt than the general patient sample to be male. Their mean IQ was in the average range and their age range and overall level of ego-conscience development did not differ significantly from the general patient sample. The bulk of these patients were at the conformity level of overall emotional development. These patients differed from the general patient sample in reporting extremely high amounts of psychosocial stressors for the year preceding their seeking psychotherapeutic intervention. All reported sleep disturbance, a major change in eating habits, major changes in financial state, changes in residence, changes in work responsibilities and work hours, major personal illnesses or injuries, changes in social activities, and changes in living conditions.

Their social histories revealed patients who had had difficulties in making friends in childhood. Almost one third reported that their children had emotional problems. They were more likely than the general patient sample to have deceased parents; they were very high in reporting histories of family members with mental problems and drug problems. They were low in histories of legal difficulties, and none had ever been arrested. They had a high incidence of reports of chronic illnesses, major handicaps, or other ongoing health problems, including: stomach problems, migraine headaches, and colitis. One patient reported a history of 17 surgeries. These patients were more likely than the general patient to have had a previous psychiatric hospitalization. Not surprisingly, the overwhelming majority (86%) were discharged on psychoactive medication. Slightly over one half were discharged receiving tricyclic antidepressants, and slightly less than half were discharged on neuroleptic medication.

Diagnostically, the majority of patients of this profile type received as their primary diagnosis an affective disorder (major depression) and, to a lesser extent, dysthymic disorder. The next major cluster was adjustment disorders with depressed mood. Over a fourth of patients of this profile type received as the primary, secondary, or tertiary diagnosis psychological factors affecting physical condition or a somatization disorder. The majority of patients of this profile type were seen as having a personality disorder in the category of anxious or fearful personality disorders (passive-aggressive or avoidant), though paranoid, schizotypal, and borderlines were also represented in this code type.

# 237 CODE

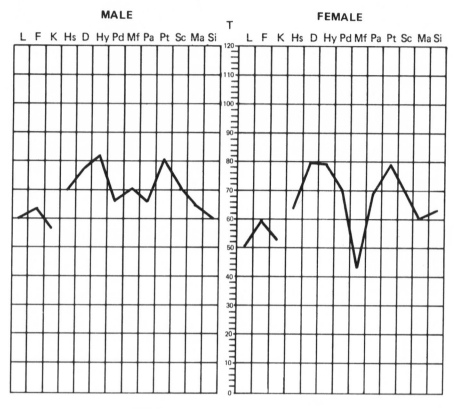

N = 12
Sex: Male 33%        Female 67%
Age: Average = 35.0   Range: 21–54
WAIS IQ:  VS  106     Range: 97–118
          PS  107     Range: 89–120
          FS  107     Range: 93–118

Modal ego level: Conformity 100%

*237 code:* Two thirds of the patients of this profile type tended to be female. Like the general sample, these patients tended to have average intelligence and their age range tended to cluster in the early 30's. All had an ego development level at the modal stage of conformity, and this was significantly different from the general sample. These patients had a higher incidence of being discharged on medication, with two thirds of the patients receiving medication at the time of discharge. The bulk of these were discharged on tricyclic antidepressants. These patients had a little lower incidence of psychosocial stressors during the previous year; they were especially apt to be low in reporting sexual difficulties or marital reconciliation. Their social histories revealed that almost half had been in psychotherapy previously, but this code type has a low incidence of previous psychiatric hospitalizations. These patients were high in recalling being abused as children. One fourth had failed a grade in school.

Diagnostically, patients with this profile type tended to be seen as having affective disorders (major depression and dysthymic). The second major diagnostic cluster was adjustment disorders with depressed mood. Slightly less than half received psychological factors affecting physical condition as a primary or secondary diagnosis. Patients of this profile type had personality disorders in the cluster of anxious or fearful personality disorders (dependent, compulsive, or passive-aggressive).

## 238 CODE

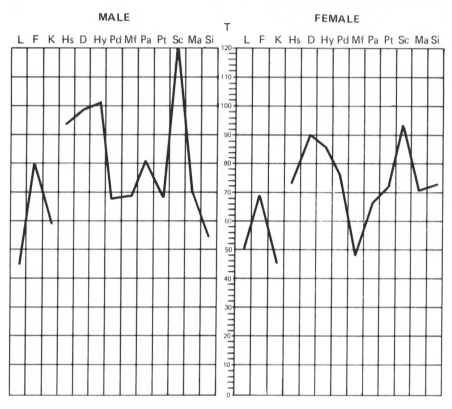

N = 7

Sex: Male 14%          Female 86%

Age: Average = 37.9    Range: 21–57

WAIS IQ:   VS 91       Range: 60–109
           PS 94       Range: 57–110
           FS 92       Range: 56–110

Modal ego level: Conformity 86%

Other ego levels:

    Self-protective/Conformist: 14%

*238 code:* The majority of patients of this profile type were female. As with the general sample, patients of this code type tended to be in their thirties. These patients were significantly lower than the general patient sample in intellect, and their mean IQ was barely in the average range. Their overall level of ego-conscience development tended to be at the conformity level, which was consistent with the general sample. These patients were quite likely to be discharged on medication; one third were on tetracyclic antidepressants, and another third were on tricyclic antidepressants. Lithium was the other medication used, making all medication given for this code type for the affective category. The patients reported a high incidence of sleep disturbance. Also, they were high in their revelation of major changes in the health or behavior of a family member, gaining a new family member, marital reconciliation, and being fired from work.

As with the general sample, they had incurred a high incidence of psychosocial stressors for the previous year. These patients were more apt to report marital unhappiness and previous marriage. They had a high incidence of career unhappiness. Almost half were reared away from their natural parents, and almost half reported having been abused as children. Their social histories also revealed that none of these patients had had any arrest records. The primary reason for seeking psychiatric assistance among these patients was depression, and this was reported significantly more often than the general sample.

Diagnostically, the overwhelming majority of patients of this profile type were seen as having affective disorders, and the majority were seen as having major affective disorders (bipolar or major depression). The underlying personality of this profile type tended to cluster in the area of anxious or fearful personality disorders (avoidant, dependent, or passive-aggressive) though a significant minority were seen as evidencing borderline personality disorders.

## 246 CODE

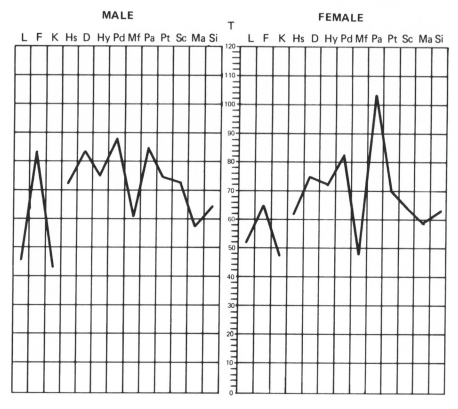

N = 7

Sex: Male 43%              Female 57%

Age: Average = 43.4        Range: 24–70

WAIS IQ:    VS  106        Range: 91–141

                PS   99        Range: 83–119

                FS  100        Range: 87–133

Modal ego level: Conformity 86%

Other ego levels:

   Self-protective/Conformist: 14%

*246 code:* Patients of this profile type tended to be a bit older than the general patient sample; their intellect was average, as was the general patient sample; they resembled the general patient sample in their overall level of ego-conscience development; namely, that the bulk of them were at the conformity level. Like the general patient sample, these patients tended to report high incidences of psychosocial stressors for the year preceding their hospitalization. They were less likely to report the death of a close friend, outstanding personal achievement, change in occupation, or change in work responsibilities in the preceding year than the general patient sample. They were more likely to experience changes in financial state, major changes in number of arguments with spouses, gaining a new family member, and major changes in social activities. Their social histories revealed high incidences of marital unhappiness and a very high incidence of problems with children. The overwhelming majority had children with physical handicaps, emotional problems, or discipline problems. These patients tended to be somewhat less likely to be employed than the general sample. They were less likely than the general sample to have problems making friends as children and teenagers. They reported getting easily upset and having crying spells as children. They had school problems, with almost one third reporting having failed a grade in school. They also reported a high incidence of health problems, but their health problems tended to cluster in areas that are not traditionally seen as psychosomatic in origin. The social history of these patients revealed they were less apt than the general patient sample to be living with spouse or children.

Diagnostically, almost half the patients of this profile type received adjustment disorders as a primary diagnosis, with depressed mood or mixed emotional features. One third were seen as having a major affective disorder (major depression). One in seven were seen as substance abusers. The majority of this profile type received the personality disorder classification of passive-aggressive personality; however, paranoid, schizoid, antisocial, and borderline classifications were also evidenced in this code type.

## 248 CODE

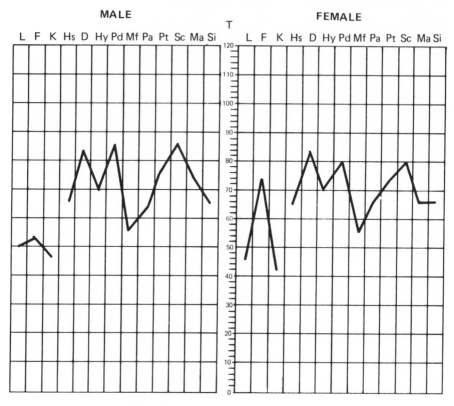

N = 10
Sex: Male 40%          Female 60%
Age: Average = 31.0    Range: 19–42
WAIS IQ:   VS  106     Range: 93–116
           PS  106     Range: 83–124
           FS  106     Range: 88–113

Modal ego level: Self-protective/Conformist 60%
Other ego levels:
   Conformist: 30%
   Conformist/Conscientious: 10%

*248 code:* Patients of this profile type were a bit more likely to be female than the average patient sample; but, like the average patient, they tended to have a mean IQ in the average range. Their age was a bit lower than the general sample. These patients as a group had a below-average ego development, with their modal level of ego development being in the transition state from hedonism to conformity. They reported a very high incidence of psychosocial stressors in the year preceding hospitalization, with more than average changes in living conditions. Additionally, they experienced changes in social activities; half reported changes in number of arguments with spouses. Nearly all told of changes in eating habits, and 100% reported sleep disturbance during the preceding year. Their social histories revealed a high incidence of temper tantrums, crying spells, and being easily upset as children. Forty percent had been adopted or raised by others than their natural parents. One third reported failing an entire grade in school. Nearly half reported a history of drug problems, and nearly two thirds reported chronic illnesses, major handicaps, or other health problems. Regarding their reasons for seeking assistance, half stated bluntly that drug problems had brought them in.

Diagnostically, patients of this profile type tend to fall into three groups: one third with an affective disorder (major depression or dysthymic); one third had adjustment disorders with either depressed mood or mixed emotional features; and one third had substance abuse as their primary diagnosis. However, when primary and secondary diagnoses are combined, 70% were diagnosed as having substance abuse problems. The personality disorders of these patients tended to cluster in the area of dramatic, emotional, or erratic personality disorders (histrionic and, to a lesser extent, borderline).

## 268 CODE

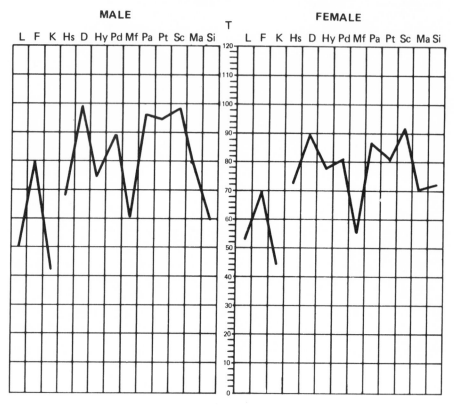

N = 6
Sex: Male 33%            Female 67%
Age: Average = 42.7      Range: 26–60
WAIS IQ:   VS  96        Range: 84–103
           PS  96        Range: 78–105
           FS  95        Range: 80–104

Modal ego level: Conformity 50%
Other ego levels:
    Self-protective/Conformist: 33%
    Conformist-Conscientious: 17%

*Code type 268:* Patients of this profile type were slightly more apt to be female than the general patients sample. The intellect tended to be a bit below-average than the general patient sample, but still within the average range. These patients were a bit less likely than the general sample to be at the conformity level, with only half reporting an overall level of emotional development at the conformity level. One third were seen as below average and one third above the conformity level. These patients had a high incidence of medication usage, with 80% discharged on medication. The primary medications were in the antidepressant category, either tetracyclics or tricyclics. These patients reported a marked incidence of psychosocial stressors for the year preceding their hospitalization and were especially likely to have experienced sleep difficulties, death of a close friend, change in number of arguments with spouse, change in living conditions, change in their eating habits, problems with their bosses, major change in work hours, major change in health or behavior of a family member, revision of personal habits, and gaining a new family member. In other words, a change had occurred in high rates in all major life areas–marriage and family, occupational, and interpersonal. The social histories of these patients revealed that they had a higher incidence of previous marriages. One of these patients reported difficulties in caring for the children; one in six had physically handicapped children. Only half the patients of this profile type reported working outside the home. They were also quite likely to have had childhood histories of crying spells and sickness. These patients had a higher-than-average amount of school difficulties and were high in reporting learning problems, difficulty making friends at school, and histories of school failure. Half the patient sample had an arrest record, and a half had had previous psychiatric hospitalization.

Diagnostically, half the patients of this profile type were seen as having adjustment disorders with depressed mood; the next major cluster was major affective disorders. Their underlying personality was bimodally distributed between histrionic or avoidant personalitites.

## 278 CODE

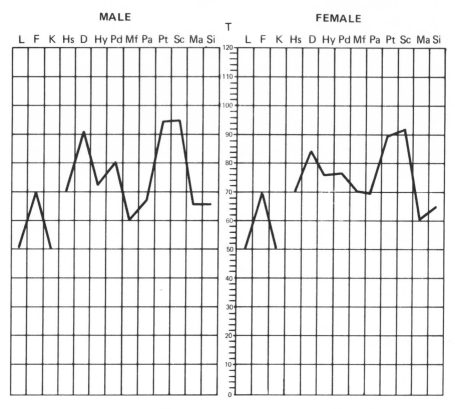

N = 25
Sex: Male 60 %              Female 40%
Age: Average = 38.96       Range: 18–67
WAIS IQ:   VS  100         Range: 70–125
           PS  100         Range: 72–123
           FS  100         Range: 74–122

Modal ego level: Conformity 92%
Other ego levels:
    Self-protective/Conformist: 8%

*278 code:* Patients of this profile type were a bit more apt to be male than female. Their mean intellect was in the average range, as was the general patient sample, and they did not differ significantly on the basis of age from the general patient sample. These patients were a bit more apt to be conformists than anything else, with only a small minority seen as below average in their overall level of ego-conscience development. As a general patient sample, these patients had incurred a high amount of psychosocial stressors in the year preceding their hospitalization; but regarding the nature of the stressors, they were only significantly different from the general patient sample in reporting a very high incidence of sleep disturbance. The social histories of these patients was, by and large, not significant from the general patient sample regarding history and problem areas. A full third of these patients reported depression or suicide attempts as the reason for seeking psychotherapeutic assistance. The overwhelming majority of patients of this profile type (80%) were discharged on medication, with slightly over half discharged on tricyclic antidepressants. The bulk of the remainder were on neuroleptics.

Diagnostically, roughly two thirds of the patients of this profile type were seen as psychotic, evidencing major depression, bipolar disorder, or schizoaffective disorder. One in eight received either a substance abuse disorder as either their primary or secondary disorder classification. The remainder were seen as anxiety or adjustment disorders. The overwhelming majority of patients of this profile type tend to cluster in the personality disorder category of anxious or fearful personality disorders (compulsive, avoidant, dependent, or passive-aggressive). In general, this profile type is a remarkably consistent profile, with these patients being seen as moderately to severely depressed individuals who are chronically anxious and worried.

## 289 CODE

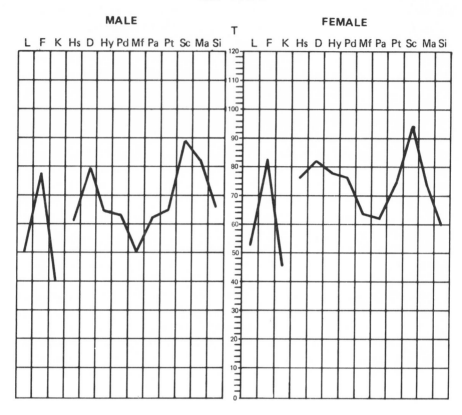

N = 7
Sex: Male 71%              Female 29%
Age: Average = 30.7        Range: 18–38
WAIS IQ:   VS  104         Range: 87–117
           PS   99         Range: 74–120
           FS  102         Range: 81–120

Modal ego level: Conformity 43%
Other ego levels:
    Conformist-Conscientious: 14%
    Self-protective/Conformist: 43%

*289 code:* Patients of this profile type were more apt to be male and almost half were below average in their overall level of ego-conscience development. These patients tended to resemble the general sample in that their IQ was in the average range, but their age level was a bit lower than the general sample. Like the general patient sample, these patients reported a high incidence of psychosocial stressors during the year preceding their hospitalization. They were more apt to report a change in living conditions, pregnancy in themselves or spouse; all reported sleep disturbance. They were less likely than the general sample to have problems with their bosses in the preceding year. The social histories of these patients revealed a significant minority on disability. These patients were quite apt to have had few friends as children and adolescents and no dating as teenagers. They had frequent temper tantrums and crying spells as children, as well as easily becoming upset. All these patients were reared by their natural parents. They were somewhat high in reporting histories of being arrested. They were also high in reporting health problems; their health complaints included back problems, asthma, and gynecological problems. The overwhelming majority of patients of this profile type were discharged on psychoactive medication, with almost half discharged on neuroleptics and a third discharged on tricyclic antidepressants.

Diagnostically, almost half the patients of this profile type were seen as psychotic and evidencing a schizoaffective disorder or major depression. Almost a third were seen as having an organic mental disorder as the primary diagnosis; one fourth received substance abuse disorder as their primary or secondary diagnostic category. Over half the patients of this profile type had their personality disorder deferred because it was obscured by, or their problems limited to, their primary disorder. The remainder were all seen as clustering in the personality disorder category of anxious and fearful personality disorders (avoidant, dependent, or passive-aggressive).

# 468 CODE

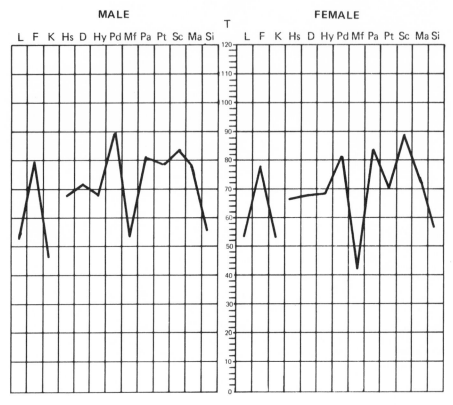

N = 7
Sex: Male 14%            Female 86%
Age:Average =  33.4      Range: 25–45
WAIS IQ:   VS  110       Range: 83–102
           PS  113       Range: 89–101
           FS  111       Range: 90–100

Modal ego level: Conformity 86%
Other ego levels:
   Self-protective/Conformist: 14%

*468 code:* Patients of this profile type are primarily female and tended to be a bit higher in intellect than the general sample, with their average IQ in the bright–normal range. These patients tended to resemble the general sample, with the average age range in the late 30's. Their overall level of emotional development is generally at the conformity level, and this is not generally significant from the general sample. Slightly more than a third were discharged on medication, and this resembled the general sample. These patients tended to report a very high amount of psychosocial stressors for the preceding year over and above that of the average patient; they were especially high in reporting occupational difficulties, i.e., trouble with the boss and major change in working hours or conditions. They also revealed a high incidence of revision of personal habits, change in number of arguments with spouse, and major personal illness or injury for the year preceding seeking psychiatric assistance. Their social histories included a high incidence of marital unhappiness; nearly a third of these patients reported a history of recent affairs. All were employed. Their childhood histories revealed frequent temper tantrums and difficulty making friends as children. Almost one half the patients of this profile type also revealed a history of school failure; this same number reported having been raised away from their natural parents. Over one half reported suicidal ideation or a suicide attempt as their reason for seeking psychiatric assistance.

Diagnostically, 42% of the patients of this profile type received substance abuse as their primary, secondary, or tertiary diagnosis. The modal primary diagnostic category was, however, adjustment disorder with either depressed mood or mixed emotional features; one third of the patients were seen as having a major affective disorder (bipolar disorder). These patients were homogenous in their personality disorders; all contained the common element of wariness, but ran the gamut of major personality clusters and included paranoid, schizotypal, borderline, and avoidant.

## 469 CODE

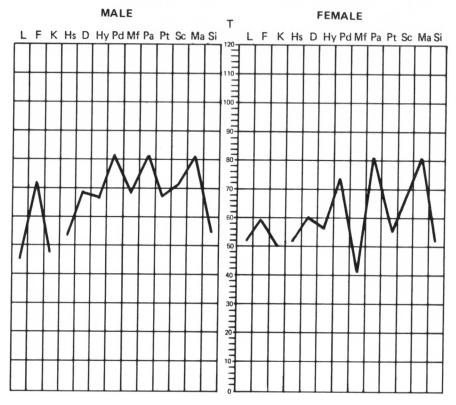

N = 8
Sex: Male 37%            Female 63%
Age: Average = 31.1      Range: 18–42
WAIS IQ:  VS  113        Range: 97–113
          PS  111        Range: 89–145
          FS  113        Range: 93–140

Modal ego level: Conformity 75%
Other ego levels:
   Conformist-Conscientious: 12%
   Self-protective/Conformist: 12%

*469 code:* Patients of this profile type tend to be a bit brighter than the average sample, having a mean IQ in the bright-normal range. They were slightly more likely to be female and, as with the general sample, these patients tended to have as their average level of ego development the conformity level. Their mean age a bit below the general patient sample and was in the early 30's. These patients were slightly more apt to be discharged on psychoactive medication; their primary medication category was that of neuroleptics. As with the general sample, these patients had high incidences of psychosocial stressors in the past year and were especially likely to report marital separation and marital reconciliation as psychosocial stressors. Their social histories revealed a low incidence of difficulty making friends in adolescence, as well as hyperactivity; otherwise, their social histories were unremarkable.

Diagnostically, half the patients of this profile type were seen as evidencing adjustment disorders with depressed mood or mixed emotional features. One third of the patients of this profile type were seen as having alcohol abuse problems. The underlying personality disorder was bimodal, in that these patients were seen as either paranoid or having personality disorders clustering in the anxious or fearful category (dependent or passive-aggressive).

## 478 CODE

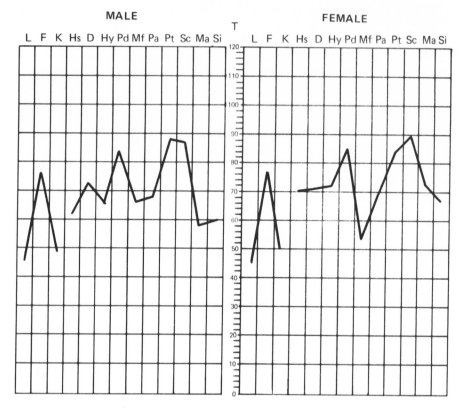

N = 15
Sex: Male 47%            Female 53%
Age: Average = 27.1      Range: 18-62
WAIS IQ:   VS  105       Range: 96-113
           PS  102       Range: 74-117
           FS  104       Range: 86-112

Modal ego level: Conformity 67%
Other ego levels:
    Self-protective/Conformist: 33%

*478 code:* Patients of this profile type were about evenly divided between men and women; in this factor as well as intellect, they resembled the general patient sample. They were much younger than the general patient sample and were of average intelligence. Their overall level of ego development was a bit below average, though this was not significant. Two thirds of the patients of this profile type tended to fall into the conformity level category of overall ego-emotional development, with the remaining two thirds falling at the transition state between hedonism and conformity. As with the general population, these patients were high in their incidences of psychosocial stressors for the year preceding seeking psychiatric assistance. They were especially apt to be newly weds, have job changes, experience changes in the health or behavior of a family member, and have sleep disturbances. They were low in reporting a history of outstanding personal achievements in the recent past. Their social histories revealed high incidences of marital unhappiness; however, these patients were less likely to have previous marriages. They were more apt than the general patient sample to be unemployed; not surprisingly, one third of the patients of this profile type experienced problems holding a job. They were also apt to have been sickly as children. The majority of this profile type reported histories of previous arrests. They were more apt than the general patient sample to have been on medication at the time of discharge, though no significant pattern of type of medication emerges.

Diagnostically, slightly over one fourth of the patients of this profile type were seen as psychotic and evidencing schizoaffective disorders or major depressions; one third were seen as having adjustment disorders with either depressed mood or mixed emotional features; another one third were diagnosed as having substance abuse as their primary or secondary diagnosis. The primary personality category of patients of this profile type was a cluster of dramatic, emotional, or erratic personality disorders (histrionic, antisocial, or borderline).

# 489 CODE

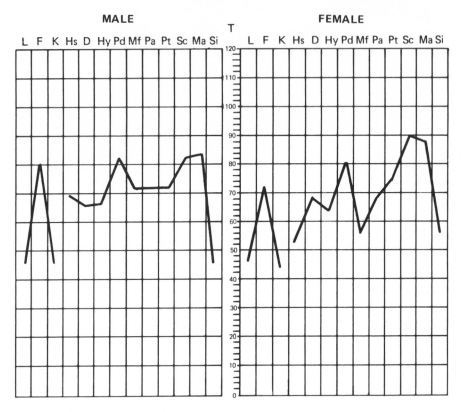

MALE      T      FEMALE

L  F  K  Hs  D  Hy Pd Mf Pa Pt Sc Ma Si     L  F  K  Hs  D  Hy Pd Mf Pa Pt Sc Ma Si

N = 6
Sex: Male 50%          Female 50%
Age: Average = 26.7    Range: 22-34
WAIS IQ:   VS  97      Range: 80-113
           PS  97      Range: 85-107
           FS  97      Range: 81-111

Modal ego level: Conformity 50%
Other ego levels:
    Self-protective/Conformist: 50%

*489 code:* Patients of this profile type were about evenly divided between men and women; they tended to be lower in age than the general sample. They were also a bit low in intellect, but were still within the average range as a mean. They were significantly lower in their overall level of ego-conscience development, with, half the patients below average in emotional development. One third were discharged on medication, which was not significantly different from the general patient sample. They reported a very high incidence of psychosocial stressors for the past year (higher than most patients). They were especially apt to report marital separations, foreclosure on a mortgage or loan, change in health or behavior of a family member, change in financial state, and change in working hours or conditions during the year preceding seeking psychotherapeutic assistance. Their social histories revealed a high incidence of arrests, with half these patients having an arrest record. They recalled frequent crying spells and being easily upset as children. The overwhelming majority of patients of this profile type had a history of family members with drinking problems and drug problems, as well as nervous breakdowns. None had been reared away from their natural parents. None were living with their spouses at the time of testing.

Diagnostically, these patients were bimodal in their primary diagnosis, with a third being seen as psychotic and evidencing either a major affective disorder (major depression) or a schizoaffective disorder. One third were seen as having adjustment disorders with mixed emotional features; one third received a diagnosis of drug abuse as their primary or secondary diagnosis. The modal personality category for patients of this profile type was dramatic, emotional, or erratic personality disorders (histrionic or antisocial).

# 678 CODE

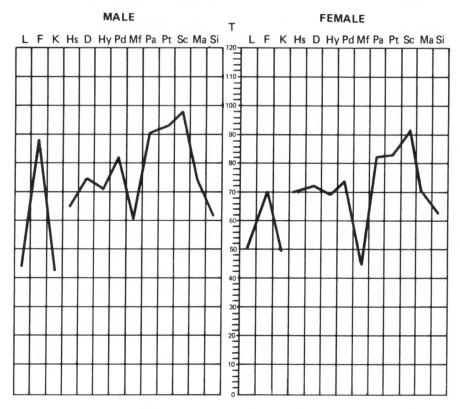

N = 9
Sex: Male 44%          Female 56%
Age: Average = 32.3    Range: 18-50
WAIS IQ:   VS  96      Range: 69-112
           PS  97      Range: 82-112
           FS  96      Range: 73-112

Modal ego level: Conformity 67%
Other ego levels:
   Self-protective/Conformist: 33%

*678 code:* Patients of this profile type were about evenly divided between men and women, with a mean age in the early 30's, which was somewhat lower than the general patient sample. They were, however, slightly lower in intellect than the general patient sample; however, their mean IQ was still within the average range. Like the general patient sample, these patients tended to have conformity levels of ego development. These patients had incurred a large amount of psychosocial stressors for the past year, especially in the area of work; the majority of these patients reported trouble with the boss, and major change in work responsibilities and a significant number reported a major change in working hours or conditions. These patients were also more apt than the general patient sample to have sleep disturbances, marital separations, change in number of arguments with spouses, and revision of personal habits within the preceding year. They were low, however, in revealing a change in financial state. Half the patients of this profile type again reported marital unhappiness on their social histories. All were employed. They were, however, quite apt to have failed a grade in school. None of these patients had ever been arrested. Few reported a major handicap or chronic illness. Over half stated their reason for seeking help as depression or suicide attempts.

Diagnostically, this was a bimodal distribution, with roughly half the patients of this profile type receiving a major affective disorder (major depression) as their primary diagnosis, with the other half receiving adjustment disorders with either depressed mood or mixed emotional features as their primary diagnosis. In terms of personality, this was a diffuse sample, with the majority being seen as either histrionic or passive-aggressive; however, schizotypal, paranoid, or avoidant personality disorders were reported in patients of this profile type.

## 689 CODE

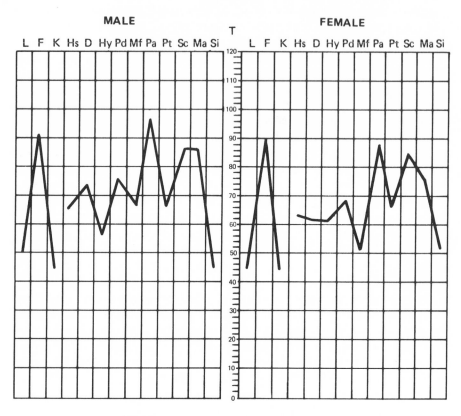

MALE   T   FEMALE

L F K Hs D Hy Pd Mf Pa Pt Sc Ma Si  L F K Hs D Hy Pd Mf Pa Pt Sc Ma Si

N = 8
Sex: Male 37%   Female 63%
Age: Average = 43.0  Range:
WAIS IQ: VS 87  Range: 71–106
    PS 85  Range: 72–99
    FS 87  Range: 75–98

Modal ego level: Conformity 63%
Other ego levels:
 Self-protective/Conformist: 25%
 Self-protective: 12%

*689 code:* Patients of this profile type were more apt to be female and somewhat older than the general patient sample. Their intellect was significantly lower than the general patient sample, with the mean IQ being in the dull-normal range. These patients were also apt to be a bit below average in their overall level of ego development, though the majority of these patients were still at the average-conformity level. These patients were apt to report slightly fewer psychosocial stressors for the preceding year than the general patient sample, though their overall level of psychosocial stressors was still fairly high. They tended to report a high number of deaths of close family members, gaining new family members, and in-law troubles during the year preceding psychiatric assistance. They were, however, low in revealing sexual difficulties, outstanding personal achievements, changes in financial state, and changes in residence. Patients of this profile type tended to be unemployed, though this may be partly because a significant number of females were in the sample. Few had been married previously, but they tended to have a high incidence of affairs, with one fourth seeing someone else outside their marriage at the time of seeking assistance. These patients were quite apt to have first and second-degree relatives with a history of mental illness. One third of these patients had been abused as children. A significant minority indicated they were seeking help at the request of family or friends.

Diagnostically, these patients tended to cluster into three main groups: one third were diagnosed with an organic mental disorder as their primary or secondary diagnostic category; one third received a diagnostic of adjustment disorder with either depressed mood or mixed emotional features as their primary or secondary diagnostic category. The majority of patients of this profile type had their personality disorder deferred, primarily because it was obscured by their primary diagnosis. The personality disorder classifications given were heterogeneous and spanned all three major clusters; they included schizotypal, histrionic, and passive-aggressive.

## 789 CODE

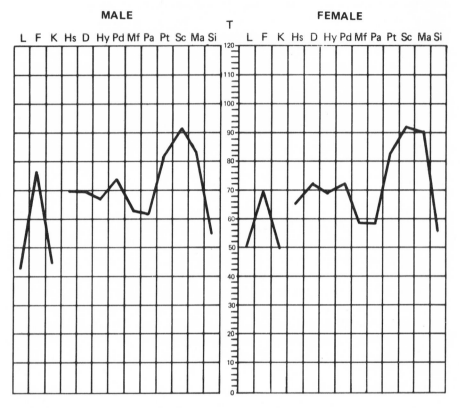

N = 6
Sex: Male 67%              Female 33%
Age: Average = 24.7       Range: 18–30
WAIS IQ:   VS  107         Range: 84–124
           PS  104         Range: 88–127
           FS  106         Range: 85–119

Modal ego level: Conformity 67%
Other ego levels:
   Self-protective/Conformist: 33%

*789 code:* Patients of this profile type were slightly more apt to be male. The mean age was significantly below that of the average patient, with these patients being in their twenties. Like the general patient sample, they tended to have average intelligence. Though the majority of patients of this profile type were seen as having an overall emotional maturity level at the conformity level, a fair minority were below average in their overall level of ego development. Patients of this profile type were quite apt to be discharged on medication, with a third being discharged on tricyclic antidepressants; one third were discharged on tricyclic antidepressants and one third on neuroleptics. These patients tended to have a high incidence of psychosocial stressors during the year preceding psychotherapeutic assistance, more so than the average patient. They were especially apt to experience trouble with the boss and change into a different line of work; they were also quite apt to report changes in number of arguments with their spouse. One half reported detention in jail or other institution; all revealed a change in financial state in the year preceding psychotherapeutic intervention. They were also high in reporting changes in eating habits and personal habits, as well as changes in the health or behavior of a family member. Two thirds of the patients of this profile type had sexual difficulties. Their social histories revealed low incidences of employment, with only one half working outside the home. These patients tended not to report being sickly as children. None had been reared away from their natural parents. They had a significant amount of drug abuse histories in the family of origin. Half these patients had been arrested. They were high in reporting drinking and drug problems in their histories. Half had been in psychotherapy on an outpatient basis in the past.

Diagnostically, the overwhelming majority of patients of this profile type received substance abuse as their primary or secondary diagnosis. The other major diagnostic category was adjustment disorder with depressed mood or mixed emotional features. This code had a bimodal distribution regarding personality disorders, with dramatic, emotional, or erratic personality disorders represented (antisocial or borderline). Anxious and fearful personality disorders were also represented in this code type, namely, avoidant or passive-aggressive.

(Use with The Psychological Corporation scoring keys)

# Raw Scale Score Conversion for the MMPI-168 for Adults[1]

### Table A1  Raw Scale Score Conversion For the MMPI-168[a]

| 168 Score | L | F | K | Hs | D | Hy | Pd | Mf | Pa | Pt | Sc | Ma | Si | 168 Score |
|---|---|---|---|---|---|---|---|---|---|---|---|---|---|---|
| 1 | 2 | 3 | 4 | 2 | 6 | 8 | 7 | 7 | 4 | 3 | 7 | 3 | 5 | 1 |
| 2 | 3 | 5 | 6 | 3 | 7 | 10 | 8 | 9 | 6 | 6 | 10 | 5 | 9 | 2 |
| 3 | 4 | 7 | 8 | 5 | 8 | 11 | 10 | 11 | 8 | 8 | 14 | 7 | 13 | 3 |
| 4 | 5 | 9 | 10 | 6 | 10 | 12 | 11 | 12 | 10 | 10 | 17 | 9 | 17 | 4 |
| 5 | 7 | 10 | 12 | 8 | 11 | 14 | 13 | 14 | 12 | 13 | 21 | 10 | 20 | 5 |
| 6 | 8 | 12 | 14 | 9 | 12 | 15 | 14 | 16 | 14 | 15 | 24 | 12 | 24 | 6 |
| 7 | 9 | 14 | 16 | 10 | 13 | 16 | 15 | 18 | 17 | 18 | 28 | 14 | 28 | 7 |
| 8 | 11 | 16 | 17 | 12 | 15 | 18 | 17 | 19 | 19 | 20 | 33 | 16 | 32 | 8 |
| 9 | 12 | 17 | 19 | 13 | 16 | 19 | 18 | 21 | 21 | 22 | 35 | 17 | 35 | 9 |
| 10 | 13 | 19 | 21 | 15 | 17 | 21 | 19 | 23 | 23 | 25 | 38 | 19 | 40 | 10 |
| 11 | 15 | 21 | 23 | 16 | 18 | 22 | 21 | 25 | 25 | 27 | 42 | 22 | 43 | 11 |
| 12 | | 23 | 25 | 17 | 20 | 23 | 22 | 27 | 27 | 29 | 45 | 23 | 47 | 12 |
| 13 | | 25 | | 19 | 21 | 25 | 23 | 28 | 29 | 34 | 49 | 25 | 51 | 13 |
| 14 | | 26 | | 20 | 22 | 26 | 25 | 30 | 33 | 34 | 53 | 26 | 54 | 14 |
| 15 | | 29 | | 22 | 24 | 27 | 26 | 32 | 34 | 37 | 56 | 28 | 58 | 15 |
| 16 | | 30 | | 23 | 25 | 29 | 28 | 34 | 36 | 40 | 60 | 30 | 61 | 16 |
| 17 | | 32 | | 24 | 26 | 30 | 29 | 35 | 38 | 41 | 63 | 31 | | 17 |
| 18 | | 33 | | 26 | 27 | 32 | 30 | 37 | | 44 | 67 | 33 | | 18 |
| 19 | | 35 | | 27 | 29 | 33 | 32 | 39 | | 46 | | 35 | | 19 |
| 20 | | 37 | | 28 | 30 | 34 | 33 | 41 | | | | 37 | | 20 |
| 21 | | 39 | | 30 | 31 | 36 | 34 | 43 | | | | 39 | | 21 |
| 22 | | 40 | | 31 | 32 | 37 | 36 | 44 | | | | 41 | | 22 |
| 23 | | 42 | | 33 | 34 | 38 | 37 | 46 | | | | 42 | | 23 |
| 24 | | 44 | | | 35 | 40 | 39 | 48 | | | | | | 24 |
| 25 | | 46 | | | 36 | 41 | 40 | 50 | | | | | | 25 |
| 26 | | 47 | | | 37 | 42 | 41 | 51 | | | | | | 26 |
| 27 | | 49 | | | 39 | 44 | 43 | 53 | | | | | | 27 |
| 28 | | 51 | | | 40 | 45 | 44 | 55 | | | | | | 28 |
| 29 | | 53 | | | 41 | 47 | | 57 | | | | | | 29 |
| 30 | | 54 | | | 42 | 48 | | 59 | | | | | | 30 |
| 31 | | 56 | | | 44 | 49 | | | | | | | | 31 |
| 32 | | | | | 45 | 50 | | | | | | | | 32 |
| 33 | | | | | 46 | 52 | | | | | | | | 33 |
| 34 | | | | | | 53 | | | | | | | | 34 |
| 35 | | | | | | 55 | | | | | | | | 35 |
| 36 | | | | | | 56 | | | | | | | | 36 |

[a] Equivalent MMPI Raw Scale Scores rounded to the nearest whole number.

[1] Overall, Higgins, & DeSchweintz, A. (1976, p. 244; reprinted with permission).

(Use with NCS scoring keys)

# Raw Scale Score Conversion for the MMPI-168 for Adults[1,2]

### Table A-1.1  Raw Scale Score Conversion for the MMPI-168[a]

| 168 Score | L | F | K | Hs | D | Hy | Pd | Mf | Pa | Pt | Sc | Ma | Si | 168 Score |
|---|---|---|---|---|---|---|---|---|---|---|---|---|---|---|
| 1 | 2 | 3 | 4 | 2 | 6 | 8 | 7 | 7 | 4 | 3 | 3 | 3 | 5 | 1 |
| 2 | 3 | 5 | 6 | 3 | 7 | 10 | 8 | 9 | 6 | 6 | 5 | 5 | 9 | 2 |
| 3 | 4 | 7 | 8 | 5 | 8 | 11 | 10 | 11 | 8 | 8 | 8 | 7 | 13 | 3 |
| 4 | 5 | 9 | 10 | 6 | 10 | 12 | 11 | 12 | 10 | 10 | 10 | 9 | 17 | 4 |
| 5 | 7 | 10 | 12 | 8 | 11 | 14 | 13 | 14 | 11 | 13 | 12 | 10 | 20 | 5 |
| 6 | 8 | 12 | 14 | 9 | 12 | 15 | 14 | 16 | 13 | 15 | 15 | 12 | 24 | 6 |
| 7 | 9 | 14 | 16 | 10 | 13 | 16 | 15 | 18 | 15 | 18 | 17 | 14 | 28 | 7 |
| 8 | 11 | 16 | 17 | 12 | 15 | 18 | 17 | 19 | 17 | 20 | 19 | 16 | 32 | 8 |
| 9 | 12 | 17 | 19 | 13 | 16 | 19 | 18 | 21 | 19 | 22 | 21 | 17 | 35 | 9 |
| 10 | 13 | 19 | 21 | 15 | 17 | 21 | 19 | 23 | 21 | 25 | 24 | 19 | 40 | 10 |
| 11 | 15 | 21 | 23 | 16 | 18 | 22 | 21 | 25 | 23 | 27 | 26 | 22 | 43 | 11 |
| 12 | | 23 | 25 | 17 | 20 | 23 | 22 | 27 | 24 | 29 | 28 | 23 | 47 | 12 |
| 13 | | 25 | | 19 | 21 | 25 | 23 | 28 | 26 | 34 | 31 | 25 | 51 | 13 |
| 14 | | 26 | | 20 | 22 | 26 | 25 | 30 | 28 | 34 | 33 | 26 | 54 | 14 |
| 15 | | 29 | | 22 | 24 | 27 | 26 | 32 | 30 | 37 | 35 | 28 | 58 | 15 |
| 16 | | 30 | | 23 | 25 | 29 | 28 | 34 | 32 | 40 | 38 | 30 | 61 | 16 |
| 17 | | 32 | | 24 | 26 | 30 | 29 | 35 | 34 | 41 | 40 | 31 | | 17 |
| 18 | | 33 | | 26 | 27 | 32 | 30 | 37 | 36 | 44 | 42 | 33 | | 18 |
| 19 | | 35 | | 27 | 29 | 33 | 32 | 39 | 38 | 46 | 44 | 35 | | 19 |
| 20 | | 37 | | 28 | 30 | 34 | 33 | 41 | | | 47 | 37 | | 20 |
| 21 | | 39 | | 30 | 31 | 36 | 34 | 43 | | | 49 | 39 | | 21 |
| 22 | | 40 | | 31 | 32 | 37 | 36 | 44 | | | 51 | 41 | | 22 |
| 23 | | 42 | | 33 | 34 | 38 | 37 | 46 | | | 54 | 42 | | 23 |
| 24 | | 44 | | | 35 | 40 | 39 | 48 | | | 56 | | | 24 |
| 25 | | 46 | | | 36 | 41 | 40 | 50 | | | 58 | | | 25 |
| 26 | | 47 | | | 37 | 42 | 41 | 51 | | | 61 | | | 26 |
| 27 | | 49 | | | 39 | 44 | 43 | 53 | | | 63 | | | 27 |
| 28 | | 51 | | | 40 | 45 | 44 | 55 | | | 65 | | | 28 |
| 29 | | 53 | | | 41 | 47 | | 57 | | | | | | 29 |
| 30 | | 54 | | | 42 | 48 | | 59 | | | | | | 30 |
| 31 | | 56 | | | 44 | 49 | | | | | | | | 31 |
| 32 | | | | | 45 | 50 | | | | | | | | 32 |
| 33 | | | | | 46 | 52 | | | | | | | | 33 |
| 34 | | | | | | 53 | | | | | | | | 34 |
| 35 | | | | | | 55 | | | | | | | | 35 |
| 36 | | | | | | 56 | | | | | | | | 36 |

[a] Equivalent MMPI Raw Scale Scores rounded to the nearest whole number.

[1] Overall, Higgins, & DeSchweintz, A. (1976, p. 244; reprinted with permission).
[2] Pa and Sc conversions courtesy of Dr. L. Charles Ward.

# APPENDIX B

### (Use with The Psychological Corporation scoring keys)

# Raw Scale Score Conversion Tables for the MMPI-168 for Adolescents Ages 17 and Below (without K corrections)[1]

**Table B1  Raw Scale Score Conversion for the MMPI-168 for Female Adolescents Age 14 and Below (Without K Corrections)[a]**

| 168 Score | L | F | K | Hs | D | Hy | Pd | Mf | Pa | Pt | Sc | Ma | Si | 168 Score |
|---|---|---|---|---|---|---|---|---|---|---|---|---|---|---|
| 33 | | | | | 108 | | | | | | | | | 33 |
| 32 | | | | | 106 | 120 | | | | | | | | 32 |
| 31 | | | | | 104 | 115 | | | | | | | | 31 |
| 30 | | | | | 99 | 113 | | | | | | | | 30 |
| 29 | | | | | 97 | 111 | | | | | | | | 29 |
| 28 | | | | | 95 | 106 | 109 | | | | | | | 28 |
| 27 | | | | | 93 | 104 | 107 | | | | | | | 27 |
| 26 | | | | | 89 | 100 | 104 | | | | | | | 26 |
| 25 | | | | | 87 | 98 | 100 | | | | | | | 25 |
| 24 | | | | | 85 | 95 | 98 | 22 | | | | 104 | | 24 |
| 23 | | 118 | | | 83 | 91 | 94 | 26 | | | | 104 | | 23 |
| 22 | | 113 | | | 78 | 89 | 92 | 31 | | | | 102 | | 22 |
| 21 | | 111 | | | 76 | 86 | 87 | 33 | | | | 98 | | 21 |
| 20 | | 106 | | | 74 | 82 | 85 | 37 | | | | 94 | | 20 |
| 19 | | 104 | | | 72 | 80 | 83 | 42 | | 94 | | 89 | | 19 |
| 18 | | 119 | | 101 | 68 | 78 | 79 | 46 | | 92 | 144 | 85 | | 18 |
| 17 | | 114 | | 96 | 66 | 73 | 76 | 51 | 110 | 87 | 109 | 83 | | 17 |
| 16 | | 111 | | 94 | 64 | 71 | 74 | 53 | 106 | 84 | 106 | 79 | 92 | 16 |
| 15 | | 106 | | 91 | 62 | 66 | 70 | 57 | 102 | 80 | 101 | 77 | 87 | 15 |
| 14 | | 101 | | 86 | 57 | 64 | 68 | 62 | 99 | 77 | 97 | 70 | 82 | 14 |
| 13 | | 99 | | 84 | 55 | 62 | 64 | 66 | 91 | 77 | 92 | 68 | 78 | 13 |
| 12 | | 94 | 76 | 79 | 53 | 58 | 61 | 68 | 86 | 72 | 87 | 64 | 73 | 12 |
| 11 | 101 | 89 | 71 | 76 | 49 | 55 | 59 | 73 | 82 | 67 | 84 | 60 | 68 | 11 |
| 10 | 97 | 84 | 67 | 74 | 47 | 53 | 55 | 77 | 78 | 64 | 79 | 56 | 63 | 10 |
| 9 | 87 | 79 | 62 | 69 | 45 | 49 | 53 | 81 | 73 | 60 | 75 | 51 | 58 | 9 |
| 8 | 83 | 76 | 58 | 66 | 43 | 46 | 51 | 86 | 69 | 57 | 73 | 49 | 54 | 8 |
| 7 | 73 | 71 | 56 | 61 | 38 | 42 | 46 | 88 | 65 | 54 | 67 | 45 | 49 | 7 |
| 6 | 69 | 66 | 51 | 59 | 36 | 40 | 44 | 92 | 58 | 50 | 62 | 41 | 44 | 6 |
| 5 | 64 | 61 | 47 | 56 | 34 | 38 | 42 | 97 | 54 | 47 | 58 | 37 | 39 | 5 |
| 4 | 55 | 59 | 42 | 51 | 32 | 33 | 38 | 100 | 49 | 43 | 53 | 35 | 35 | 4 |
| 3 | 50 | 54 | 38 | 49 | 28 | 31 | 36 | 102 | 45 | 40 | 49 | 30 | 30 | 3 |
| 2 | 46 | 49 | 33 | 44 | 26 | 29 | 31 | 107 | 40 | 37 | 45 | 26 | 25 | 2 |
| 1 | 41 | 44 | 29 | 41 | 24 | 24 | 29 | 111 | 36 | 33 | 41 | 22 | 20 | 1 |

[a] Equivalent MMPI T-Scores rounded to the nearest whole number.

[1] Vincent (1980c)

# Raw Scale Score Conversion Tables for the MMPI-168 for Adolescents Ages 17 and Below (without K corrections)

Table B-1.1  Raw Scale Score Conversion for the MMPI-168 for Female Adolescents Age 14 and Below (Without K Corrections)[a]

| 168 Score | L | F | K | Hs | D | Hy | Pd | Mf | Pa | Pt | Sc | Ma | Si | 168 Score |
|---|---|---|---|---|---|---|---|---|---|---|---|---|---|---|
| 33 |  |  |  |  | 108 |  |  |  |  |  |  |  |  | 33 |
| 32 |  |  |  |  | 106 | 120 |  |  |  |  |  |  |  | 32 |
| 31 |  |  |  |  | 104 | 115 |  |  |  |  |  |  |  | 31 |
| 30 |  |  |  |  | 99 | 113 |  |  |  |  |  |  |  | 30 |
| 29 |  |  |  |  | 97 | 111 |  |  |  |  |  |  |  | 29 |
| 28 |  |  |  |  | 95 | 106 | 109 |  |  |  | 112 |  |  | 28 |
| 27 |  |  |  |  | 93 | 104 | 107 |  |  |  | 109 |  |  | 27 |
| 26 |  |  |  |  | 89 | 100 | 104 |  |  |  | 107 |  |  | 26 |
| 25 |  |  |  |  | 87 | 98 | 100 |  |  |  | 103 |  |  | 25 |
| 24 |  |  |  |  | 85 | 95 | 98 | 22 |  |  | 101 |  |  | 24 |
| 23 |  |  |  | 118 | 83 | 91 | 94 | 26 |  |  | 98 | 104 |  | 23 |
| 22 |  |  |  | 113 | 78 | 89 | 92 | 31 |  |  | 95 | 102 |  | 22 |
| 21 |  |  |  | 111 | 76 | 86 | 87 | 33 |  |  | 92 | 98 |  | 21 |
| 20 |  |  |  | 106 | 74 | 82 | 85 | 37 |  |  | 90 | 94 |  | 20 |
| 19 |  |  |  | 104 | 72 | 80 | 83 | 42 | 110 | 94 | 86 | 89 |  | 19 |
| 18 |  | 119 |  | 101 | 68 | 78 | 79 | 46 | 106 | 92 | 84 | 85 |  | 18 |
| 17 |  | 114 |  | 96 | 66 | 73 | 76 | 51 | 102 | 87 | 81 | 83 |  | 17 |
| 16 |  | 111 |  | 94 | 64 | 71 | 74 | 53 | 97 | 84 | 79 | 79 | 92 | 16 |
| 15 |  | 106 |  | 91 | 62 | 66 | 70 | 57 | 93 | 80 | 75 | 77 | 87 | 15 |
| 14 |  | 101 |  | 86 | 57 | 64 | 68 | 62 | 89 | 77 | 73 | 70 | 82 | 14 |
| 13 |  | 99 |  | 84 | 55 | 62 | 64 | 66 | 84 | 77 | 70 | 68 | 78 | 13 |
| 12 |  | 94 | 76 | 79 | 53 | 58 | 61 | 68 | 80 | 72 | 67 | 64 | 73 | 12 |
| 11 | 101 | 89 | 71 | 76 | 49 | 55 | 59 | 73 | 78 | 67 | 64 | 60 | 68 | 11 |
| 10 | 97 | 84 | 67 | 74 | 47 | 53 | 55 | 77 | 73 | 64 | 62 | 56 | 63 | 10 |
| 9 | 87 | 79 | 62 | 69 | 45 | 49 | 53 | 81 | 69 | 60 | 58 | 51 | 58 | 9 |
| 8 | 83 | 76 | 58 | 66 | 43 | 46 | 51 | 86 | 65 | 57 | 56 | 49 | 54 | 8 |
| 7 | 73 | 71 | 56 | 61 | 38 | 42 | 46 | 88 | 60 | 54 | 53 | 45 | 49 | 7 |
| 6 | 69 | 66 | 51 | 59 | 36 | 40 | 44 | 92 | 56 | 50 | 51 | 41 | 44 | 6 |
| 5 | 64 | 61 | 47 | 56 | 34 | 38 | 42 | 97 | 51 | 47 | 47 | 37 | 39 | 5 |
| 4 | 55 | 59 | 42 | 51 | 32 | 33 | 38 | 100 | 49 | 43 | 43 | 35 | 35 | 4 |
| 3 | 50 | 54 | 38 | 49 | 28 | 31 | 36 | 102 | 45 | 40 | 42 | 30 | 30 | 3 |
| 2 | 46 | 49 | 33 | 44 | 26 | 29 | 31 | 107 | 40 | 37 | 38 | 26 | 25 | 2 |
| 1 | 41 | 44 | 29 | 41 | 24 | 24 | 29 | 111 | 36 | 33 | 36 | 22 | 20 | 1 |

[a] Equivalent MMPI T-Scores rounded to the nearest whole number.

Table B-2  Raw Scale Score Conversion for the MMPI-168
for Male Adolescents Age 14 and Below
(Without K Corrections)[a]—Psychological Corporation Scoring Keys

| 168 Score | L | F | K | Hs | D | Hy | Pd | Mf | Pa | Pt | Sc | Ma | Si | 168 Score |
|---|---|---|---|---|---|---|---|---|---|---|---|---|---|---|
| 33 | | | | | 112 | | | | | | | | | 33 |
| 32 | | | | | 110 | | | | | | | | | 32 |
| 31 | | | | | 108 | 120 | | | | | | | | 31 |
| 30 | | | | | 103 | 118 | | | | | | | | 30 |
| 29 | | | | | 101 | 115 | | | | | | | | 29 |
| 28 | | | | | 99 | 111 | 111 | | | | | | | 28 |
| 27 | | | | | 97 | 109 | 109 | | | | | | | 27 |
| 26 | | | | | 92 | 104 | 104 | | | | | | | 26 |
| 25 | | | | | 90 | 102 | 102 | 119 | | | | | | 25 |
| 24 | | | | | 88 | 100 | 100 | 114 | | | | | | 24 |
| 23 | | 119 | | | 86 | 95 | 95 | 109 | | | | 98 | | 23 |
| 22 | | 115 | | | 81 | 93 | 93 | 105 | | | | 96 | | 22 |
| 21 | | 113 | | 123 | 79 | 91 | 88 | 102 | | | | 92 | | 21 |
| 20 | | 109 | | 117 | 77 | 87 | 86 | 98 | | | | 88 | | 20 |
| 19 | | 105 | | 114 | 75 | 84 | 83 | 93 | | 93 | | 84 | | 19 |
| 18 | | 101 | | 111 | 70 | 82 | 79 | 88 | | 91 | 104 | 80 | | 18 |
| 17 | | 97 | | 105 | 68 | 78 | 76 | 83 | | 86 | 100 | 78 | | 17 |
| 16 | | 95 | | 102 | 66 | 75 | 74 | 81 | 120 | 84 | 97 | 74 | 95 | 16 |
| 15 | | 91 | | 99 | 63 | 73 | 69 | 76 | 114 | 80 | 92 | 70 | 89 | 15 |
| 14 | | 87 | | 93 | 59 | 69 | 67 | 72 | 112 | 77 | 89 | 66 | 84 | 14 |
| 13 | | 85 | | 90 | 57 | 67 | 62 | 67 | 101 | 77 | 85 | 65 | 80 | 13 |
| 12 | | 81 | 74 | 84 | 55 | 62 | 60 | 65 | 95 | 71 | 81 | 60 | 75 | 12 |
| 11 | 105 | 77 | 70 | 82 | 50 | 60 | 58 | 60 | 90 | 67 | 77 | 56 | 69 | 11 |
| 10 | 95 | 73 | 66 | 79 | 48 | 58 | 53 | 55 | 84 | 65 | 73 | 52 | 64 | 10 |
| 9 | 90 | 70 | 62 | 73 | 46 | 53 | 51 | 50 | 79 | 60 | 70 | 49 | 58 | 9 |
| 8 | 85 | 68 | 58 | 70 | 43 | 51 | 49 | 46 | 74 | 58 | 68 | 47 | 54 | 8 |
| 7 | 76 | 64 | 56 | 64 | 39 | 47 | 44 | 43 | 68 | 55 | 62 | 43 | 49 | 7 |
| 6 | 71 | 60 | 52 | 61 | 37 | 44 | 42 | 38 | 60 | 51 | 58 | 39 | 43 | 6 |
| 5 | 66 | 56 | 48 | 58 | 35 | 42 | 39 | 34 | 55 | 48 | 55 | 35 | 38 | 5 |
| 4 | 56 | 54 | 43 | 52 | 32 | 38 | 35 | 29 | 49 | 44 | 51 | 33 | 34 | 4 |
| 3 | 51 | 50 | 39 | 49 | 28 | 36 | 32 | 27 | 44 | 41 | 47 | 29 | 28 | 3 |
| 2 | 46 | 46 | 35 | 43 | 26 | 33 | 28 | 22 | 38 | 38 | 43 | 25 | 23 | 2 |
| 1 | 42 | 42 | 31 | 40 | 23 | 29 | 25 | 20 | 33 | 34 | 40 | 21 | 20 | 1 |

[a]Equivalent MMPI T-Scores rounded to the nearest whole number.

Table B-1.2  Raw Scale Score Conversion for the MMPI-168
for Male Adolescents Age 14 and Below (Without K Corrections)[a]
—NCS Scoring Keys

| 168 Score | L | F | K | Hs | D | Hy | Pd | Mf | Pa | Pt | Sc | Ma | Si | 168 Score |
|---|---|---|---|---|---|---|---|---|---|---|---|---|---|---|
| 33 | | | | 112 | | | | | | | | | | 33 |
| 32 | | | | 110 | | | | | | | | | | 32 |
| 31 | | | | 108 | 120 | | | | | | | | | 31 |
| 30 | | | | 103 | 118 | | | | | | | | | 30 |
| 29 | | | | 101 | 115 | | | | | | | | | 29 |
| 28 | | | | 99 | 111 | 111 | | | | | 102 | | | 28 |
| 27 | | | | 97 | 109 | 109 | | | | | 100 | | | 27 |
| 26 | | | | 92 | 104 | 104 | | | | | 98 | | | 26 |
| 25 | | | | 90 | 102 | 102 | 119 | | | | 95 | | | 25 |
| 24 | | | | 88 | 100 | 100 | 114 | | | | 92 | | | 24 |
| 23 | | 119 | | 86 | 95 | 95 | 109 | | | | 90 | 98 | | 23 |
| 22 | | 115 | | 81 | 93 | 93 | 105 | | | | 87 | 96 | | 22 |
| 21 | | 113 | | 123 | 79 | 91 | 88 | 102 | | | 85 | 92 | | 21 |
| 20 | | 109 | | 117 | 77 | 87 | 86 | 98 | | | 83 | 88 | | 20 |
| 19 | | 105 | | 114 | 75 | 84 | 83 | 93 | | 93 | 80 | 84 | | 19 |
| 18 | | 101 | | 111 | 70 | 82 | 79 | 88 | 120 | 91 | 77 | 80 | | 18 |
| 17 | | 97 | | 105 | 68 | 78 | 76 | 83 | 114 | 86 | 75 | 78 | | 17 |
| 16 | | 95 | | 102 | 66 | 75 | 74 | 81 | 109 | 84 | 73 | 74 | 95 | 16 |
| 15 | | 91 | | 99 | 63 | 73 | 69 | 76 | 104 | 80 | 70 | 70 | 89 | 15 |
| 14 | | 87 | | 93 | 59 | 69 | 67 | 72 | 98 | 77 | 68 | 66 | 84 | 14 |
| 13 | | 85 | | 90 | 57 | 67 | 62 | 67 | 93 | 77 | 66 | 65 | 80 | 13 |
| 12 | | 81 | 74 | 84 | 55 | 62 | 60 | 65 | 87 | 71 | 62 | 60 | 75 | 12 |
| 11 | 105 | 77 | 70 | 82 | 50 | 60 | 58 | 60 | 84 | 67 | 60 | 56 | 69 | 11 |
| 10 | 95 | 73 | 66 | 79 | 48 | 58 | 53 | 55 | 79 | 65 | 58 | 52 | 64 | 10 |
| 9 | 90 | 70 | 62 | 73 | 46 | 53 | 51 | 50 | 74 | 60 | 55 | 49 | 58 | 9 |
| 8 | 85 | 68 | 58 | 70 | 43 | 51 | 49 | 46 | 68 | 58 | 53 | 47 | 54 | 8 |
| 7 | 76 | 64 | 56 | 64 | 39 | 47 | 44 | 43 | 63 | 55 | 51 | 43 | 49 | 7 |
| 6 | 71 | 60 | 52 | 61 | 37 | 44 | 42 | 38 | 57 | 51 | 48 | 39 | 43 | 6 |
| 5 | 66 | 56 | 48 | 58 | 35 | 42 | 39 | 34 | 52 | 48 | 45 | 35 | 38 | 5 |
| 4 | 56 | 54 | 43 | 52 | 32 | 38 | 35 | 29 | 49 | 44 | 43 | 33 | 34 | 4 |
| 3 | 51 | 50 | 39 | 49 | 28 | 36 | 32 | 27 | 44 | 41 | 41 | 29 | 28 | 3 |
| 2 | 46 | 46 | 35 | 43 | 26 | 33 | 28 | 22 | 38 | 38 | 37 | 25 | 23 | 2 |
| 1 | 42 | 42 | 31 | 40 | 23 | 29 | 25 | 20 | 33 | 34 | 34 | 21 | 20 | 1 |

[a]Equivalent MMPI T-Scores rounded to the nearest whole number.

Table B-3  Raw Scale Score Conversion for the MMPI-168
for Female Adolescents Age 15
(Without K Corrections)[a]—Psychological Corporation Scoring Keys

| 168 Score | L | F | K | Hs | D | Hy | Pd | Mf | Pa | Pt | Sc | Ma | Si | 168 Score |
|---|---|---|---|---|---|---|---|---|---|---|---|---|---|---|
| 33 |  |  |  | 108 | 115 |  |  |  |  |  |  |  |  | 33 |
| 32 |  |  |  | 106 | 113 |  |  |  |  |  |  |  |  | 32 |
| 31 |  |  |  | 103 | 111 |  |  |  |  |  |  |  |  | 31 |
| 30 |  |  |  | 99 | 107 |  |  |  |  |  |  |  |  | 30 |
| 29 |  |  |  | 97 | 105 |  |  |  |  |  |  |  |  | 29 |
| 28 |  |  |  | 95 | 101 | 105 |  |  |  |  |  |  |  | 28 |
| 27 |  |  |  | 93 | 99 | 103 |  |  |  |  |  |  |  | 27 |
| 26 |  |  |  | 88 | 95 | 99 |  |  |  |  |  |  |  | 26 |
| 25 |  |  |  | 86 | 93 | 97 |  |  |  |  |  |  |  | 25 |
| 24 |  |  |  |  | 84 | 91 | 95 | 22 |  |  |  |  |  | 24 |
| 23 |  |  |  | 110 | 82 | 87 | 90 | 26 |  |  |  | 96 |  | 23 |
| 22 |  |  |  | 106 | 78 | 85 | 88 | 30 |  |  |  | 95 |  | 22 |
| 21 |  |  |  | 104 | 75 | 83 | 84 | 32 |  |  |  | 91 |  | 21 |
| 20 |  | 120 |  | 99 | 73 | 79 | 82 | 36 |  |  |  | 87 |  | 20 |
| 19 |  | 116 |  | 97 | 71 | 76 | 80 | 40 |  | 91 |  | 83 |  | 19 |
| 18 |  | 111 |  | 95 | 67 | 74 | 76 | 45 |  | 89 | 105 | 80 |  | 18 |
| 17 |  | 107 |  | 90 | 65 | 70 | 74 | 49 | 110 | 85 | 101 | 78 |  | 17 |
| 16 |  | 104 |  | 88 | 62 | 68 | 71 | 51 | 106 | 82 | 98 | 74 | 93 | 16 |
| 15 |  | 100 |  | 86 | 60 | 64 | 67 | 55 | 101 | 78 | 93 | 70 | 88 | 15 |
| 14 |  | 95 |  | 81 | 56 | 62 | 65 | 59 | 99 | 75 | 90 | 67 | 82 | 14 |
| 13 |  | 93 |  | 79 | 54 | 60 | 61 | 63 | 90 | 75 | 86 | 65 | 79 | 13 |
| 12 |  | 89 | 75 | 75 | 52 | 56 | 59 | 65 | 86 | 70 | 82 | 61 | 73 | 12 |
| 11 | 96 | 84 | 71 | 72 | 47 | 54 | 57 | 69 | 82 | 66 | 78 | 57 | 68 | 11 |
| 10 | 88 | 79 | 67 | 70 | 45 | 52 | 53 | 73 | 77 | 63 | 74 | 54 | 63 | 10 |
| 9 | 83 | 75 | 62 | 66 | 43 | 48 | 51 | 77 | 73 | 59 | 71 | 50 | 58 | 9 |
| 8 | 79 | 73 | 58 | 64 | 41 | 46 | 48 | 82 | 68 | 56 | 69 | 48 | 54 | 8 |
| 7 | 70 | 68 | 56 | 59 | 37 | 42 | 44 | 84 | 64 | 53 | 63 | 44 | 49 | 7 |
| 6 | 66 | 63 | 51 | 57 | 34 | 39 | 42 | 88 | 58 | 49 | 59 | 41 | 44 | 6 |
| 5 | 62 | 59 | 47 | 55 | 32 | 37 | 40 | 92 | 53 | 47 | 56 | 37 | 39 | 5 |
| 4 | 53 | 47 | 42 | 50 | 30 | 33 | 36 | 96 | 49 | 43 | 51 | 35 | 35 | 4 |
| 3 | 49 | 52 | 38 | 48 | 26 | 31 | 34 | 98 | 44 | 40 | 48 | 31 | 30 | 3 |
| 2 | 45 | 47 | 34 | 43 | 24 | 29 | 30 | 101 | 40 | 37 | 44 | 28 | 24 | 2 |
| 1 | 40 | 43 | 29 | 41 | 21 | 25 | 27 | 105 | 36 | 33 | 41 | 24 | 21 | 1 |

[a] Equivalent MMPI T-Scores rounded to the nearest whole number.

**B-1.3  Raw Scale Score Conversion for the MMPI-168 for Female Adolescents Age 15 (Without K Corrections)[a]—NCS Scoring Keys**

| 168 Score | L | F | K | Hs | D | Hy | Pd | Mf | Pa | Pt | Sc | Ma | Si | 168 Score |
|---|---|---|---|---|---|---|---|---|---|---|---|---|---|---|
| 33 | | | | | 108 | 115 | | | | | | | | 33 |
| 32 | | | | | 106 | 113 | | | | | | | | 32 |
| 31 | | | | | 103 | 111 | | | | | | | | 31 |
| 30 | | | | | 99 | 107 | | | | | | | | 30 |
| 29 | | | | | 97 | 105 | | | | | | | | 29 |
| 28 | | | | | 95 | 101 | 105 | | | | 103 | | | 28 |
| 27 | | | | | 93 | 99 | 103 | | | | 101 | | | 27 |
| 26 | | | | | 88 | 95 | 99 | | | | 99 | | | 26 |
| 25 | | | | | 86 | 93 | 97 | | | | 95 | | | 25 |
| 24 | | | | | 84 | 91 | 95 | 22 | | | 93 | | | 24 |
| 23 | | | | 110 | 82 | 87 | 90 | 26 | | | 91 | 96 | | 23 |
| 22 | | | | 106 | 78 | 85 | 88 | 30 | | | 88 | 95 | | 22 |
| 21 | | | | 104 | 75 | 83 | 84 | 32 | | | 86 | 91 | | 21 |
| 20 | | 120 | | 99 | 73 | 79 | 82 | 36 | | | 84 | 87 | | 20 |
| 19 | | 116 | | 97 | 71 | 76 | 80 | 40 | 110 | 91 | 80 | 83 | | 19 |
| 18 | | 111 | | 95 | 67 | 74 | 76 | 45 | 106 | 89 | 78 | 80 | | 18 |
| 17 | | 107 | | 90 | 65 | 70 | 74 | 49 | 101 | 85 | 76 | 78 | | 17 |
| 16 | | 104 | | 88 | 62 | 68 | 71 | 51 | 97 | 82 | 74 | 74 | 93 | 16 |
| 15 | | 100 | | 86 | 60 | 64 | 67 | 55 | 93 | 78 | 71 | 70 | 88 | 15 |
| 14 | | 95 | | 81 | 56 | 62 | 65 | 59 | 88 | 75 | 69 | 67 | 82 | 14 |
| 13 | | 93 | | 79 | 54 | 60 | 61 | 63 | 84 | 75 | 66 | 65 | 79 | 13 |
| 12 | | 89 | 75 | 75 | 52 | 56 | 59 | 65 | 79 | 70 | 63 | 61 | 73 | 12 |
| 11 | 96 | 84 | 71 | 72 | 47 | 54 | 57 | 69 | 77 | 66 | 61 | 57 | 68 | 11 |
| 10 | 88 | 79 | 67 | 70 | 45 | 52 | 53 | 73 | 73 | 63 | 59 | 54 | 63 | 10 |
| 9 | 83 | 75 | 62 | 66 | 43 | 48 | 51 | 77 | 68 | 59 | 56 | 50 | 58 | 9 |
| 8 | 79 | 73 | 58 | 64 | 41 | 46 | 48 | 82 | 64 | 56 | 54 | 48 | 54 | 8 |
| 7 | 70 | 68 | 56 | 59 | 37 | 42 | 44 | 84 | 60 | 53 | 51 | 44 | 49 | 7 |
| 6 | 66 | 63 | 51 | 57 | 34 | 39 | 42 | 88 | 55 | 49 | 49 | 41 | 44 | 6 |
| 5 | 62 | 59 | 47 | 55 | 32 | 37 | 40 | 92 | 51 | 47 | 46 | 37 | 39 | 5 |
| 4 | 53 | 47 | 42 | 50 | 30 | 33 | 36 | 96 | 49 | 43 | 44 | 35 | 35 | 4 |
| 3 | 49 | 52 | 38 | 48 | 26 | 31 | 34 | 98 | 44 | 40 | 42 | 31 | 30 | 3 |
| 2 | 45 | 47 | 34 | 43 | 24 | 29 | 30 | 101 | 38 | 37 | 39 | 28 | 24 | 2 |
| 1 | 40 | 43 | 29 | 41 | 21 | 25 | 27 | 105 | 33 | 33 | 36 | 24 | 21 | 1 |

[a] Equivalent MMPI T-Scores rounded to the nearest whole number.

Table B-4  Raw Scale Score Conversion for the MMPI-168
for Male Adolescents Age 15 (Without K Corrections)[a]
—Psychological Corporation Scoring Keys

| 168 Score | L | F | K | Hs | D | Hy | Pd | Mf | Pa | Pt | Sc | Ma | Si | 168 Score |
|---|---|---|---|---|---|---|---|---|---|---|---|---|---|---|
| 33 |  |  |  |  | 113 | 120 |  |  |  |  |  |  |  | 33 |
| 32 |  |  |  |  | 111 | 118 |  |  |  |  |  |  |  | 32 |
| 31 |  |  |  |  | 108 | 114 |  |  |  |  |  |  |  | 31 |
| 30 |  |  |  |  | 104 | 112 |  |  |  |  |  |  |  | 30 |
| 29 |  |  |  |  | 101 | 110 |  |  |  |  |  |  |  | 29 |
| 28 |  |  |  |  | 99 | 106 | 105 | 120 |  |  |  |  |  | 28 |
| 27 |  | 120 |  |  | 97 | 104 | 103 | 116 |  |  |  |  |  | 27 |
| 26 |  | 115 |  |  | 92 | 100 | 99 | 112 |  |  |  |  |  | 26 |
| 25 |  | 114 |  |  | 90 | 98 | 96 | 110 |  |  |  |  |  | 25 |
| 24 |  | 110 |  |  | 88 | 96 | 94 | 106 |  |  |  |  |  | 24 |
| 23 |  | 107 |  | 114 | 86 | 91 | 90 | 101 |  |  |  | 95 |  | 23 |
| 22 |  | 103 |  | 109 | 81 | 89 | 88 | 97 |  |  |  | 93 |  | 22 |
| 21 |  | 102 |  | 107 | 79 | 87 | 84 | 95 |  |  |  | 89 |  | 21 |
| 20 |  | 98 |  | 102 | 77 | 83 | 81 | 91 |  |  |  | 86 |  | 20 |
| 19 |  | 95 |  | 100 | 74 | 81 | 79 | 87 |  | 95 |  | 82 |  | 19 |
| 18 |  | 92 |  | 98 | 70 | 79 | 75 | 83 |  | 92 | 100 | 78 |  | 18 |
| 17 |  | 88 |  | 93 | 67 | 75 | 73 | 79 | 106 | 88 | 96 | 76 |  | 17 |
| 16 |  | 87 |  | 91 | 65 | 73 | 71 | 76 | 102 | 85 | 93 | 72 | 93 | 16 |
| 15 |  | 83 |  | 88 | 63 | 69 | 66 | 72 | 98 | 81 | 89 | 68 | 91 | 15 |
| 14 |  | 80 |  | 84 | 58 | 67 | 64 | 68 | 96 | 78 | 86 | 65 | 83 | 14 |
| 13 |  | 78 |  | 81 | 56 | 65 | 60 | 64 | 88 | 78 | 82 | 63 | 79 | 13 |
| 12 |  | 75 | 74 | 76 | 54 | 61 | 58 | 62 | 83 | 72 | 78 | 59 | 74 | 12 |
| 11 | 98 | 72 | 70 | 74 | 49 | 59 | 56 | 58 | 79 | 68 | 75 | 55 | 69 | 11 |
| 10 | 89 | 68 | 66 | 72 | 47 | 57 | 52 | 53 | 75 | 65 | 71 | 51 | 63 | 10 |
| 9 | 85 | 65 | 62 | 67 | 45 | 52 | 49 | 49 | 71 | 61 | 68 | 47 | 58 | 9 |
| 8 | 80 | 63 | 58 | 65 | 43 | 50 | 47 | 45 | 67 | 58 | 66 | 45 | 54 | 8 |
| 7 | 72 | 60 | 55 | 60 | 38 | 46 | 43 | 43 | 63 | 55 | 61 | 42 | 48 | 7 |
| 6 | 67 | 57 | 51 | 58 | 36 | 44 | 41 | 39 | 56 | 51 | 57 | 38 | 43 | 6 |
| 5 | 63 | 53 | 47 | 55 | 33 | 42 | 39 | 35 | 52 | 48 | 54 | 34 | 38 | 5 |
| 4 | 55 | 52 | 43 | 51 | 31 | 38 | 34 | 31 | 48 | 44 | 50 | 32 | 34 | 4 |
| 3 | 50 | 48 | 39 | 48 | 27 | 36 | 32 | 28 | 44 | 41 | 47 | 28 | 28 | 3 |
| 2 | 46 | 45 | 34 | 44 | 24 | 30 | 28 | 24 | 40 | 38 | 43 | 24 | 23 | 2 |
| 1 | 42 | 41 | 30 | 41 | 22 | 28 | 26 | 20 | 35 | 34 | 40 | 21 | 20 | 1 |

[a] Equivalent MMPI T-Scores rounded to nearest whole number.

Table B-1.4  Raw Scale Score Conversion for the MMPI-168 for Male Adolescents Age 15 (Without K Corrections)[a]—NCS Scoring Keys

| 168 Score | L | F | K | Hs | D | Hy | Pd | Mf | Pa | Pt | Sc | Ma | Si | 168 Score |
|---|---|---|---|---|---|---|---|---|---|---|---|---|---|---|
| 33 |  |  |  | 113 | 120 |  |  |  |  |  |  |  |  | 33 |
| 32 |  |  |  | 111 | 118 |  |  |  |  |  |  |  |  | 32 |
| 31 |  |  |  | 108 | 114 |  |  |  |  |  |  |  |  | 31 |
| 30 |  |  |  | 104 | 112 |  |  |  |  |  |  |  |  | 30 |
| 29 |  |  |  | 101 | 110 |  |  |  |  |  |  |  |  | 29 |
| 28 |  |  |  | 99 | 106 | 105 | 120 |  |  |  | 103 |  |  | 28 |
| 27 |  | 120 |  | 97 | 104 | 103 | 116 |  |  |  | 101 |  |  | 27 |
| 26 |  | 115 |  | 92 | 100 | 99 | 112 |  |  |  | 99 |  |  | 26 |
| 25 |  | 114 |  | 90 | 98 | 96 | 110 |  |  |  | 95 |  |  | 25 |
| 24 |  | 110 |  | 88 | 96 | 94 | 106 |  |  |  | 93 |  |  | 24 |
| 23 |  | 107 | 114 | 86 | 91 | 90 | 101 |  |  |  | 87 | 95 |  | 23 |
| 22 |  | 103 | 109 | 81 | 89 | 88 | 97 |  |  |  | 84 | 93 |  | 22 |
| 21 |  | 102 | 107 | 79 | 87 | 84 | 95 |  |  |  | 82 | 89 |  | 21 |
| 20 |  | 98 | 102 | 77 | 83 | 81 | 91 |  |  |  | 80 | 86 |  | 20 |
| 19 |  | 95 | 100 | 74 | 81 | 79 | 87 |  |  | 95 | 77 | 82 |  | 19 |
| 18 |  | 92 | 98 | 70 | 79 | 75 | 83 |  |  | 92 | 75 | 78 |  | 18 |
| 17 |  | 88 | 93 | 67 | 75 | 73 | 79 |  | 111 | 88 | 73 | 76 |  | 17 |
| 16 |  | 87 | 91 | 65 | 73 | 71 | 76 |  | 106 | 85 | 71 | 72 | 93 | 16 |
| 15 |  | 83 | 88 | 63 | 69 | 66 | 72 |  | 100 | 81 | 68 | 68 | 91 | 15 |
| 14 |  | 80 | 84 | 58 | 67 | 64 | 68 |  | 96 | 78 | 66 | 65 | 83 | 14 |
| 13 |  | 78 | 81 | 56 | 65 | 60 | 64 |  | 92 | 78 | 64 | 63 | 79 | 13 |
| 12 |  | 75 | 74 | 76 | 54 | 61 | 58 | 62 | 86 | 72 | 61 | 59 | 74 | 12 |
| 11 | 98 | 72 | 70 | 74 | 49 | 59 | 56 | 58 | 81 | 68 | 59 | 55 | 69 | 11 |
| 10 | 89 | 68 | 66 | 72 | 47 | 57 | 52 | 53 | 77 | 65 | 57 | 51 | 63 | 10 |
| 9 | 85 | 65 | 62 | 67 | 45 | 52 | 49 | 49 | 71 | 61 | 54 | 47 | 58 | 9 |
| 8 | 80 | 63 | 58 | 65 | 43 | 50 | 47 | 45 | 67 | 58 | 52 | 45 | 54 | 8 |
| 7 | 72 | 60 | 55 | 60 | 38 | 46 | 43 | 43 | 63 | 55 | 50 | 42 | 48 | 7 |
| 6 | 67 | 57 | 51 | 58 | 36 | 44 | 41 | 39 | 58 | 51 | 48 | 38 | 43 | 6 |
| 5 | 63 | 53 | 47 | 55 | 33 | 42 | 39 | 35 | 52 | 48 | 45 | 34 | 38 | 5 |
| 4 | 55 | 52 | 43 | 51 | 31 | 38 | 34 | 31 | 48 | 44 | 43 | 32 | 34 | 4 |
| 3 | 50 | 48 | 39 | 48 | 27 | 36 | 32 | 28 | 44 | 41 | 41 | 28 | 28 | 3 |
| 2 | 46 | 45 | 34 | 44 | 24 | 30 | 28 | 24 | 37 | 38 | 38 | 24 | 23 | 2 |
| 1 | 42 | 41 | 30 | 41 | 22 | 28 | 26 | 20 | 33 | 34 | 36 | 21 | 20 | 1 |

[a] Equivalent MMPI T-Scores rounded to nearest whole number.

Table B-5  Raw Scale Score Conversion for the MMPI-168
for Female Adolescents Age 16 (Without K Corrections)[a]
—Psychological Corporation Scoring Keys

| 168 Score | L | F | K | Hs | D | Hy | Pd | Mf | Pa | Pt | Sc | Ma | Si | 168 Score |
|---|---|---|---|---|---|---|---|---|---|---|---|---|---|---|
| 33 | | | | | 102 | 113 | | | | | | | | 33 |
| 32 | | | | | 100 | 111 | | | | | | | | 32 |
| 31 | | | | | 98 | 109 | | | | | | | | 31 |
| 30 | | | | | 94 | 105 | | | | | | | | 30 |
| 29 | | | | | 92 | 103 | | | | | | | | 29 |
| 28 | | | | | 89 | 99 | 108 | | | | | | | 28 |
| 27 | | | | | 87 | 97 | 106 | | | | | | | 27 |
| 26 | | | | | 83 | 93 | 101 | | | | | | | 26 |
| 25 | | | | | 81 | 91 | 99 | | | | | | | 25 |
| 24 | | | | | 79 | 89 | 97 | | | | | | | 24 |
| 23 | | | | 112 | 77 | 85 | 92 | 22 | | | | 106 | | 23 |
| 22 | | | | 107 | 73 | 83 | 90 | 27 | | | | 104 | | 22 |
| 21 | | | | 105 | 71 | 81 | 86 | 29 | | | | 100 | | 21 |
| 20 | | 118 | | 100 | 69 | 77 | 84 | 34 | | | | 95 | | 20 |
| 19 | | 113 | | 98 | 67 | 75 | 82 | 38 | | 89 | | 91 | | 19 |
| 18 | | 109 | | 95 | 63 | 73 | 77 | 43 | | 86 | 103 | 86 | | 18 |
| 17 | | 104 | | 91 | 61 | 69 | 75 | 47 | 120 | 82 | 99 | 84 | | 17 |
| 16 | | 102 | | 88 | 59 | 67 | 73 | 50 | 115 | 79 | 95 | 80 | 88 | 16 |
| 15 | | 98 | | 86 | 57 | 63 | 68 | 54 | 110 | 75 | 91 | 75 | 83 | 15 |
| 14 | | 93 | | 81 | 53 | 61 | 66 | 59 | 107 | 73 | 88 | 71 | 78 | 14 |
| 13 | | 91 | | 79 | 51 | 59 | 62 | 64 | 97 | 73 | 84 | 68 | 74 | 13 |
| 12 | | 86 | 93 | 74 | 49 | 56 | 60 | 66 | 92 | 67 | 80 | 64 | 69 | 12 |
| 11 | 95 | 82 | 88 | 72 | 45 | 54 | 57 | 70 | 87 | 64 | 77 | 59 | 64 | 11 |
| 10 | 86 | 77 | 84 | 70 | 43 | 52 | 53 | 75 | 81 | 61 | 72 | 55 | 59 | 10 |
| 9 | 82 | 73 | 63 | 65 | 40 | 48 | 51 | 80 | 76 | 57 | 69 | 50 | 54 | 9 |
| 8 | 78 | 71 | 59 | 63 | 38 | 46 | 49 | 84 | 71 | 54 | 67 | 48 | 51 | 8 |
| 7 | 69 | 66 | 57 | 58 | 34 | 42 | 44 | 87 | 66 | 52 | 62 | 44 | 46 | 7 |
| 6 | 64 | 62 | 52 | 56 | 32 | 40 | 42 | 91 | 58 | 48 | 58 | 39 | 41 | 6 |
| 5 | 60 | 57 | 48 | 54 | 30 | 38 | 40 | 96 | 53 | 45 | 54 | 35 | 36 | 5 |
| 4 | 51 | 55 | 44 | 49 | 28 | 34 | 36 | 100 | 48 | 41 | 50 | 32 | 32 | 4 |
| 3 | 47 | 50 | 39 | 47 | 24 | 32 | 33 | 102 | 42 | 38 | 47 | 28 | 27 | 3 |
| 2 | 42 | 46 | 35 | 42 | 22 | 30 | 29 | 106 | 37 | 36 | 43 | 23 | 22 | 2 |
| 1 | 38 | 41 | 30 | 40 | 20 | 26 | 27 | 111 | 32 | 32 | 40 | 21 | 20 | 1 |

[a] Equivalent MMPI T-Scores rounded to the nearest whole number.

**Table B-1.5  Raw Scale Score Conversion for the MMPI-168 for Female Adolescents Age 16 (Without K Corrections)[a]–NCS Scoring Keys**

| 168 Score | L | F | K | Hs | D | Hy | Pd | Mf | Pa | Pt | Sc | Ma | Si | 168 Score |
|---|---|---|---|---|---|---|---|---|---|---|---|---|---|---|
| 33 | | | | | 102 | 113 | | | | | | | | 33 |
| 32 | | | | | 100 | 111 | | | | | | | | 32 |
| 31 | | | | | 98 | 109 | | | | | | | | 31 |
| 30 | | | | | 94 | 105 | | | | | | | | 30 |
| 29 | | | | | 92 | 103 | | | | | | | | 29 |
| 28 | | | | | 89 | 99 | 108 | | | | 101 | | | 28 |
| 27 | | | | | 87 | 97 | 106 | | | | 99 | | | 27 |
| 26 | | | | | 83 | 93 | 101 | | | | 97 | | | 26 |
| 25 | | | | | 81 | 91 | 99 | | | | 93 | | | 25 |
| 24 | | | | | 79 | 89 | 97 | | | | 91 | | | 24 |
| 23 | | | | 112 | 77 | 85 | 92 | 22 | | | 89 | 106 | | 23 |
| 22 | | | | 107 | 73 | 83 | 90 | 27 | | | 86 | 104 | | 22 |
| 21 | | | | 105 | 71 | 81 | 86 | 29 | | | 84 | 100 | | 21 |
| 20 | | 118 | | 100 | 69 | 77 | 84 | 34 | | | 82 | 95 | | 20 |
| 19 | | 113 | | 98 | 67 | 75 | 82 | 38 | 120 | 89 | 79 | 91 | | 19 |
| 18 | | 109 | | 95 | 63 | 73 | 77 | 43 | 115 | 86 | 77 | 86 | | 18 |
| 17 | | 104 | | 91 | 61 | 69 | 75 | 47 | 110 | 82 | 74 | 84 | | 17 |
| 16 | | 102 | | 88 | 59 | 67 | 73 | 50 | 105 | 79 | 72 | 80 | 88 | 16 |
| 15 | | 98 | | 86 | 57 | 63 | 68 | 54 | 99 | 75 | 69 | 75 | 83 | 15 |
| 14 | | 93 | | 81 | 53 | 61 | 66 | 59 | 94 | 73 | 67 | 71 | 78 | 14 |
| 13 | | 91 | | 79 | 51 | 59 | 62 | 64 | 89 | 73 | 65 | 68 | 74 | 13 |
| 12 | | 86 | 93 | 74 | 49 | 56 | 60 | 66 | 84 | 67 | 62 | 64 | 69 | 12 |
| 11 | 95 | 82 | 88 | 72 | 45 | 54 | 57 | 70 | 81 | 64 | 60 | 59 | 64 | 11 |
| 10 | 86 | 77 | 84 | 70 | 43 | 52 | 53 | 75 | 76 | 61 | 58 | 55 | 59 | 10 |
| 9 | 82 | 73 | 63 | 65 | 40 | 48 | 51 | 80 | 71 | 57 | 54 | 50 | 54 | 9 |
| 8 | 78 | 71 | 59 | 63 | 38 | 46 | 49 | 84 | 66 | 54 | 52 | 48 | 51 | 8 |
| 7 | 69 | 66 | 57 | 58 | 34 | 42 | 44 | 87 | 61 | 52 | 50 | 44 | 46 | 7 |
| 6 | 64 | 62 | 52 | 56 | 32 | 40 | 42 | 91 | 55 | 48 | 48 | 39 | 41 | 6 |
| 5 | 60 | 57 | 48 | 54 | 30 | 38 | 40 | 96 | 50 | 45 | 45 | 35 | 36 | 5 |
| 4 | 51 | 55 | 44 | 49 | 28 | 34 | 36 | 100 | 48 | 41 | 43 | 32 | 32 | 4 |
| 3 | 47 | 50 | 39 | 47 | 24 | 32 | 33 | 102 | 42 | 38 | 41 | 28 | 27 | 3 |
| 2 | 42 | 46 | 35 | 42 | 22 | 30 | 29 | 106 | 37 | 36 | 38 | 23 | 22 | 2 |
| 1 | 38 | 41 | 30 | 40 | 20 | 26 | 27 | 111 | 32 | 32 | 35 | 21 | 20 | 1 |

[a] Equivalent MMPI T-Scores rounded to the nearest whole number.

Table B-6  Raw Scale Score Conversion for the MMPI-168
for Male Adolescents Age 16 (Without K Corrections)[a]
—Psychological Corporation Scoring Keys

| 168 Score | L | F | K | Hs | D | Hy | Pd | Mf | Pa | Pt | Sc | Ma | Si | 168 Score |
|---|---|---|---|---|---|---|---|---|---|---|---|---|---|---|
| 33 |  |  |  | 112 |  |  |  |  |  |  |  |  |  | 33 |
| 32 |  |  |  | 110 |  |  |  |  |  |  |  |  |  | 32 |
| 31 |  |  |  | 107 | 120 |  |  |  |  |  |  |  |  | 31 |
| 30 |  |  |  | 103 | 115 |  |  |  |  |  |  |  |  | 30 |
| 29 |  |  |  | 101 | 113 |  |  |  |  |  |  |  |  | 29 |
| 28 |  |  |  | 98 | 109 | 105 |  |  |  |  |  |  |  | 28 |
| 27 |  | 120 |  | 96 | 106 | 103 |  |  |  |  |  |  |  | 27 |
| 26 |  | 117 |  | 92 | 102 | 99 |  |  |  |  |  |  |  | 26 |
| 25 |  | 115 |  | 89 | 100 | 97 | 119 |  |  |  |  |  |  | 25 |
| 24 |  | 112 |  | 87 | 98 | 95 | 114 |  |  |  |  |  |  | 24 |
| 23 |  | 108 |  | 85 | 93 | 90 | 110 |  |  |  |  | 100 |  | 23 |
| 22 |  | 105 |  | 80 | 91 | 88 | 105 |  |  |  |  | 98 |  | 22 |
| 21 |  | 103 | 118 | 78 | 89 | 84 | 103 |  |  |  |  | 94 |  | 21 |
| 20 |  | 99 | 112 | 76 | 85 | 82 | 98 |  |  |  |  | 90 |  | 20 |
| 19 |  | 96 | 109 | 74 | 82 | 79 | 93 |  |  | 96 |  | 85 |  | 19 |
| 18 |  | 92 | 107 | 69 | 80 | 75 | 88 |  |  | 93 | 104 | 81 |  | 18 |
| 17 |  | 89 | 101 | 67 | 76 | 73 | 84 |  | 89 | 89 | 99 | 79 |  | 17 |
| 16 |  | 87 | 98 | 65 | 74 | 71 | 81 |  | 86 | 86 | 96 | 75 | 96 | 16 |
| 15 |  | 84 | 95 | 63 | 69 | 66 | 76 |  | 83 | 82 | 92 | 70 | 90 | 15 |
| 14 |  | 80 | 90 | 58 | 67 | 64 | 72 |  | 82 | 79 | 89 | 66 | 85 | 14 |
| 13 |  | 79 | 87 | 56 | 65 | 60 | 67 |  | 76 | 79 | 84 | 64 | 81 | 13 |
| 12 |  | 75 | 76 | 81 | 54 | 61 | 58 | 65 | 73 | 73 | 80 | 60 | 75 | 12 |
| 11 | 99 | 72 | 72 | 78 | 49 | 58 | 56 | 60 | 70 | 68 | 77 | 55 | 69 | 11 |
| 10 | 89 | 68 | 67 | 76 | 47 | 56 | 51 | 55 | 67 | 65 | 72 | 51 | 63 | 10 |
| 9 | 85 | 65 | 63 | 70 | 45 | 52 | 49 | 50 | 64 | 61 | 69 | 47 | 58 | 9 |
| 8 | 80 | 63 | 58 | 67 | 42 | 50 | 47 | 46 | 61 | 58 | 67 | 45 | 54 | 8 |
| 7 | 71 | 60 | 56 | 62 | 38 | 45 | 43 | 43 | 58 | 55 | 62 | 40 | 48 | 7 |
| 6 | 67 | 56 | 51 | 59 | 36 | 43 | 41 | 39 | 54 | 51 | 57 | 36 | 42 | 6 |
| 5 | 62 | 53 | 47 | 56 | 33 | 41 | 38 | 34 | 51 | 48 | 54 | 32 | 37 | 5 |
| 4 | 53 | 51 | 42 | 50 | 31 | 37 | 34 | 29 | 48 | 43 | 50 | 30 | 32 | 4 |
| 3 | 49 | 47 | 38 | 47 | 27 | 34 | 32 | 27 | 45 | 40 | 46 | 28 | 27 | 3 |
| 2 | 44 | 44 | 33 | 42 | 24 | 32 | 28 | 22 | 42 | 37 | 42 | 21 | 21 | 2 |
| 1 | 40 | 40 | 29 | 39 | 22 | 28 | 25 | 20 | 39 | 33 | 39 | 21 | 20 | 1 |

[a] Equivalent MMPI T-Scores rounded to the nearest whole number.

**Table B-1.6  Raw Scale Score Conversion for the MMPI-168 for Male Adolescents Age 16 (Without K Corrections)[a]—NCS Scoring Keys**

| 168 Score | L | F | K | Hs | D | Hy | Pd | Mf | Pa | Pt | Sc | Ma | Si | 168 Score |
|---|---|---|---|---|---|---|---|---|---|---|---|---|---|---|
| 33 |  |  |  | 112 |  |  |  |  |  |  |  |  |  | 33 |
| 32 |  |  |  | 110 |  |  |  |  |  |  |  |  |  | 32 |
| 31 |  |  |  | 107 | 120 |  |  |  |  |  |  |  |  | 31 |
| 30 |  |  |  | 103 | 115 |  |  |  |  |  |  |  |  | 30 |
| 29 |  |  |  | 101 | 113 |  |  |  |  |  |  |  |  | 29 |
| 28 |  |  |  | 98 | 109 | 105 |  |  |  |  | 102 |  |  | 28 |
| 27 |  | 120 |  | 96 | 106 | 103 |  |  |  |  | 99 |  |  | 27 |
| 26 |  | 117 |  | 92 | 102 | 99 |  |  |  |  | 97 |  |  | 26 |
| 25 |  | 115 |  | 89 | 100 | 97 | 119 |  |  |  | 94 |  |  | 25 |
| 24 |  | 112 |  | 87 | 98 | 95 | 114 |  |  |  | 92 |  |  | 24 |
| 23 |  | 108 |  | 85 | 93 | 90 | 110 |  |  |  | 90 | 100 |  | 23 |
| 22 |  | 105 |  | 80 | 91 | 88 | 105 |  |  |  | 86 | 98 |  | 22 |
| 21 |  | 103 | 118 | 78 | 89 | 84 | 103 |  |  |  | 84 | 94 |  | 21 |
| 20 |  | 99 | 112 | 76 | 85 | 82 | 98 |  |  |  | 82 | 90 |  | 20 |
| 19 |  | 96 | 109 | 74 | 82 | 79 | 93 |  | 89 | 96 | 79 | 85 |  | 19 |
| 18 |  | 92 | 107 | 69 | 80 | 75 | 88 |  | 86 | 93 | 77 | 81 |  | 18 |
| 17 |  | 89 | 101 | 67 | 76 | 73 | 84 |  | 83 | 89 | 75 | 79 |  | 17 |
| 16 |  | 87 | 98 | 65 | 74 | 71 | 81 |  | 80 | 86 | 72 | 75 | 96 | 16 |
| 15 |  | 84 | 95 | 63 | 69 | 66 | 76 |  | 77 | 82 | 69 | 70 | 90 | 15 |
| 14 |  | 80 | 90 | 58 | 67 | 64 | 72 |  | 74 | 79 | 67 | 66 | 85 | 14 |
| 13 |  | 79 | 87 | 56 | 65 | 60 | 67 |  | 71 | 79 | 65 | 64 | 81 | 13 |
| 12 |  | 75 | 76 | 81 | 54 | 61 | 58 | 65 | 68 | 73 | 62 | 60 | 75 | 12 |
| 11 | 99 | 72 | 72 | 78 | 49 | 58 | 56 | 60 | 67 | 68 | 59 | 55 | 69 | 11 |
| 10 | 89 | 68 | 67 | 76 | 47 | 56 | 51 | 55 | 64 | 65 | 57 | 51 | 63 | 10 |
| 9 | 85 | 65 | 63 | 70 | 45 | 52 | 49 | 50 | 61 | 61 | 54 | 47 | 58 | 9 |
| 8 | 80 | 63 | 58 | 67 | 42 | 50 | 47 | 46 | 58 | 58 | 52 | 45 | 54 | 8 |
| 7 | 71 | 60 | 56 | 62 | 38 | 45 | 43 | 43 | 55 | 55 | 50 | 40 | 48 | 7 |
| 6 | 67 | 56 | 51 | 59 | 36 | 43 | 41 | 39 | 52 | 51 | 48 | 36 | 42 | 6 |
| 5 | 62 | 53 | 47 | 56 | 33 | 41 | 38 | 34 | 49 | 48 | 44 | 32 | 37 | 5 |
| 4 | 53 | 51 | 42 | 50 | 31 | 37 | 34 | 29 | 48 | 43 | 42 | 30 | 32 | 4 |
| 3 | 49 | 47 | 38 | 47 | 27 | 34 | 32 | 27 | 45 | 40 | 40 | 28 | 27 | 3 |
| 2 | 44 | 44 | 33 | 42 | 24 | 32 | 28 | 22 | 42 | 37 | 37 | 21 | 21 | 2 |
| 1 | 40 | 40 | 29 | 39 | 22 | 28 | 25 | 20 | 39 | 33 | 35 | 21 | 20 | 1 |

[a] Equivalent MMPI T-Scores rounded to the nearest whole number.

Table B-7  Raw Scale Score Conversion for the MMPI-168
for Female Adolescents Age 17 (Without K Corrections)[a]
—Psychological Corporation Scoring Keys

| 168 Score | L | F | K | Hs | D | Hy | Pd | Mf | Pa | Pt | Sc | Ma | Si | 168 Score |
|---|---|---|---|---|---|---|---|---|---|---|---|---|---|---|
| 33 | | | | | 103 | 111 | | | | | | | | 33 |
| 32 | | | | | 101 | 109 | | | | | | | | 32 |
| 31 | | | | | 99 | 105 | | | | | | | | 31 |
| 30 | | | | | 95 | 103 | | | | | | | | 30 |
| 29 | | | | | 93 | 101 | | | | | | | | 29 |
| 28 | | | | | 90 | 97 | 109 | | | | | | | 28 |
| 27 | | | | | 90 | 95 | 107 | | | | | | | 27 |
| 26 | | | | | 88 | 91 | 102 | | | | | | | 26 |
| 25 | | | | | 87 | 89 | 100 | | | | | | | 25 |
| 24 | | | | | 86 | 87 | 98 | | | | | | | 24 |
| 23 | | | | 107 | 85 | 83 | 93 | 22 | | | | 106 | | 23 |
| 22 | | | | 103 | 84 | 81 | 91 | 27 | | | | 104 | | 22 |
| 21 | | | | 100 | 82 | 79 | 86 | 29 | | | | 99 | | 21 |
| 20 | | | | 96 | 78 | 75 | 84 | 33 | | | | 95 | | 20 |
| 19 | | 118 | | 93 | 75 | 73 | 81 | 38 | | 93 | | 91 | | 19 |
| 18 | | 113 | | 91 | 73 | 71 | 77 | 42 | | 90 | 106 | 86 | | 18 |
| 17 | | 109 | | 87 | 69 | 67 | 74 | 47 | | 85 | 102 | 84 | | 17 |
| 16 | | 106 | | 84 | 67 | 65 | 72 | 49 | | 82 | 98 | 80 | 90 | 16 |
| 15 | | 101 | | 82 | 62 | 61 | 67 | 53 | 119 | 78 | 94 | 76 | 85 | 15 |
| 14 | | 96 | | 77 | 60 | 59 | 65 | 58 | 116 | 75 | 90 | 71 | 79 | 14 |
| 13 | | 94 | | 75 | 58 | 57 | 61 | 62 | 105 | 75 | 86 | 69 | 75 | 13 |
| 12 | | 89 | 81 | 71 | 54 | 53 | 58 | 65 | 99 | 69 | 81 | 65 | 70 | 12 |
| 11 | 91 | 84 | 76 | 68 | 52 | 51 | 56 | 69 | 93 | 65 | 78 | 60 | 65 | 11 |
| 10 | 83 | 79 | 71 | 66 | 50 | 49 | 51 | 74 | 87 | 62 | 73 | 56 | 59 | 10 |
| 9 | 79 | 74 | 66 | 61 | 45 | 45 | 49 | 78 | 82 | 58 | 70 | 52 | 54 | 9 |
| 8 | 74 | 72 | 61 | 59 | 43 | 43 | 47 | 83 | 76 | 55 | 68 | 50 | 50 | 8 |
| 7 | 66 | 67 | 59 | 55 | 39 | 39 | 42 | 85 | 70 | 52 | 62 | 45 | 45 | 7 |
| 6 | 62 | 62 | 54 | 52 | 37 | 37 | 40 | 89 | 61 | 47 | 57 | 41 | 39 | 6 |
| 5 | 58 | 57 | 49 | 50 | 35 | 35 | 37 | 94 | 56 | 44 | 54 | 37 | 34 | 5 |
| 4 | 49 | 54 | 44 | 45 | 30 | 31 | 33 | 98 | 50 | 40 | 49 | 34 | 30 | 4 |
| 3 | 45 | 49 | 38 | 43 | 28 | 29 | 31 | 100 | 44 | 37 | 46 | 30 | 25 | 3 |
| 2 | 41 | 45 | 33 | 38 | 26 | 27 | 26 | 104 | 38 | 34 | 41 | 26 | 21 | 2 |
| 1 | 37 | 40 | 28 | 36 | 22 | 23 | 24 | 108 | 33 | 30 | 37 | 22 | 21 | 1 |

[a] Equivalent MMPI T-Scores rounded to the nearest whole number.

Table B-1.7  Raw Scale Score Conversion for the MMPI-168 for Female Adolescents Age 17 (Without K Corrections)[a]—NCS Scoring Keys

| 168 Score | L | F | K | Hs | D | Hy | Pd | Mf | Pa | Pt | Sc | Ma | Si | 168 Score |
|---|---|---|---|---|---|---|---|---|---|---|---|---|---|---|
| 33 | | | | | 103 | 111 | | | | | | | | 33 |
| 32 | | | | | 101 | 109 | | | | | | | | 32 |
| 31 | | | | | 99 | 105 | | | | | | | | 31 |
| 30 | | | | | 95 | 103 | | | | | | | | 30 |
| 29 | | | | | 93 | 101 | | | | | | | | 29 |
| 28 | | | | | 90 | 97 | 109 | | | | 104 | | | 28 |
| 27 | | | | | 90 | 95 | 107 | | | | 102 | | | 27 |
| 26 | | | | | 88 | 91 | 102 | | | | 100 | | | 26 |
| 25 | | | | | 87 | 89 | 100 | | | | 96 | | | 25 |
| 24 | | | | | 86 | 87 | 98 | | | | 94 | | | 24 |
| 23 | | | | 107 | 85 | 83 | 93 | 22 | | | 92 | 106 | | 23 |
| 22 | | | | 103 | 84 | 81 | 91 | 27 | | | 88 | 104 | | 22 |
| 21 | | | | 100 | 82 | 79 | 86 | 29 | | | 86 | 99 | | 21 |
| 20 | | | | 96 | 78 | 75 | 84 | 33 | | | 84 | 95 | | 20 |
| 19 | | 118 | | 93 | 75 | 73 | 81 | 38 | | 93 | 80 | 91 | | 19 |
| 18 | | 113 | | 91 | 73 | 71 | 77 | 42 | | 90 | 78 | 86 | | 18 |
| 17 | | 109 | | 87 | 69 | 67 | 74 | 47 | 119 | 85 | 76 | 84 | | 17 |
| 16 | | 106 | | 84 | 67 | 65 | 72 | 49 | 113 | 82 | 73 | 80 | 90 | 16 |
| 15 | | 101 | | 82 | 62 | 61 | 67 | 53 | 108 | 78 | 70 | 76 | 85 | 15 |
| 14 | | 96 | | 77 | 60 | 59 | 65 | 58 | 102 | 75 | 68 | 71 | 79 | 14 |
| 13 | | 94 | | 75 | 58 | 57 | 61 | 62 | 96 | 75 | 65 | 69 | 75 | 13 |
| 12 | | 89 | 81 | 71 | 54 | 53 | 58 | 65 | 90 | 69 | 62 | 65 | 70 | 12 |
| 11 | 91 | 84 | 76 | 68 | 52 | 51 | 56 | 69 | 87 | 65 | 60 | 60 | 65 | 11 |
| 10 | 83 | 79 | 71 | 66 | 50 | 49 | 51 | 74 | 82 | 62 | 57 | 56 | 59 | 10 |
| 9 | 79 | 74 | 66 | 61 | 45 | 45 | 49 | 78 | 76 | 58 | 54 | 52 | 54 | 9 |
| 8 | 74 | 72 | 61 | 59 | 43 | 43 | 47 | 83 | 70 | 55 | 52 | 50 | 50 | 8 |
| 7 | 66 | 67 | 59 | 55 | 39 | 39 | 42 | 85 | 64 | 52 | 49 | 45 | 45 | 7 |
| 6 | 62 | 62 | 54 | 52 | 37 | 37 | 40 | 89 | 59 | 47 | 47 | 41 | 39 | 6 |
| 5 | 58 | 57 | 49 | 50 | 35 | 35 | 37 | 94 | 53 | 44 | 44 | 37 | 34 | 5 |
| 4 | 49 | 54 | 44 | 45 | 30 | 31 | 33 | 98 | 50 | 40 | 41 | 34 | 30 | 4 |
| 3 | 45 | 49 | 38 | 43 | 28 | 29 | 31 | 100 | 44 | 37 | 39 | 30 | 25 | 3 |
| 2 | 41 | 45 | 33 | 38 | 26 | 27 | 26 | 104 | 38 | 34 | 36 | 26 | 21 | 2 |
| 1 | 37 | 40 | 28 | 36 | 22 | 23 | 24 | 108 | 31 | 30 | 33 | 22 | 21 | 1 |

[a] Equivalent MMPI T-Scores rounded to the nearest whole number.

Table B-8  Raw Scale Score Conversion for the MMPI-168
for Male Adolescents Age 17 (Without K Corrections)[a]
—Psychological Corporation Scoring Keys

| 168 Score | L | F | K | Hs | D | Hy | Pd | Mf | Pa | Pt | Sc | Ma | Si | 168 Score |
|---|---|---|---|---|---|---|---|---|---|---|---|---|---|---|
| 33 |   |   |   |   | 99 | 112 |   |   |   |   |   |   |   | 33 |
| 32 |   |   |   |   | 97 | 110 |   |   |   |   |   |   |   | 32 |
| 31 |   |   |   |   | 95 | 107 |   |   |   |   |   |   |   | 31 |
| 30 |   |   |   |   | 92 | 105 |   |   |   |   |   |   |   | 30 |
| 29 |   |   |   |   | 90 | 103 |   |   |   |   |   |   |   | 29 |
| 28 |   |   |   |   | 88 | 99 | 109 |   |   |   |   |   |   | 28 |
| 27 |   |   |   |   | 86 | 97 | 107 | 120 |   |   |   |   |   | 27 |
| 26 |   |   |   |   | 83 | 93 | 102 | 116 |   |   |   |   |   | 26 |
| 25 |   |   |   |   | 81 | 91 | 100 | 114 |   |   |   |   |   | 25 |
| 24 |   |   |   |   | 79 | 89 | 98 | 109 |   |   |   |   |   | 24 |
| 23 |   |   |   | 118 | 77 | 86 | 93 | 105 |   |   |   | 101 |   | 23 |
| 22 |   | 119 |   | 113 | 73 | 84 | 91 | 100 |   |   |   | 99 |   | 22 |
| 21 |   | 117 |   | 110 | 72 | 82 | 86 | 98 |   |   |   | 94 |   | 21 |
| 20 |   | 113 |   | 105 | 70 | 78 | 84 | 94 |   |   |   | 90 |   | 20 |
| 19 |   | 108 |   | 103 | 68 | 76 | 81 | 90 |   | 98 |   | 86 |   | 19 |
| 18 |   | 104 |   | 100 | 64 | 74 | 77 | 85 |   | 95 | 104 | 82 |   | 18 |
| 17 |   | 100 |   | 95 | 63 | 70 | 74 | 81 |   | 90 | 100 | 79 |   | 17 |
| 16 |   | 97 |   | 93 | 61 | 68 | 72 | 79 |   | 87 | 96 | 75 | 100 | 16 |
| 15 |   | 93 |   | 90 | 59 | 65 | 67 | 74 | 120 | 82 | 92 | 71 | 94 | 15 |
| 14 |   | 89 |   | 85 | 55 | 63 | 64 | 70 | 117 | 79 | 89 | 67 | 88 | 14 |
| 13 |   | 87 |   | 83 | 54 | 61 | 59 | 66 | 105 | 79 | 84 | 65 | 83 | 13 |
| 12 |   | 82 | 75 | 78 | 52 | 57 | 57 | 63 | 99 | 73 | 80 | 60 | 77 | 12 |
| 11 | 93 | 78 | 71 | 75 | 48 | 55 | 55 | 59 | 93 | 69 | 77 | 56 | 71 | 11 |
| 10 | 84 | 73 | 67 | 73 | 46 | 53 | 50 | 55 | 87 | 65 | 72 | 52 | 65 | 10 |
| 9 | 80 | 69 | 62 | 68 | 44 | 49 | 48 | 50 | 81 | 61 | 69 | 48 | 59 | 9 |
| 8 | 76 | 67 | 58 | 65 | 43 | 48 | 46 | 46 | 75 | 58 | 67 | 45 | 55 | 8 |
| 7 | 68 | 63 | 56 | 60 | 39 | 44 | 41 | 44 | 70 | 55 | 61 | 41 | 49 | 7 |
| 6 | 63 | 58 | 51 | 58 | 37 | 42 | 39 | 40 | 61 | 50 | 57 | 37 | 42 | 6 |
| 5 | 59 | 54 | 47 | 55 | 35 | 40 | 36 | 35 | 55 | 47 | 53 | 33 | 36 | 5 |
| 4 | 51 | 52 | 42 | 50 | 34 | 36 | 32 | 31 | 49 | 42 | 49 | 31 | 32 | 4 |
| 3 | 47 | 47 | 38 | 48 | 30 | 34 | 29 | 29 | 43 | 39 | 46 | 26 | 26 | 3 |
| 2 | 43 | 43 | 34 | 43 | 28 | 32 | 25 | 24 | 37 | 36 | 41 | 22 | 20 | 2 |
| 1 | 38 | 39 | 29 | 40 | 26 | 29 | 23 | 20 | 31 | 32 | 38 | 20 | 20 | 1 |

[a] Equivalent MMPI T-Scores rounded to the nearest whole number.

Table B-1.8  Raw Scale Score Conversion for the MMPI-168
for Male Adolescents Age 17 (Without K Corrections)[a]–NCS Scoring Keys

| 168 Score | L | F | K | Hs | D | Hy | Pd | Mf | Pa | Pt | Sc | Ma | Si | 168 Score |
|---|---|---|---|---|---|---|---|---|---|---|---|---|---|---|
| 33 | | | | | 99 | 112 | | | | | | | | 33 |
| 32 | | | | | 97 | 110 | | | | | | | | 32 |
| 31 | | | | | 95 | 107 | | | | | | | | 31 |
| 30 | | | | | 92 | 105 | | | | | | | | 30 |
| 29 | | | | | 90 | 103 | | | | | | | | 29 |
| 28 | | | | | 88 | 99 | 109 | | | | 102 | | | 28 |
| 27 | | | | | 86 | 97 | 107 | 120 | | | 100 | | | 27 |
| 26 | | | | | 83 | 93 | 102 | 116 | | | 97 | | | 26 |
| 25 | | | | | 81 | 91 | 100 | 114 | | | 94 | | | 25 |
| 24 | | | | | 79 | 89 | 98 | 109 | | | 92 | | | 24 |
| 23 | | | | 118 | 77 | 86 | 93 | 105 | | | 90 | 101 | | 23 |
| 22 | | 119 | | 113 | 73 | 84 | 91 | 100 | | | 86 | 99 | | 22 |
| 21 | | 117 | | 110 | 72 | 82 | 86 | 98 | | | 84 | 94 | | 21 |
| 20 | | 113 | | 105 | 70 | 78 | 84 | 94 | | | 82 | 90 | | 20 |
| 19 | | 108 | | 103 | 68 | 76 | 81 | 90 | | 98 | 79 | 86 | | 19 |
| 18 | | 104 | | 100 | 64 | 74 | 77 | 85 | | 95 | 77 | 82 | | 18 |
| 17 | | 100 | | 95 | 63 | 70 | 74 | 81 | 120 | 90 | 74 | 79 | | 17 |
| 16 | | 97 | | 93 | 61 | 68 | 72 | 79 | 114 | 87 | 72 | 75 | 100 | 16 |
| 15 | | 93 | | 90 | 59 | 65 | 67 | 74 | 108 | 82 | 69 | 71 | 94 | 15 |
| 14 | | 89 | | 85 | 55 | 63 | 64 | 70 | 102 | 79 | 67 | 67 | 88 | 14 |
| 13 | | 87 | | 83 | 54 | 61 | 59 | 66 | 96 | 79 | 64 | 65 | 83 | 13 |
| 12 | | 82 | 75 | 78 | 52 | 57 | 57 | 63 | 90 | 73 | 61 | 60 | 77 | 12 |
| 11 | 93 | 78 | 71 | 75 | 48 | 55 | 55 | 59 | 87 | 69 | 59 | 56 | 71 | 11 |
| 10 | 84 | 73 | 67 | 73 | 46 | 53 | 50 | 55 | 81 | 65 | 57 | 52 | 65 | 10 |
| 9 | 80 | 69 | 62 | 68 | 44 | 49 | 48 | 50 | 75 | 61 | 53 | 48 | 59 | 9 |
| 8 | 76 | 67 | 58 | 65 | 43 | 48 | 46 | 46 | 70 | 58 | 51 | 45 | 55 | 8 |
| 7 | 68 | 63 | 56 | 60 | 39 | 44 | 41 | 44 | 64 | 55 | 49 | 41 | 49 | 7 |
| 6 | 63 | 58 | 51 | 58 | 37 | 42 | 39 | 40 | 58 | 50 | 47 | 37 | 42 | 6 |
| 5 | 59 | 54 | 47 | 55 | 35 | 40 | 36 | 35 | 52 | 47 | 44 | 33 | 36 | 5 |
| 4 | 51 | 52 | 42 | 50 | 34 | 36 | 32 | 31 | 49 | 42 | 44 | 31 | 32 | 4 |
| 3 | 47 | 47 | 38 | 48 | 30 | 34 | 29 | 29 | 43 | 39 | 39 | 26 | 26 | 3 |
| 2 | 43 | 43 | 34 | 43 | 28 | 32 | 25 | 24 | 37 | 36 | 36 | 22 | 20 | 2 |
| 1 | 38 | 39 | 29 | 40 | 26 | 29 | 23 | 20 | 31 | 32 | 34 | 20 | 20 | 1 |

[a] Equivalent MMPI T-Scores rounded to the nearest whole number.

# Responses by Code Types to the Social Readjustment Rating Scale[1] (Items)

### Table C1  Social Readjustment Rating Scale Item: Marriage

| Comparison Data | Frequency (%) |
|---|---|
| Mythical Average Patient Code: | 10 |
| L greater than T-score 70: | 14 |
| F greater than Raw Score 15: | 0 |
| K greater than T-score 70: | 0 |
| False Normal Code: | 2 |

| Code Type | Frequency (%) | Code Type | Frequency (%) | Code Type | Frequency (%) |
|---|---|---|---|---|---|
| 1 code | 0 | 26 code | 0 | 128 code | 0 |
| 2 code | 7 | 27 code | 0 | 237 code | 17 |
| 3 code | 10 | 28 code | 7 | 238 code | 14 |
| 4 code | 6 | 36 code | 0 | 246 code | 0 |
| 5 code | 0 | 37 code | 9 | 248 code | 0 |
| Low 5 female | 7 | 38 code | 0 | 268 code | 0 |
| 6 code | 0 | 46 code | 0 | 278 code | 4 |
| 7 code | 12 | 47 code | 21 | 289 code | 0 |
| 8 code | 10 | 48 code | 14 | 468 code | 0 |
| 9 code | 5 | 49 code | 0 | 469 code | 0 |
| 12 code | 14 | 68 code | 0 | 478 code | 40 |
| 13 code | 0 | 69 code | 13 | 489 code | 0 |
| 18 code | 0 | 78 code | 8 | 678 code | 11 |
| 23 code | 14 | 89 code | 0 | 689 code | 0 |
| 24 code | 0 | 123 code | 14 | 789 code | 0 |

[1] The Social Readjustment Rating Scale may be purchsed from: Thomas H. Holmes, M.D., Department of Medicine and Behavioral Science, School of Medicine, University of Washington, Seattle, WA 98195.

### Table C2  Social Readjustment Rating Scale Item: Trouble with the Boss

| Comparison Data | Frequency (%) |
|---|---|
| Mythical Average Patient Code: | 32 |
| L greater than T-score 70: | 14 |
| F greater than Raw Score 15: | 38 |
| K greater than T-score 70: | 10 |
| False Normal Code: | 20 |

| Code Type | Frequency (%) | Code Type | Frequency (%) | Code Type | Frequency (%) |
|---|---|---|---|---|---|
| 1 code | 27 | 26 code | 57 | 128 code | 43 |
| 2 code | 47 | 27 code | 14 | 237 code | 8 |
| 3 code | 0 | 28 code | 41 | 238 code | 14 |
| 4 code | 63 | 36 code | 0 | 246 code | 14 |
| 5 code | 43 | 37 code | 0 | 248 code | 20 |
| Low 5 female | 23 | 38 code | 14 | 268 code | 67 |
| 6 code | 44 | 46 code | 35 | 278 code | 40 |
| 7 code | 18 | 47 code | 50 | 289 code | 0 |
| 8 code | 38 | 48 code | 50 | 468 code | 57 |
| 9 code | 38 | 49 code | 14 | 469 code | 25 |
| 12 code | 14 | 68 code | 41 | 478 code | 33 |
| 13 code | 15 | 69 code | 38 | 489 code | 50 |
| 18 code | 14 | 78 code | 37 | 678 code | 67 |
| 23 code | 29 | 89 code | 36 | 689 code | 38 |
| 24 code | 14 | 123 code | 14 | 789 code | 67 |

### Table C3  Social Readjustment Rating Scale Item: Detention in Jail or Other Institution

| Comparison Data | Frequency (%) |
|---|---|
| Mythical Average Patient Code: | 10 |
| L greater than T-score 70: | 0 |
| F greater than Raw Score 15: | 13 |
| K greater than T-score 70: | 0 |
| False Normal Code: | 7 |

| Code Type | Frequency (%) | Code Type | Frequency (%) | Code Type | Frequency (%) |
|---|---|---|---|---|---|
| 1 code | 0 | 26 code | 0 | 128 code | 0 |
| 2 code | 13 | 27 code | 0 | 237 code | 0 |
| 3 code | 0 | 28 code | 3 | 238 code | 0 |
| 4 code | 19 | 36 code | 0 | 246 code | 0 |
| 5 code | 14 | 37 code | 9 | 248 code | 0 |
| Low 5 female | 5 | 38 code | 0 | 268 code | 0 |
| 6 code | 6 | 46 code | 12 | 278 code | 4 |
| 7 code | 12 | 47 code | 7 | 289 code | 14 |
| 8 code | 9 | 48 code | 29 | 468 code | 14 |
| 9 code | 10 | 49 code | 0 | 469 code | 0 |
| 12 code | 14 | 68 code | 18 | 478 code | 20 |
| 13 code | 0 | 69 code | 0 | 489 code | 17 |
| 18 code | 14 | 78 code | 13 | 678 code | 0 |
| 23 code | 7 | 89 code | 9 | 689 code | 25 |
| 24 code | 14 | 123 code | 0 | 789 code | 50 |

### Table C4  Social Readjustment Rating Scale Item: Death of a Spouse

| Comparison Data | Frequency (%) |
|---|---|
| Mythical Average Patient Code: | 0 |
| L greater than T-score 70: | 0 |
| F greater than Raw Score 15: | 0 |
| K greater than T-score 70: | 0 |
| False Normal Code: | 2 |

| Code Type | Frequency (%) | Code Type | Frequency (%) | Code Type | Frequency (%) |
|---|---|---|---|---|---|
| 1 code | 0 | 26 code | 0 | 128 code | 0 |
| 2 code | 0 | 27 code | 0 | 237 code | 0 |
| 3 code | 0 | 28 code | 0 | 238 code | 0 |
| 4 code | 0 | 36 code | 0 | 246 code | 0 |
| 5 code | 14 | 37 code | 0 | 248 code | 0 |
| Low 5 female | 2 | 38 code | 0 | 268 code | 0 |
| 6 code | 0 | 46 code | 0 | 278 code | 0 |
| 7 code | 0 | 47 code | 0 | 289 code | 0 |
| 8 code | 3 | 48 code | 7 | 468 code | 0 |
| 9 code | 5 | 49 code | 0 | 469 code | 0 |
| 12 code | 0 | 68 code | 0 | 478 code | 0 |
| 13 code | 0 | 69 code | 0 | 489 code | 0 |
| 18 code | 0 | 78 code | 3 | 678 code | 0 |
| 23 code | 0 | 89 code | 0 | 689 code | 0 |
| 24 code | 0 | 123 code | 0 | 789 code | 0 |

### Table C5  Social Readjustment Rating Scale Item: Sleep Disturbance (Much More or Much Less)

| Comparison Data | Frequency (%) |
|---|---|
| Mythical Average Patient Code: | 68 |
| L greater than T-score 70: | 71 |
| F greater than Raw Score 15: | 50 |
| K greater than T-score 70: | 60 |
| False Normal Code: | 51 |

| Code Type | Frequency (%) | Code Type | Frequency (%) | Code Type | Frequency (%) |
|---|---|---|---|---|---|
| 1 code | 64 | 26 code | 71 | 128 code | 100 |
| 2 code | 87 | 27 code | 79 | 237 code | 83 |
| 3 code | 90 | 28 code | 87 | 238 code | 100 |
| 4 code | 63 | 36 code | 50 | 246 code | 86 |
| 5 code | 71 | 37 code | 55 | 248 code | 100 |
| Low 5 female | 73 | 38 code | 86 | 268 code | 100 |
| 6 code | 91 | 46 code | 65 | 278 code | 88 |
| 7 code | 94 | 47 code | 79 | 289 code | 100 |
| 8 code | 74 | 48 code | 86 | 468 code | 86 |
| 9 code | 76 | 49 code | 43 | 469 code | 50 |
| 12 code | 71 | 68 code | 76 | 478 code | 87 |
| 13 code | 77 | 69 code | 50 | 489 code | 67 |
| 18 code | 100 | 78 code | 79 | 678 code | 89 |
| 23 code | 86 | 89 code | 68 | 689 code | 75 |
| 24 code | 100 | 123 code | 57 | 789 code | 83 |

## Table C6  Social Readjustment Rating Scale Item:
## Death of a Close Family Member

| Comparison Data | Frequency (%) |
|---|---|
| Mythical Average Patient Code: | 24 |
| L greater than T-score 70: | 43 |
| F greater than Raw Score 15: | 25 |
| K greater than T-score 70: | 10 |
| False Normal Code: | 13 |

| Code Type | Frequency (%) | Code Type | Frequency (%) | Code Type | Frequency (%) |
|---|---|---|---|---|---|
| 1 code | 27 | 26 code | 0 | 128 code | 43 |
| 2 code | 13 | 27 code | 29 | 237 code | 25 |
| 3 code | 10 | 28 code | 14 | 238 code | 0 |
| 4 code | 25 | 36 code | 17 | 246 code | 14 |
| 5 code | 29 | 37 code | 0 | 248 code | 30 |
| Low 5 female | 27 | 38 code | 14 | 268 code | 17 |
| 6 code | 25 | 46 code | 12 | 278 code | 20 |
| 7 code | 24 | 47 code | 14 | 289 code | 29 |
| 8 code | 26 | 48 code | 7 | 468 code | 29 |
| 9 code | 33 | 49 code | 29 | 469 code | 12 |
| 12 code | 14 | 68 code | 35 | 478 code | 13 |
| 13 code | 23 | 69 code | 13 | 489 code | 17 |
| 18 code | 57 | 78 code | 21 | 678 code | 22 |
| 23 code | 21 | 89 code | 18 | 689 code | 50 |
| 24 code | 29 | 123 code | 0 | 789 code | 0 |

## Table C7  Social Readjustment Rating Scale Item: Major Change in
## Eating Habits (Less/More Food Intake, Different Hours, Surroundings, etc.)

| Comparison Data | Frequency (%) |
|---|---|
| Mythical Average Patient Code: | 62 |
| L greater than T-score 70: | 29 |
| F greater than Raw Score 15: | 50 |
| K greater than T-score 70: | 30 |
| False Normal Code: | 33 |

| Code Type | Frequency (%) | Code Type | Frequency (%) | Code Type | Frequency (%) |
|---|---|---|---|---|---|
| 1 code | 82 | 26 code | 100 | 128 code | 100 |
| 2 code | 47 | 27 code | 36 | 237 code | 42 |
| 3 code | 10 | 28 code | 79 | 238 code | 71 |
| 4 code | 63 | 36 code | 17 | 246 code | 57 |
| 5 code | 14 | 37 code | 64 | 248 code | 90 |
| Low 5 female | 45 | 38 code | 29 | 268 code | 83 |
| 6 code | 44 | 46 code | 59 | 278 code | 64 |
| 7 code | 59 | 47 code | 50 | 289 code | 71 |
| 8 code | 68 | 48 code | 57 | 468 code | 43 |
| 9 code | 48 | 49 code | 43 | 469 code | 50 |
| 12 code | 57 | 68 code | 47 | 478 code | 53 |
| 13 code | 54 | 69 code | 38 | 489 code | 83 |
| 18 code | 71 | 78 code | 66 | 678 code | 67 |
| 23 code | 50 | 89 code | 64 | 689 code | 64 |
| 24 code | 71 | 123 code | 57 | 789 code | 83 |

### Table C8  Social Readjustment Rating Scale Item: Foreclosure on a Mortgage or Loan

| Comparison Data | Frequency (%) |
|---|---|
| Mythical Average Patient Code: | 2 |
| L greater than T-score 70: | 0 |
| F greater than Raw Score 15: | 0 |
| K greater than T-score 0: | 0 |
| False Normal Code: | 0 |

| Code Type | Frequency (%) | Code Type | Frequency (%) | Code Type | Frequency (%) |
|---|---|---|---|---|---|
| 1 code | 0 | 26 code | 0 | 128 code | 0 |
| 2 code | 7 | 27 code | 0 | 237 code | 10 |
| 3 code | 0 | 28 code | 7 | 238 code | 0 |
| 4 code | 0 | 36 code | 0 | 246 code | 0 |
| 5 code | 0 | 37 code | 9 | 248 code | 10 |
| Low 5 female | 5 | 38 code | 0 | 268 code | 0 |
| 6 code | 0 | 46 code | 41 | 278 code | 8 |
| 7 code | 0 | 47 code | 0 | 289 code | 0 |
| 8 code | 0 | 48 code | 7 | 468 code | 0 |
| 9 code | 0 | 49 code | 0 | 469 code | 0 |
| 12 code | 0 | 68 code | 0 | 478 code | 0 |
| 13 code | 8 | 69 code | 0 | 489 code | 33 |
| 18 code | 0 | 78 code | 0 | 678 code | 0 |
| 23 code | 7 | 89 code | 18 | 689 code | 0 |
| 24 code | 29 | 123 code | 0 | 789 code | 0 |

### Table C9  Social Readjustment Rating Scale Item: Revision of Personal Habits (Dress, Friends, Manners, etc.)

| Comparison Data | Frequency (%) |
|---|---|
| Mythical Average Patient Code: | 34 |
| L greater than T-score 70: | 14 |
| F greater than Raw Score 15: | 50 |
| K greater than T-score 70: | 20 |
| False Normal Code: | 24 |

| Code Type | Frequency (%) | Code Type | Frequency (%) | Code Type | Frequency (%) |
|---|---|---|---|---|---|
| 1 code | 9 | 26 code | 71 | 128 code | 57 |
| 2 code | 40 | 27 code | 29 | 237 code | 33 |
| 3 code | 20 | 28 code | 41 | 238 code | 43 |
| 4 code | 19 | 36 code | 0 | 246 code | 43 |
| 5 code | 29 | 37 code | 18 | 248 code | 40 |
| Low 5 female | 20 | 38 code | 43 | 268 code | 67 |
| 6 code | 19 | 38 code | 0 | 278 code | 28 |
| 7 code | 35 | 47 code | 36 | 289 code | 43 |
| 8 code | 45 | 48 code | 36 | 468 code | 57 |
| 9 code | 43 | 49 code | 29 | 469 code | 38 |
| 12 code | 57 | 68 code | 35 | 478 code | 27 |
| 13 code | 8 | 69 code | 13 | 489 code | 50 |
| 18 code | 43 | 78 code | 37 | 678 code | 56 |
| 23 code | 29 | 89 code | 32 | 689 code | 38 |
| 24 code | 29 | 123 code | 29 | 789 code | 67 |

## Table C10  Social Readjustment Rating Scale Item: Death of a Close Friend

| Comparison Data | Frequency (%) |
|---|---|
| Mythical Average Patient Code: | 28 |
| L greater than T-score 70: | 29 |
| F greater than Raw Score 15: | 38 |
| K greater than T-score: | 10 |
| False Normal Code: | 9 |

| Code Type | Frequency (%) | Code Type | Frequency (%) | Code Type | Frequency (%) |
|---|---|---|---|---|---|
| 1 code | 18 | 26 code | 29 | 128 code | 43 |
| 2 code | 20 | 27 code | 14 | 237 code | 8 |
| 3 code | 6 | 28 code | 14 | 238 code | 0 |
| 4 code | 6 | 36 code | 0 | 246 code | 0 |
| 5 code | 0 | 37 code | 0 | 248 code | 0 |
| Low 5 female | 7 | 38 code | 29 | 268 code | 50 |
| 6 code | 6 | 46 code | 6 | 278 code | 8 |
| 7 code | 18 | 47 code | 14 | 289 code | 0 |
| 8 code | 17 | 48 code | 7 | 468 code | 0 |
| 9 code | 10 | 49 code | 0 | 469 code | 12 |
| 12 code | 57 | 68 code | 6 | 478 code | 13 |
| 13 code | 15 | 69 code | 13 | 489 code | 17 |
| 18 code | 29 | 78 code | 13 | 678 code | 11 |
| 23 code | 7 | 89 code | 14 | 689 code | 12 |
| 24 code | 0 | 123 code | 14 | 789 code | 0 |

## Table C11  Social Readjustment Rating Scale Item: Minor Violations of Law (Traffic Tickets. Jay Walking, Disturbing the Peace, etc.)

| Comparison Data | Frequency (%) |
|---|---|
| Mythical Average Patient Code: | 16 |
| L greater than T-score 70: | 0 |
| F greater than Raw Score 15: | 13 |
| K greater than T-score 70: | 30 |
| False Normal Code: | 20 |

| Code Type | Frequency (%) | Code Type | Frequency (%) | Code Type | Frequency (%) |
|---|---|---|---|---|---|
| 1 code | 0 | 26 code | 29 | 128 code | 14 |
| 2 code | 13 | 27 code | 7 | 237 code | 8 |
| 3 code | 0 | 28 code | 10 | 238 code | 0 |
| 4 code | 25 | 36 code | 17 | 246 code | 14 |
| 5 code | 14 | 37 code | 0 | 248 code | 30 |
| Low 5 female | 7 | 38 code | 0 | 268 code | 0 |
| 6 code | 6 | 46 code | 24 | 278 code | 4 |
| 7 code | 29 | 47 code | 21 | 289 code | 14 |
| 8 code | 12 | 48 code | 14 | 468 code | 29 |
| 9 code | 10 | 49 code | 14 | 469 code | 25 |
| 12 code | 0 | 68 code | 12 | 478 code | 13 |
| 13 code | 0 | 69 code | 0 | 489 code | 50 |
| 18 code | 14 | 78 code | 13 | 678 code | 11 |
| 23 code | 14 | 89 code | 32 | 689 code | 0 |
| 24 code | 14 | 123 code | 0 | 789 code | 33 |

### Table C12  Social Readjustment Rating Scale Item: Outstanding Personal Achievement

| Comparison Data | Frequency (%) |
|---|---|
| Mythical Average Patient Code: | 30 |
| L greater than T-score 70: | 0 |
| F greater than Raw Score 15: | 25 |
| K greater than T-score 70: | 30 |
| False Normal Code: | 7 |

| Code Type | Frequency (%) | Code Type | Frequency (%) | Code Type | Frequency (%) |
|---|---|---|---|---|---|
| 1 code | 36 | 26 code | 0 | 128 code | 14 |
| 2 code | 27 | 27 code | 21 | 237 code | 8 |
| 3 code | 20 | 28 code | 17 | 238 code | 14 |
| 4 code | 19 | 36 code | 0 | 246 code | 0 |
| 5 code | 29 | 37 code | 0 | 248 code | 30 |
| Low 5 female | 34 | 38 code | 0 | 268 code | 0 |
| 6 code | 0 | 46 code | 6 | 278 code | 28 |
| 7 code | 24 | 47 code | 21 | 289 code | 43 |
| 8 code | 22 | 48 code | 36 | 468 code | 14 |
| 9 code | 43 | 49 code | 29 | 469 code | 25 |
| 12 code | 29 | 68 code | 24 | 478 code | 7 |
| 13 code | 31 | 69 code | 13 | 489 code | 17 |
| 18 code | 13 | 78 code | 26 | 678 code | 44 |
| 23 code | 36 | 89 code | 36 | 689 code | 0 |
| 24 code | 14 | 123 code | 43 | 789 code | 33 |

### Table C13  Social Readjustment Rating Scale Item: Pregnancy

| Comparison Data | Frequency (%) |
|---|---|
| Mythical Average Patient Code: | 6 |
| L greater than T-score 70: | 0 |
| F greater than Raw Score 15: | 0 |
| K greater than T-score 70: | 10 |
| False Normal Code: | 4 |

| Code Type | Frequency (%) | Code Type | Frequency (%) | Code Type | Frequency (%) |
|---|---|---|---|---|---|
| 1 code | 0 | 26 code | 14 | 128 code | 0 |
| 2 code | 7 | 27 code | 0 | 237 code | 0 |
| 3 code | 10 | 28 code | 3 | 238 code | 14 |
| 4 code | 13 | 36 code | 0 | 246 code | 0 |
| 5 code | 29 | 37 code | 0 | 248 code | 0 |
| Low 5 female | 2 | 38 code | 14 | 268 code | 0 |
| 6 code | 6 | 46 code | 12 | 278 code | 0 |
| 7 code | 12 | 47 code | 21 | 289 code | 29 |
| 8 code | 5 | 48 code | 0 | 468 code | 14 |
| 9 code | 14 | 49 code | 14 | 469 code | 12 |
| 12 code | 0 | 68 code | 6 | 478 code | 20 |
| 13 code | 0 | 69 code | 0 | 489 code | 0 |
| 18 code | 0 | 78 code | 3 | 678 code | 0 |
| 23 code | 7 | 89 code | 14 | 689 code | 0 |
| 24 code | 0 | 123 code | 0 | 789 code | 0 |

### Table C14  Social Readjustment Rating Scale Item: Major Change in Health or Behavior of a Family Member

| Comparison Data | Frequency (%) |
|---|---|
| Mythical Average Patient Code: | 26 |
| L greater than T-score 70: | 14 |
| F greater than Raw Score 15: | 25 |
| K greater than T-score 70: | 20 |
| False Normal Code: | 29 |

| Code Type | Frequency (%) | Code Type | Frequency (%) | Code Type | Frequency (%) |
|---|---|---|---|---|---|
| 1 code | 27 | 26 code | 57 | 128 code | 43 |
| 2 code | 29 | 27 code | 14 | 237 code | 17 |
| 3 code | 20 | 28 code | 38 | 238 code | 71 |
| 4 code | 38 | 36 code | 33 | 246 code | 29 |
| 5 code | 14 | 37 code | 18 | 248 code | 30 |
| Low 5 female | 34 | 38 code | 29 | 268 code | 83 |
| 6 code | 38 | 46 code | 35 | 278 code | 28 |
| 7 code | 29 | 47 code | 29 | 289 code | 14 |
| 8 code | 47 | 48 code | 57 | 468 code | 29 |
| 9 code | 48 | 49 code | 29 | 469 code | 38 |
| 12 code | 29 | 68 code | 12 | 478 code | 47 |
| 13 code | 38 | 69 code | 38 | 489 code | 67 |
| 18 code | 71 | 78 code | 45 | 678 code | 33 |
| 23 code | 50 | 89 code | 27 | 689 code | 25 |
| 24 code | 0 | 123 code | 43 | 789 code | 50 |

### Table C15  Social Readjustment Rating Scale Item:  Sexual Difficulties

| Comparison Data | Frequency (%) |
|---|---|
| Mythical Average Patient Code: | 40 |
| L greater than T-score 70: | 14 |
| F greater than Raw Score 15: | 38 |
| K greater than T-score 70: | 30 |
| False Normal Code: | 20 |

| Code Type | Frequency (%) | Code Type | Frequency (%) | Code Type | Frequency (%) |
|---|---|---|---|---|---|
| 1 code | 36 | 26 code | 43 | 128 code | 29 |
| 2 code | 13 | 27 code | 14 | 237 code | 8 |
| 3 code | 30 | 28 code | 34 | 238 code | 43 |
| 4 code | 50 | 36 code | 33 | 246 code | 29 |
| 5 code | 14 | 37 code | 18 | 248 code | 50 |
| Low 5 female | 32 | 38 code | 43 | 268 code | 17 |
| 6 code | 31 | 46 code | 41 | 278 code | 28 |
| 7 code | 35 | 47 code | 50 | 289 code | 43 |
| 8 code | 38 | 48 code | 43 | 468 code | 43 |
| 9 code | 52 | 49 code | 29 | 469 code | 12 |
| 12 code | 43 | 68 code | 24 | 478 code | 47 |
| 13 code | 46 | 69 code | 25 | 489 code | 33 |
| 18 code | 71 | 78 code | 39 | 678 code | 33 |
| 23 code | 29 | 89 code | 50 | 689 code | 0 |
| 24 code | 43 | 123 code | 43 | 789 code | 67 |

### Table C16  Social Readjustment Rating Scale Item: In-Law Troubles

| Comparison Data | Frequency (%) |
|---|---|
| Mythical Average Patient Code: | 16 |
| L greater than T-score 70: | 0 |
| F greater than Raw Score 15: | 38 |
| K greater than T-score: | 0 |
| False Normal Code: | 4 |

| Code Type | Frequency (%) | Code Type | Frequency (%) | Code Type | Frequency (%) |
|---|---|---|---|---|---|
| 1 code | 27 | 26 code | 14 | 128 code | 29 |
| 2 code | 13 | 27 code | 7 | 237 code | 33 |
| 3 code | 10 | 28 code | 17 | 238 code | 29 |
| 4 code | 13 | 36 code | 0 | 246 code | 14 |
| 5 code | 0 | 37 code | 9 | 248 code | 30 |
| Low 5 female | 16 | 38 code | 14 | 268 code | 17 |
| 6 code | 19 | 46 code | 12 | 278 code | 8 |
| 7 code | 12 | 47 code | 14 | 289 code | 0 |
| 8 code | 21 | 48 code | 21 | 468 code | 29 |
| 9 code | 19 | 49 code | 0 | 469 code | 0 |
| 12 code | 0 | 68 code | 35 | 478 code | 20 |
| 13 code | 15 | 69 code | 0 | 489 code | 17 |
| 18 code | 14 | 78 code | 16 | 678 code | 44 |
| 23 code | 21 | 89 code | 9 | 689 code | 38 |
| 24 code | 71 | 123 code | 0 | 789 code | 0 |

### Table C17  Social Readjustment Rating Scale Item:  Major Change in Number of Family Get-togethers

| Comparison Data | Frequency (%) |
|---|---|
| Mythical Average Patient Code: | 18 |
| L greater than T-score 70: | 0 |
| F greater than Raw Score 15: | 25 |
| K greater than T-score 70: | 0 |
| False Normal Code: | 7 |

| Code Type | Frequency (%) | Code Type | Frequency (%) | Code Type | Frequency (%) |
|---|---|---|---|---|---|
| 1 code | 0 | 26 code | 14 | 128 code | 43 |
| 2 code | 20 | 27 code | 21 | 237 code | 8 |
| 3 code | 10 | 28 code | 24 | 238 code | 43 |
| 4 code | 31 | 36 code | 17 | 246 code | 29 |
| 5 code | 0 | 37 code | 9 | 248 code | 10 |
| Low 5 female | 16 | 38 code | 14 | 268 code | 0 |
| 6 code | 13 | 46 code | 41 | 278 code | 12 |
| 7 code | 12 | 47 code | 43 | 289 code | 14 |
| 8 code | 14 | 48 code | 14 | 468 code | 0 |
| 9 code | 19 | 49 code | 0 | 469 code | 25 |
| 12 code | 29 | 68 code | 6 | 478 code | 20 |
| 13 code | 0 | 69 code | 0 | 489 code | 33 |
| 18 code | 14 | 78 code | 8 | 678 code | 0 |
| 23 code | 21 | 89 code | 18 | 689 code | 0 |
| 24 code | 0 | 123 code | 14 | 789 code | 33 |

### Table C18  Social Readjustment Rating Scale Item: Major Change in Financial State (Much Worse Off, Much Better Off)

| Comparison Data | Frequency (%) |
|---|---|
| Mythical Average Patient Code: | 50 |
| L greater than T-score 70: | 14 |
| F greater than Raw Score 15: | 50 |
| K greater than T-score 70: | 10 |
| False Normal Code: | 33 |

| Code Type | Frequency (%) | Code Type | Frequency (%) | Code Type | Frequency (%) |
|---|---|---|---|---|---|
| 1 code | 36 | 26 code | 71 | 128 code | 71 |
| 2 code | 53 | 27 code | 50 | 237 code | 71 |
| 3 code | 40 | 28 code | 41 | 238 code | 43 |
| 4 code | 44 | 36 code | 33 | 246 code | 71 |
| 5 code | 71 | 37 code | 36 | 248 code | 50 |
| Low 5 female | 48 | 38 code | 43 | 268 code | 68 |
| 6 code | 31 | 46 code | 57 | 278 code | 52 |
| 7 code | 41 | 47 code | 57 | 289 code | 57 |
| 8 code | 52 | 48 code | 50 | 468 code | 43 |
| 9 code | 43 | 49 code | 43 | 469 code | 50 |
| 12 code | 43 | 68 code | 24 | 478 code | 53 |
| 13 code | 31 | 69 code | 13 | 489 code | 100 |
| 18 code | 43 | 78 code | 47 | 678 code | 22 |
| 23 code | 64 | 89 code | 82 | 689 code | 12 |
| 24 code | 71 | 123 code | 43 | 789 code | 100 |

### Table C19  Social Readjustment Rating Scale Item: Gaining New Family Member (Birth, Adoption, Oldster Moving In, etc.)

| Comparison Data | Frequency (%) |
|---|---|
| Mythical Average Patient Code: | 8 |
| L greater than T-score 70: | 0 |
| F greater than Raw Score 15: | 13 |
| K greater than T-score 70: | 10 |
| False Normal Code: | 4 |

| Code Type | Frequency (%) | Code Type | Frequency (%) | Code Type | Frequency (%) |
|---|---|---|---|---|---|
| 1 code | 18 | 26 code | 43 | 128 code | 0 |
| 2 code | 13 | 27 code | 0 | 237 code | 25 |
| 3 code | 10 | 28 code | 10 | 238 code | 71 |
| 4 code | 13 | 36 code | 17 | 246 code | 29 |
| 5 code | 43 | 37 code | 36 | 248 code | 20 |
| Low 5 female | 20 | 38 code | 29 | 268 code | 50 |
| 6 code | 31 | 46 code | 35 | 278 code | 0 |
| 7 code | 0 | 47 code | 0 | 289 code | 0 |
| 8 code | 12 | 48 code | 7 | 468 code | 29 |
| 9 code | 10 | 49 code | 14 | 469 code | 12 |
| 12 code | 14 | 68 code | 29 | 478 code | 13 |
| 13 code | 15 | 69 code | 25 | 489 code | 0 |
| 18 code | 0 | 78 code | 11 | 678 code | 0 |
| 23 code | 14 | 89 code | 9 | 689 code | 38 |
| 24 code | 29 | 123 code | 0 | 789 code | 17 |

### Table C20 Social Readjustment Scale Item: Change in Residence

| Comparison Data | Frequency (%) |
|---|---|
| Mythical Average Patient Code: | 50 |
| L greater than T-score 70: | 0 |
| F greater than Raw Score 15: | 38 |
| K greater than T-score 70: | 20 |
| False Normal Code: | 24 |

| Code Type | Frequency (%) | Code Type | Frequency (%) | Code Type | Frequency (%) |
|---|---|---|---|---|---|
| 1 code | 45 | 26 code | 57 | 128 code | 71 |
| 2 code | 47 | 27 code | 21 | 237 code | 33 |
| 3 code | 0 | 28 code | 52 | 238 code | 14 |
| 4 code | 25 | 36 code | 0 | 246 code | 43 |
| 5 code | 5 | 37 code | 36 | 248 code | 70 |
| Low 5 female | 36 | 38 code | 14 | 268 code | 67 |
| 6 code | 19 | 46 code | 41 | 278 code | 40 |
| 7 code | 41 | 47 code | 36 | 289 code | 43 |
| 8 code | 40 | 48 code | 43 | 468 code | 14 |
| 9 code | 24 | 49 code | 14 | 469 code | 38 |
| 12 code | 71 | 68 code | 24 | 478 code | 60 |
| 13 code | 23 | 69 code | 13 | 489 code | 50 |
| 18 code | 43 | 78 code | 37 | 678 code | 44 |
| 23 code | 50 | 89 code | 36 | 689 code | 25 |
| 24 code | 57 | 123 code | 57 | 789 code | 33 |

### Table C21 Social Readjustment Rating Scale Item: Son or Daughter Leaving Home (Marriage, College, etc.)

| Comparison Data | Frequency (%) |
|---|---|
| Mythical Average Patient Code: | 10 |
| L greater than T-score 70: | 0 |
| F greater than Raw Score 15: | 13 |
| K greater than T-score 70: | 0 |
| False Normal Code: | 9 |

| Code Type | Frequency (%) | Code Type | Frequency (%) | Code Type | Frequency (%) |
|---|---|---|---|---|---|
| 1 code | 27 | 26 code | 0 | 128 code | 14 |
| 2 code | 20 | 27 code | 14 | 237 code | 17 |
| 3 code | 10 | 28 code | 7 | 238 code | 0 |
| 4 code | 6 | 36 code | 17 | 246 code | 14 |
| 5 code | 0 | 37 code | 18 | 248 code | 10 |
| Low 5 female | 23 | 38 code | 0 | 268 code | 0 |
| 6 code | 6 | 46 code | 18 | 278 code | 24 |
| 7 code | 24 | 47 code | 0 | 289 code | 0 |
| 8 code | 9 | 48 code | 0 | 468 code | 14 |
| 9 code | 5 | 49 code | 0 | 469 code | 25 |
| 12 code | 14 | 68 code | 12 | 478 code | 7 |
| 13 code | 23 | 69 code | 0 | 489 code | 0 |
| 18 code | 14 | 78 code | 11 | 678 code | 0 |
| 23 code | 21 | 89 code | 14 | 689 code | 25 |
| 24 code | 14 | 123 code | 0 | 789 code | 0 |

### Table C22 Social Readjustment Rating Scale Item: Marital Separation from Mate

| Comparison Data | Frequency (%) |
|---|---|
| Mythical Average Patient Code: | 14 |
| L greater than T-score 70: | 0 |
| F greater than Raw Score 15: | 63 |
| K greater than T-score: | 10 |
| False Normal Code: | 13 |

| Code Type | Frequency (%) | Code Type | Frequency (%) | Code Type | Frequency (%) |
|---|---|---|---|---|---|
| 1 code | 9 | 26 code | 29 | 128 code | 29 |
| 2 code | 47 | 27 code | 0 | 237 code | 8 |
| 3 code | 0 | 28 code | 24 | 238 code | 29 |
| 4 code | 31 | 36 code | 0 | 246 code | 29 |
| 5 code | 0 | 37 code | 27 | 248 code | 20 |
| Low 5 female | 7 | 38 code | 14 | 268 code | 17 |
| 6 code | 6 | 46 code | 24 | 278 code | 12 |
| 7 code | 18 | 47 code | 21 | 289 code | 14 |
| 8 code | 14 | 48 code | 29 | 468 code | 29 |
| 9 code | 14 | 49 code | 29 | 469 code | 64 |
| 12 code | 14 | 68 code | 18 | 478 code | 27 |
| 13 code | 15 | 69 code | 25 | 489 code | 33 |
| 18 code | 29 | 78 code | 16 | 678 code | 44 |
| 23 code | 14 | 89 code | 23 | 689 code | 25 |
| 24 code | 57 | 123 code | 29 | 789 code | 17 |

### Table C23 Social Readjustment Rating Scale Item: Major Change in Church Activities (much more, much less than usual)

| Comparison Data | Frequency (%) |
|---|---|
| Mythical Average Patient Code: | 8 |
| L greater than T-score 70: | 0 |
| F greater than Raw Score 15: | 0 |
| K greater than T-score: | 0 |
| False Normal Code: | 9 |

| Code Type | Frequency (%) | Code Type | Frequency (%) | Code Type | Frequency (%) |
|---|---|---|---|---|---|
| 1 code | 18 | 26 code | 14 | 128 code | 14 |
| 2 code | 13 | 27 code | 7 | 237 code | 8 |
| 3 code | 0 | 28 code | 3 | 238 code | 0 |
| 4 code | 44 | 36 code | 17 | 246 code | 29 |
| 5 code | 14 | 37 code | 0 | 248 code | 0 |
| Low 5 female | 16 | 38 code | 0 | 268 code | 0 |
| 6 code | 0 | 46 code | 6 | 278 code | 0 |
| 7 code | 0 | 47 code | 21 | 289 code | 0 |
| 8 code | 5 | 48 code | 21 | 468 code | 0 |
| 9 code | 10 | 49 code | 29 | 469 code | 12 |
| 12 code | 0 | 68 code | 0 | 478 code | 13 |
| 13 code | 8 | 69 code | 0 | 489 code | 0 |
| 18 code | 0 | 78 code | 8 | 678 code | 11 |
| 23 code | 7 | 89 code | 18 | 689 code | 0 |
| 24 code | 0 | 123 code | 0 | 789 code | 33 |

### Table C24 Social Readjustment Rating Scale Item: Marital Reconciliation with Mate

| Comparison Data | Frequency (%) |
|---|---|
| Mythical Average Patient Code: | 6 |
| L greater than T-score 70: | 0 |
| F greater than Raw Score 15: | 25 |
| K greater than T-score: | 10 |
| False Normal Code: | 4 |

| Code Type | Frequency (%) | Code Type | Frequency (%) | Code Type | Frequency (%) |
|---|---|---|---|---|---|
| 1 code | 0 | 26 code | 14 | 128 code | 0 |
| 2 code | 27 | 27 code | 0 | 237 code | 0 |
| 3 code | 0 | 28 code | 14 | 238 code | 29 |
| 4 code | 19 | 36 code | 0 | 246 code | 29 |
| 5 code | 0 | 37 code | 9 | 248 code | 10 |
| Low 5 female | 2 | 38 code | 14 | 268 code | 17 |
| 6 code | 0 | 46 code | 12 | 278 code | 4 |
| 7 code | 6 | 47 code | 7 | 289 code | 0 |
| 8 code | 9 | 48 code | 21 | 468 code | 14 |
| 9 code | 10 | 49 code | 14 | 469 code | 38 |
| 12 code | 0 | 68 code | 6 | 478 code | 13 |
| 13 code | 0 | 69 code | 13 | 489 code | 0 |
| 18 code | 0 | 78 code | 8 | 678 code | 22 |
| 23 code | 7 | 89 code | 0 | 689 code | 12 |
| 24 code | 29 | 123 code | 0 | 789 code | 0 |

### Table C25  Social Readjustment Rating Scale Item: Being Fired from Work

| Comparison Data | Frequency (%) |
|---|---|
| Mythical Average Patient Code: | 4 |
| L greater than T-score 70: | 14 |
| F greater than Raw Score 15: | 25 |
| K greater than T-score 70: | 0 |
| False Normal Code: | 2 |

| Code Type | Frequency (%) | Code Type | Frequency (%) | Code Type | Frequency (%) |
|---|---|---|---|---|---|
| 1 code | 0 | 26 code | 14 | 128 code | 14 |
| 2 code | 7 | 27 code | 0 | 237 code | 0 |
| 3 code | 0 | 28 code | 7 | 238 code | 29 |
| 4 code | 13 | 36 code | 0 | 246 code | 0 |
| 5 code | 0 | 37 code | 0 | 248 code | 10 |
| Low 5 female | 2 | 38 code | 14 | 268 code | 0 |
| 6 code | 6 | 46 code | 0 | 278 code | 0 |
| 7 code | 6 | 47 code | 7 | 289 code | 0 |
| 8 code | 5 | 48 code | 29 | 468 code | 0 |
| 9 code | 10 | 49 code | 0 | 469 code | 0 |
| 12 code | 0 | 68 code | 0 | 478 code | 7 |
| 13 code | 0 | 69 code | 0 | 489 code | 0 |
| 18 code | 0 | 78 code | 3 | 678 code | 0 |
| 23 code | 0 | 89 code | 14 | 689 code | 0 |
| 24 code | 0 | 123 code | 0 | 789 code | 17 |

### Table C26 Social Readjustment Rating Scale Item: Divorce

| Comparison Data | Frequency (%) |
| --- | --- |
| Mythical Average Patient Code: | 0 |
| L greater than T-score 70: | 0 |
| F greater than Raw Score 15: | 0 |
| K greater than T-score: | 0 |
| False Normal Code: | 7 |

| Code Type | Frequency (%) | Code Type | Frequency (%) | Code Type | Frequency (%) |
| --- | --- | --- | --- | --- | --- |
| 1 code | 9 | 26 code | 0 | 128 code | 0 |
| 2 code | 0 | 27 code | 0 | 237 code | 8 |
| 3 code | 0 | 28 code | 3 | 238 code | 0 |
| 4 code | 0 | 36 code | 0 | 246 code | 0 |
| 5 code | 0 | 37 code | 9 | 248 code | 10 |
| Low 5 female | 0 | 38 code | 0 | 268 code | 0 |
| 6 code | 0 | 46 code | 6 | 278 code | 0 |
| 7 code | 0 | 47 code | 0 | 289 code | 0 |
| 8 code | 0 | 48 code | 0 | 468 code | 0 |
| 9 code | 0 | 49 code | 0 | 469 code | 12 |
| 12 code | 0 | 68 code | 0 | 478 code | 0 |
| 13 code | 8 | 69 code | 0 | 489 code | 0 |
| 18 code | 0 | 78 code | 3 | 678 code | 11 |
| 23 code | 0 | 89 code | 0 | 689 code | 0 |
| 24 code | 14 | 123 code | 0 | 789 code | 0 |

### Table C27 Social Readjustment Rating Scale Item: Change to a Different Line of Work

| Comparison Data | Frequency (%) |
| --- | --- |
| Mythical Average Patient Code: | 22 |
| L greater than T-score 70: | 0 |
| F greater than Raw Score 15: | 38 |
| K greater than T-score 70: | 10 |
| False Normal Code: | 11 |

| Code Type | Frequency (%) | Code Type | Frequency (%) | Code Type | Frequency (%) |
| --- | --- | --- | --- | --- | --- |
| 1 code | 9 | 26 code | 29 | 128 code | 29 |
| 2 code | 13 | 27 code | 21 | 237 code | 8 |
| 3 code | 0 | 28 code | 21 | 238 code | 29 |
| 4 code | 25 | 36 code | 17 | 246 code | 0 |
| 5 code | 43 | 37 code | 18 | 248 code | 20 |
| Low 5 female | 16 | 38 code | 0 | 268 code | 33 |
| 6 code | 19 | 46 code | 29 | 278 code | 12 |
| 7 code | 29 | 47 code | 36 | 289 code | 29 |
| 8 code | 17 | 48 code | 29 | 468 code | 29 |
| 9 code | 38 | 49 code | 14 | 469 code | 38 |
| 12 code | 14 | 68 code | 18 | 478 code | 40 |
| 13 code | 15 | 69 code | 13 | 489 code | 33 |
| 18 code | 14 | 78 code | 24 | 678 code | 33 |
| 23 code | 0 | 89 code | 36 | 689 code | 12 |
| 24 code | 0 | 123 code | 0 | 789 code | 50 |

Table C28  Social Readjustment Rating Scale Item: Major Change in Number of Arguments with Spouse

| Comparison Data | Frequency (%) |
|---|---|
| Mythical Average Patient Code: | 22 |
| L greater than T-score 70: | 0 |
| F greater than Raw Score 15: | 38 |
| K greater than T-score 70: | 20 |
| False Normal Code: | 27 |

| Code Type | Frequency (%) | Code Type | Frequency (%) | Code Type | Frequency (%) |
|---|---|---|---|---|---|
| 1 code | 18 | 26 code | 43 | 128 code | 29 |
| 2 code | 47 | 27 code | 7 | 237 code | 33 |
| 3 code | 20 | 28 code | 34 | 238 code | 14 |
| 4 code | 31 | 36 code | 67 | 246 code | 43 |
| 5 code | 14 | 37 code | 36 | 248 code | 50 |
| Low 5 female | 25 | 38 code | 14 | 268 code | 50 |
| 6 code | 25 | 46 code | 35 | 278 code | 32 |
| 7 code | 29 | 47 code | 21 | 289 code | 29 |
| 8 code | 26 | 48 code | 29 | 468 code | 57 |
| 9 code | 38 | 49 code | 71 | 469 code | 38 |
| 12 code | 29 | 68 code | 35 | 478 code | 20 |
| 13 code | 15 | 69 code | 13 | 489 code | 17 |
| 18 code | 43 | 78 code | 58 | 678 code | 56 |
| 23 code | 36 | 89 code | 27 | 689 code | 12 |
| 24 code | 43 | 123 code | 43 | 789 code | 50 |

Table C29  Social Readjustment Rating Scale Item: Major Change in Work Responsibilities

| Comparison Data | Frequency (%) |
|---|---|
| Mythical Average Patient Code: | 32 |
| L greater than T-score 70: | 14 |
| F greater than Raw Score 15: | 25 |
| K greater than T-score: | 30 |
| False Normal Code: | 18 |

| Code Type | Frequency (%) | Code Type | Frequency (%) | Code Type | Frequency (%) |
|---|---|---|---|---|---|
| 1 code | 18 | 26 code | 29 | 128 code | 57 |
| 2 code | 33 | 27 code | 29 | 237 code | 17 |
| 3 code | 10 | 28 code | 31 | 238 code | 43 |
| 4 code | 31 | 36 code | 0 | 246 code | 14 |
| 5 code | 57 | 37 code | 9 | 248 code | 30 |
| Low 5 female | 25 | 38 code | 14 | 268 code | 50 |
| 6 code | 13 | 46 code | 29 | 278 code | 24 |
| 7 code | 24 | 47 code | 36 | 289 code | 14 |
| 8 code | 28 | 48 code | 14 | 468 code | 29 |
| 9 code | 38 | 49 code | 14 | 469 code | 50 |
| 12 code | 43 | 68 code | 35 | 478 code | 27 |
| 13 code | 23 | 69 code | 25 | 489 code | 17 |
| 18 code | 29 | 78 code | 37 | 678 code | 0 |
| 23 code | 29 | 89 code | 32 | 689 code | 25 |
| 24 code | 43 | 123 code | 14 | 789 code | 17 |

### Table C30  Social Readjustment Rating Scale Item:
### Wife Beginning or Ceasing Work Outside the Home

| Comparison Data | Frequency (%) |
|---|---|
| Mythical Average Patient Code: | 6 |
| L greater than T-score 70: | 0 |
| F greater than Raw Score 15: | 38 |
| K greater than T-score 70: | 10 |
| False Normal Code: | 4 |

| Code Type | Frequency (%) | Code Type | Frequency (%) | Code Type | Frequency (%) |
|---|---|---|---|---|---|
| 1 code | 18 | 26 code | 29 | 128 code | 14 |
| 2 code | 7 | 27 code | 0 | 237 code | 0 |
| 3 code | 10 | 28 code | 10 | 238 code | 0 |
| 4 code | 0 | 36 code | 17 | 246 code | 14 |
| 5 code | 0 | 37 code | 0 | 248 code | 20 |
| Low 5 female | 14 | 38 code | 14 | 268 code | 17 |
| 6 code | 19 | 46 code | 12 | 278 code | 40 |
| 7 code | 12 | 47 code | 7 | 289 code | 0 |
| 8 code | 9 | 48 code | 14 | 468 code | 0 |
| 9 code | 10 | 49 code | 0 | 469 code | 0 |
| 12 code | 0 | 68 code | 0 | 478 code | 27 |
| 13 code | 8 | 69 code | 13 | 489 code | 0 |
| 18 code | 29 | 78 code | 8 | 678 code | 67 |
| 23 code | 7 | 89 code | 5 | 689 code | 0 |
| 24 code | 14 | 123 code | 0 | 789 code | 0 |

### Table C31  Social Readjustment Rating Scale Item:
### Major Change in Working Hours or Conditions

| Comparison Data | Frequency (%) |
|---|---|
| Mythical Average Patient Code: | 32 |
| L greater than T-score 70: | 0 |
| F greater than Raw Score 15: | 38 |
| K greater than T-score 70: | 20 |
| False Normal Code: | 20 |

| Code Type | Frequency (%) | Code Type | Frequency (%) | Code Type | Frequency (%) |
|---|---|---|---|---|---|
| 1 code | 9 | 26 code | 29 | 128 code | 57 |
| 2 code | 40 | 27 code | 29 | 237 code | 33 |
| 3 code | 20 | 28 code | 31 | 238 code | 29 |
| 4 code | 44 | 36 code | 0 | 246 code | 29 |
| 5 code | 43 | 37 code | 27 | 248 code | 20 |
| Low 5 female | 23 | 38 code | 0 | 268 code | 50 |
| 6 code | 13 | 46 code | 35 | 278 code | 20 |
| 7 code | 28 | 47 code | 43 | 289 code | 14 |
| 8 code | 21 | 48 code | 29 | 468 code | 43 |
| 9 code | 24 | 49 code | 14 | 469 code | 25 |
| 12 code | 14 | 68 code | 35 | 478 code | 20 |
| 13 code | 15 | 69 code | 13 | 489 code | 50 |
| 18 code | 29 | 78 code | 11 | 678 code | 44 |
| 23 code | 29 | 89 code | 18 | 689 code | 38 |
| 24 code | 14 | 123 code | 14 | 789 code | 33 |

### Table C32 Social Readjustment Rating Scale Item: Major Change in Usual Type and/or Amount of Recreation

| Comparison Data | Frequency (%) |
|---|---|
| Mythical Average Patient Code: | 18 |
| L greater than T-score 70: | 14 |
| F greater than Raw Score 15: | 25 |
| K greater than T-score: | 0 |
| False Normal Code: | 11 |

| Code Type | Frequency (%) | Code Type | Frequency (%) | Code Type | Frequency (%) |
|---|---|---|---|---|---|
| 1 code | 27 | 26 code | 43 | 128 code | 0 |
| 2 code | 7 | 27 code | 14 | 237 code | 17 |
| 3 code | 10 | 28 code | 14 | 238 code | 43 |
| 4 code | 31 | 36 code | 33 | 246 code | 57 |
| 5 code | 14 | 37 code | 0 | 248 code | 30 |
| Low 5 female | 23 | 38 code | 14 | 268 code | 17 |
| 6 code | 0 | 46 code | 29 | 278 code | 4 |
| 7 code | 18 | 47 code | 29 | 289 code | 14 |
| 8 code | 12 | 48 code | 21 | 468 code | 14 |
| 9 code | 5 | 49 code | 0 | 469 code | 38 |
| 12 code | 14 | 68 code | 6 | 478 code | 20 |
| 13 code | 8 | 69 code | 25 | 489 code | 17 |
| 18 code | 14 | 78 code | 8 | 678 code | 0 |
| 23 code | 21 | 89 code | 9 | 689 code | 0 |
| 24 code | 14 | 123 code | 43 | 789 code | 17 |

### Table C33 Social Readjustment Rating Scale Item: Taking on a Mortgage Greater than $20,000 (Home, Business, etc.)

| Comparison Data | Frequency (%) |
|---|---|
| Mythical Average Patient Code: | 16 |
| L greater than T-score 70: | 0 |
| F greater than Raw Score 15: | 0 |
| K greater than T-score 70: | 0 |
| False Normal Code: | 7 |

| Code Type | Frequency (%) | Code Type | Frequency (%) | Code Type | Frequency (%) |
|---|---|---|---|---|---|
| 1 code | 18 | 26 code | 14 | 128 code | 0 |
| 2 code | 0 | 27 code | 7 | 237 code | 0 |
| 3 code | 0 | 28 code | 7 | 238 code | 0 |
| 4 code | 6 | 36 code | 0 | 246 code | 14 |
| 5 code | 29 | 37 code | 0 | 248 code | 20 |
| Low 5 female | 14 | 38 code | 0 | 268 code | 0 |
| 6 code | 6 | 46 code | 24 | 278 code | 8 |
| 7 code | 0 | 47 code | 0 | 289 code | 0 |
| 8 code | 5 | 48 code | 0 | 468 code | 14 |
| 9 code | 24 | 49 code | 14 | 469 code | 12 |
| 12 code | 29 | 68 code | 12 | 478 code | 7 |
| 13 code | 8 | 69 code | 0 | 489 code | 17 |
| 18 code | 0 | 78 code | 11 | 678 code | 0 |
| 23 code | 14 | 89 code | 18 | 689 code | 12 |
| 24 code | 14 | 123 code | 29 | 789 code | 17 |

## Table C34  Social Readjustment Rating Scale Item:  Taking on a Mortgage Less than $20,000 (TV, Car, etc.)

| Comparison Data | Frequency (%) |
|---|---|
| Mythical Average Patient Code: | 10 |
| L greater than T-score 70: | 14 |
| F greater than Raw Score 15: | 13 |
| K greater than T-score 70: | 0 |
| False Normal Code: | 9 |

| Code Type | Frequency (%) | Code Type | Frequency (%) | Code Type | Frequency (%) |
|---|---|---|---|---|---|
| 1 code | 9 | 26 code | 14 | 128 code | 0 |
| 2 code | 0 | 27 code | 7 | 237 code | 8 |
| 3 code | 10 | 28 code | 3 | 238 code | 0 |
| 4 code | 13 | 36 code | 0 | 246 code | 14 |
| 5 code | 0 | 37 code | 0 | 248 code | 0 |
| Low 5 female | 5 | 38 code | 14 | 268 code | 0 |
| 6 code | 6 | 46 code | 18 | 278 code | 8 |
| 7 code | 6 | 47 code | 0 | 289 code | 0 |
| 8 code | 9 | 48 code | 0 | 468 code | 14 |
| 9 code | 10 | 49 code | 14 | 469 code | 12 |
| 12 code | 14 | 68 code | 0 | 478 code | 0 |
| 13 code | 15 | 69 code | 0 | 489 code | 0 |
| 18 code | 0 | 78 code | 8 | 678 code | 0 |
| 23 code | 7 | 89 code | 14 | 689 code | 0 |
| 24 code | 0 | 123 code | 14 | 789 code | 33 |

## Table C35  Social Readjustment Rating Scale Item: Major Personal Injury or Illness

| Comparison Data | Frequency (%) |
|---|---|
| Mythical Average Patient Code: | 38 |
| L greater than T-score 70: | 14 |
| F greater than Raw Score 15: | 38 |
| K greater than T-score 70: | 40 |
| False Normal Code: | 36 |

| Code Type | Frequency (%) | Code Type | Frequency (%) | Code Type | Frequency (%) |
|---|---|---|---|---|---|
| 1 code | 55 | 26 code | 14 | 128 code | 71 |
| 2 code | 47 | 27 code | 21 | 237 code | 33 |
| 3 code | 50 | 28 code | 45 | 238 code | 43 |
| 4 code | 31 | 36 code | 0 | 246 code | 43 |
| 5 code | 14 | 37 code | 36 | 248 code | 30 |
| Low 5 female | 23 | 38 code | 29 | 268 code | 33 |
| 6 code | 38 | 46 code | 47 | 278 code | 44 |
| 7 code | 24 | 47 code | 21 | 289 code | 43 |
| 8 code | 43 | 48 code | 36 | 468 code | 57 |
| 9 code | 19 | 49 code | 29 | 469 code | 12 |
| 12 code | 71 | 68 code | 29 | 478 code | 33 |
| 13 code | 62 | 69 code | 13 | 489 code | 50 |
| 18 code | 6 | 78 code | 39 | 678 code | 33 |
| 23 code | 29 | 89 code | 36 | 689 code | 12 |
| 24 code | 43 | 123 code | 57 | 789 code | 17 |

## Table C36 Social Readjustment Rating Scale Item:
## Major Business Readjustment (Merger, Reorganization, Bankruptcy, etc.)

| Comparison Data | Frequency (%) |
|---|---|
| Mythical Average Patient Code: | 8 |
| L greater than T-score 70: | 0 |
| F greater than Raw Score 15: | 13 |
| K greater than T-score 70: | 0 |
| False Normal Code: | 4 |

| Code Type | Frequency (%) | Code Type | Frequency (%) | Code Type | Frequency (%) |
|---|---|---|---|---|---|
| 1 code | 18 | 26 code | 14 | 128 code | 0 |
| 2 code | 7 | 27 code | 21 | 237 code | 8 |
| 3 code | 10 | 28 code | 7 | 238 code | 14 |
| 4 code | 0 | 36 code | 0 | 246 code | 0 |
| 5 code | 14 | 37 code | 0 | 248 code | 0 |
| Low 5 female | 11 | 38 code | 0 | 268 code | 0 |
| 6 code | 0 | 46 code | 6 | 278 code | 8 |
| 7 code | 6 | 47 code | 7 | 289 code | 0 |
| 8 code | 7 | 48 code | 7 | 468 code | 0 |
| 9 code | 10 | 49 code | 0 | 469 code | 12 |
| 12 code | 14 | 68 code | 6 | 478 code | 0 |
| 13 code | 23 | 69 code | 0 | 489 code | 0 |
| 18 code | 0 | 78 code | 5 | 678 code | 11 |
| 23 code | 21 | 89 code | 5 | 689 code | 0 |
| 24 code | 29 | 123 code | 43 | 789 code | 17 |

## Table C37 Social Readjustment Rating Scale Item:
## Major Change in Social Activities

| Comparison Data | Frequency (%) |
|---|---|
| Mythical Average Patient Code: | 40 |
| L greater than T-score 70: | 29 |
| F greater than Raw Score 15: | 75 |
| K greater than T-score 70: | 20 |
| False Normal Code: | 27 |

| Code Type | Frequency (%) | Code Type | Frequency (%) | Code Type | Frequency (%) |
|---|---|---|---|---|---|
| 1 code | 18 | 26 code | 57 | 128 code | 71 |
| 2 code | 33 | 27 code | 43 | 237 code | 50 |
| 3 code | 30 | 28 code | 38 | 238 code | 29 |
| 4 code | 31 | 36 code | 33 | 246 code | 71 |
| 5 code | 43 | 37 code | 27 | 248 code | 60 |
| Low 5 female | 27 | 38 code | 43 | 268 code | 33 |
| 6 code | 44 | 46 code | 53 | 278 code | 36 |
| 7 code | 59 | 47 code | 36 | 289 code | 43 |
| 8 code | 34 | 48 code | 36 | 468 code | 57 |
| 9 code | 38 | 49 code | 57 | 469 code | 50 |
| 12 code | 43 | 68 code | 35 | 478 code | 33 |
| 13 code | 31 | 69 code | 38 | 489 code | 50 |
| 18 code | 57 | 78 code | 39 | 678 code | 33 |
| 23 code | 57 | 89 code | 27 | 689 code | 25 |
| 24 code | 71 | 123 code | 43 | 789 code | 50 |

### Table C38  Social Readjustment Rating Scale Item: Major Change in Living Conditions (Building New Home, Remodeling, Deterioration of Home or Neighborhood, etc.)

| Comparison Data | Frequency (%) |
|---|---|
| Mythical Average Patient Code: | 36 |
| L greater than T-score 70: | 0 |
| F greater than Raw Score 15: | 50 |
| K greater than T-score 70: | 20 |
| False Normal Code: | 18 |

| Code Type | Frequency (%) | Code Type | Frequency (%) | Code Type | Frequency (%) |
|---|---|---|---|---|---|
| 1 code | 27 | 26 code | 57 | 128 code | 57 |
| 2 code | 13 | 27 code | 21 | 237 code | 25 |
| 3 code | 10 | 28 code | 34 | 238 code | 23 |
| 4 code | 6 | 36 code | 0 | 246 code | 29 |
| 5 code | 14 | 37 code | 27 | 248 code | 80 |
| Low 5 female | 27 | 38 code | 43 | 268 code | 67 |
| 6 code | 31 | 46 code | 29 | 278 code | 32 |
| 7 code | 24 | 47 code | 21 | 289 code | 57 |
| 8 code | 36 | 48 code | 43 | 468 code | 43 |
| 9 code | 33 | 49 code | 14 | 469 code | 50 |
| 12 code | 29 | 68 code | 35 | 478 code | 53 |
| 13 code | 23 | 69 code | 25 | 489 code | 0 |
| 18 code | 29 | 78 code | 37 | 678 code | 22 |
| 23 code | 50 | 89 code | 27 | 689 code | 38 |
| 24 code | 0 | 123 code | 43 | 789 code | 50 |

### Table C39  Social Readjustment Rating Scale Item: Retirement from Work

| Comparison Data | Frequency (%) |
|---|---|
| Mythical Average Patient Code: | 2 |
| L greater than T-score 70: | 0 |
| F greater than Raw Score 15: | 0 |
| K greater than T-score 70: | 0 |
| False Normal Code: | 0 |

| Code Type | Frequency (%) | Code Type | Frequency (%) | Code Type | Frequency (%) |
|---|---|---|---|---|---|
| 1 code | 0 | 26 code | 0 | 128 code | 14 |
| 2 code | 0 | 27 code | 0 | 237 code | 0 |
| 3 code | 0 | 28 code | 0 | 238 code | 0 |
| 4 code | 0 | 36 code | 0 | 246 code | 14 |
| 5 code | 0 | 37 code | 0 | 248 code | 0 |
| Low 5 female | 0 | 38 code | 0 | 268 code | 0 |
| 6 code | 0 | 46 code | 0 | 278 code | 0 |
| 7 code | 0 | 47 code | 0 | 289 code | 0 |
| 8 code | 0 | 48 code | 0 | 468 code | 0 |
| 9 code | 0 | 49 code | 0 | 469 code | 0 |
| 12 code | 14 | 68 code | 0 | 478 code | 0 |
| 13 code | 0 | 69 code | 0 | 489 code | 0 |
| 18 code | 0 | 78 code | 0 | 678 code | 0 |
| 23 code | 0 | 89 code | 0 | 689 code | 0 |
| 24 code | 14 | 123 code | 0 | 789 code | 0 |

## Table C40  Social Readjustment Rating Scale Item: Change to a New School

| Comparison Data | Frequency (%) |
| --- | --- |
| Mythical Average Patient Code: | 4 |
| L greater than T-score 70: | 0 |
| F greater than Raw Score 15: | 0 |
| K greater than T-score 70: | 0 |
| False Normal Code: | 2 |

| Code Type | Frequency (%) | Code Type | Frequency (%) | Code Type | Frequency (%) |
| --- | --- | --- | --- | --- | --- |
| 1 code | 0 | 26 code | 14 | 128 code | 0 |
| 2 code | 0 | 27 code | 0 | 237 code | 0 |
| 3 code | 0 | 28 code | 0 | 238 code | 0 |
| 4 code | 13 | 36 code | 17 | 246 code | 0 |
| 5 code | 14 | 37 code | 0 | 248 code | 0 |
| Low 5 female | 9 | 38 code | 0 | 268 code | 0 |
| 6 code | 2 | 46 code | 6 | 278 code | 0 |
| 7 code | 0 | 47 code | 7 | 289 code | 0 |
| 8 code | 3 | 48 code | 7 | 468 code | 0 |
| 9 code | 5 | 49 code | 14 | 469 code | 12 |
| 12 code | 0 | 68 code | 6 | 478 code | 0 |
| 13 code | 0 | 69 code | 0 | 489 code | 0 |
| 18 code | 0 | 78 code | 2 | 678 code | 11 |
| 23 code | 0 | 89 code | 9 | 689 code | 0 |
| 24 code | 0 | 123 code | 0 | 789 code | 17 |

## Table C41  Social Readjustment Rating Scale Item: Beginning or Ceasing Formal Schooling

| Comparison Data | Frequency (%) |
| --- | --- |
| Mythical Average Patient Code: | 10 |
| L greater than T-score 70: | 0 |
| F greater than Raw Score 15: | 0 |
| K greater than T-score 70: | 0 |
| False Normal Code: | 4 |

| Code Type | Frequency (%) | Code Type | Frequency (%) | Code Type | Frequency (%) |
| --- | --- | --- | --- | --- | --- |
| 1 code | 0 | 26 code | 14 | 128 code | 0 |
| 2 code | 7 | 27 code | 14 | 237 code | 8 |
| 3 code | 0 | 28 code | 3 | 238 code | 0 |
| 4 code | 31 | 36 code | 17 | 246 code | 0 |
| 5 code | 14 | 37 code | 0 | 248 code | 0 |
| Low 5 female | 7 | 38 code | 14 | 268 code | 0 |
| 6 code | 6 | 46 code | 12 | 278 code | 8 |
| 7 code | 6 | 47 code | 21 | 289 code | 14 |
| 8 code | 12 | 48 code | 14 | 468 code | 0 |
| 9 code | 10 | 49 code | 0 | 469 code | 25 |
| 12 code | 0 | 68 code | 0 | 478 code | 20 |
| 13 code | 0 | 69 code | 13 | 489 code | 17 |
| 18 code | 14 | 78 code | 16 | 678 code | 0 |
| 23 code | 0 | 89 code | 14 | 689 code | 0 |
| 24 code | 14 | 123 code | 0 | 789 code | 17 |

# Responses by Code Types to the Vincent Biographical Inventory[1] (Non Open-ended Items)

### Table D1  Vincent Biographical Inventory Item: My Marriage Is Unhappy

| Comparison Data | Frequency (%) |
|---|---|
| Mythical Average Patient Code: | 26 |
| L greater than T-score 70: | 14 |
| F greater than Raw Score 15: | 50 |
| K greater than T-score 70: | 10 |
| False Normal Code: | 22 |

| Code Type | Frequency (%) | Code Type | Frequency (%) | Code Type | Frequency (%) |
|---|---|---|---|---|---|
| 1 code | 0 | 26 code | 43 | 128 code | 29 |
| 2 code | 33 | 27 code | 14 | 237 code | 17 |
| 3 code | 0 | 28 code | 28 | 238 code | 57 |
| 4 code | 44 | 36 code | 67 | 246 code | 43 |
| 5 code | 14 | 37 code | 18 | 248 code | 20 |
| Low 5 female | 23 | 38 code | 14 | 268 code | 17 |
| 6 code | 38 | 46 code | 24 | 278 code | 32 |
| 7 code | 35 | 47 code | 43 | 289 code | 14 |
| 8 code | 22 | 48 code | 36 | 468 code | 57 |
| 9 code | 19 | 49 code | 43 | 469 code | 38 |
| 12 code | 14 | 68 code | 18 | 478 code | 40 |
| 13 code | 8 | 69 code | 25 | 489 code | 17 |
| 18 code | 29 | 78 code | 26 | 678 code | 44 |
| 23 code | 43 | 89 code | 18 | 689 code | 12 |
| 24 code | 29 | 123 code | 29 | 789 code | 17 |

[1] The Vincent Biographical inventory may be purchased from Psychological Software Specialists, 1776 Fowler Street, Suite #7, Richland, WA 99352.

## Table D2 Vincent Biographical Inventory Item: My Spouse Abuses Me

| Comparison Data | Frequency (%) |
|---|---|
| Mythical Average Patient Code: | 8 |
| L greater than T-score 70: | 0 |
| F greater than Raw Score 15: | 25 |
| K greater than T-score: | 0 |
| False Normal Code: | 11 |

| Code Type | Frequency (%) | Code Type | Frequency (%) | Code Type | Frequency (%) |
|---|---|---|---|---|---|
| 1 code | 0 | 26 code | 14 | 128 code | 29 |
| 2 code | 13 | 27 code | 7 | 237 code | 0 |
| 3 code | 0 | 28 code | 10 | 238 code | 0 |
| 4 code | 0 | 36 code | 33 | 246 code | 14 |
| 5 code | 0 | 37 code | 0 | 248 code | 10 |
| Low 5 female | 9 | 38 code | 0 | 268 code | 17 |
| 6 code | 19 | 46 code | 6 | 278 code | 4 |
| 7 code | 0 | 47 code | 0 | 289 code | 0 |
| 8 code | 10 | 48 code | 7 | 468 code | 14 |
| 9 code | 5 | 49 code | 14 | 469 code | 25 |
| 12 code | 0 | 68 code | 6 | 478 code | 7 |
| 13 code | 0 | 69 code | 25 | 489 code | 17 |
| 18 code | 29 | 78 code | 5 | 678 code | 22 |
| 23 code | 7 | 89 code | 5 | 689 code | 0 |
| 24 code | 0 | 123 code | 0 | 789 code | 0 |

## Table D3 Vincent Biographical Inventory Item: I Am Currently Seeing Someone Outside My Marriage

| Comparison Data | Frequency (%) |
|---|---|
| Mythical Average Patient Code: | 6 |
| L greater than T-score 70: | 0 |
| F greater than Raw Score 15: | 25 |
| K greater than T-score: | 100 |
| False Normal Code: | 7 |

| Code Type | Frequency (%) | Code Type | Frequency (%) | Code Type | Frequency (%) |
|---|---|---|---|---|---|
| 1 code | 9 | 26 code | 0 | 128 code | 0 |
| 2 code | 0 | 27 code | 0 | 237 code | 0 |
| 3 code | 0 | 28 code | 0 | 238 code | 0 |
| 4 code | 13 | 36 code | 0 | 246 code | 0 |
| 5 code | 14 | 37 code | 0 | 248 code | 10 |
| Low 5 female | 0 | 38 code | 0 | 268 code | 0 |
| 6 code | 6 | 46 code | 6 | 278 code | 4 |
| 7 code | 0 | 47 code | 0 | 289 code | 0 |
| 8 code | 5 | 48 code | 21 | 468 code | 29 |
| 9 code | 14 | 49 code | 29 | 469 code | 12 |
| 12 code | 14 | 68 code | 12 | 478 code | 7 |
| 13 code | 0 | 69 code | 0 | 489 code | 17 |
| 18 code | 14 | 78 code | 3 | 678 code | 0 |
| 23 code | 0 | 89 code | 5 | 689 code | 25 |
| 24 code | 0 | 123 code | 14 | 789 code | 0 |

### Table D4  Vincent Biographical Inventory Item: My Spouse Is Currently Seeing Someone Else

| Comparison Data | Frequency (%) |
|---|---|
| Mythical Average Patient Code: | 6 |
| L greater than T-score 70: | 0 |
| F greater than Raw Score 15: | 38 |
| K greater than T-score: | 10 |
| False Normal Code: | 2 |

| Code Type | Frequency (%) | Code Type | Frequency (%) | Code Type | Frequency (%) |
|---|---|---|---|---|---|
| 1 code | 0 | 26 code | 0 | 128 code | 0 |
| 2 code | 7 | 27 code | 0 | 237 code | 0 |
| 3 code | 0 | 28 code | 7 | 238 code | 0 |
| 4 code | 6 | 36 code | 0 | 246 code | 14 |
| 5 code | 0 | 37 code | 0 | 248 code | 0 |
| Low 5 female | 2 | 38 code | 0 | 268 code | 0 |
| 6 code | 13 | 46 code | 6 | 278 code | 0 |
| 7 code | 6 | 47 code | 0 | 289 code | 0 |
| 8 code | 7 | 48 code | 7 | 468 code | 0 |
| 9 code | 10 | 49 code | 0 | 469 code | 12 |
| 12 code | 0 | 68 code | 6 | 478 code | 7 |
| 13 code | 0 | 69 code | 13 | 489 code | 0 |
| 18 code | 0 | 78 code | 8 | 678 code | 11 |
| 23 code | 0 | 89 code | 9 | 689 code | 12 |
| 24 code | 0 | 123 code | 0 | 789 code | 0 |

### Table D5  Vincent Biographical Inventory Item:  I Have Been Married Before

| Comparison Data | Frequency (%) |
|---|---|
| Mythical Average Patient Code: | 40 |
| L greater than T-score 70: | 14 |
| F greater than Raw Score 15: | 50 |
| K greater than T-score: | 0 |
| False Normal Code: | 38 |

| Code Type | Frequency (%) | Code Type | Frequency (%) | Code Type | Frequency (%) |
|---|---|---|---|---|---|
| 1 code | 36 | 26 code | 14 | 128 code | 43 |
| 2 code | 47 | 27 code | 21 | 237 code | 42 |
| 3 code | 30 | 28 code | 45 | 238 code | 71 |
| 4 code | 38 | 36 code | 50 | 246 code | 57 |
| 5 code | 14 | 37 code | 27 | 248 code | 50 |
| Low 5 female | 48 | 38 code | 29 | 268 code | 67 |
| 6 code | 56 | 46 code | 53 | 278 code | 32 |
| 7 code | 35 | 47 code | 36 | 289 code | 14 |
| 8 code | 47 | 48 code | 36 | 468 code | 43 |
| 9 code | 38 | 49 code | 71 | 469 code | 25 |
| 12 code | 14 | 68 code | 47 | 478 code | 20 |
| 13 code | 31 | 69 code | 50 | 489 code | 50 |
| 18 code | 43 | 78 code | 18 | 678 code | 33 |
| 23 code | 64 | 89 code | 50 | 689 code | 25 |
| 24 code | 43 | 123 code | 43 | 789 code | 17 |

#### Table D6 Vincent Biographical Inventory Item: One of My Children Has a Learning Disability

| Comparison Data | Frequency (%) |
|---|---|
| Mythical Average Patient Code: | 4 |
| L greater than T-score 70: | 0 |
| F greater than Raw Score 15: | 13 |
| K greater than T-score: | 0 |
| False Normal Code: | 2 |

| Code Type | Frequency (%) | Code Type | Frequency (%) | Code Type | Frequency (%) |
|---|---|---|---|---|---|
| 1 code | 0 | 26 code | 0 | 128 code | 0 |
| 2 code | 0 | 27 code | 0 | 237 code | 8 |
| 3 code | 10 | 28 code | 0 | 238 code | 14 |
| 4 code | 0 | 36 code | 0 | 246 code | 0 |
| 5 code | 0 | 37 code | 9 | 248 code | 0 |
| Low 5 female | 7 | 38 code | 14 | 268 code | 0 |
| 6 code | 0 | 46 code | 0 | 278 code | 0 |
| 7 code | 0 | 47 code | 0 | 289 code | 0 |
| 8 code | 7 | 48 code | 0 | 468 code | 0 |
| 9 code | 5 | 49 code | 0 | 469 code | 0 |
| 12 code | 0 | 68 code | 0 | 478 code | 0 |
| 13 code | 15 | 69 code | 0 | 489 code | 0 |
| 18 code | 14 | 78 code | 5 | 678 code | 0 |
| 23 code | 14 | 89 code | 0 | 689 code | 0 |
| 24 code | 0 | 123 code | 14 | 789 code | 17 |

#### Table D7 Vincent Biographical Inventory Item: One of My Children Is Retarded

| Comparison Data | Frequency (%) |
|---|---|
| Mythical Average Patient Code: | 0 |
| L greater than T-score 70: | 0 |
| F greater than Raw Score 15: | 0 |
| K greater than T-score: | 0 |
| False Normal Code: | 2 |

| Code Type | Frequency (%) | Code Type | Frequency (%) | Code Type | Frequency (%) |
|---|---|---|---|---|---|
| 1 code | 0 | 26 code | 0 | 128 code | 0 |
| 2 code | 0 | 27 code | 0 | 237 code | 8 |
| 3 code | 10 | 28 code | 0 | 238 code | 0 |
| 4 code | 0 | 36 code | 0 | 246 code | 0 |
| 5 code | 0 | 37 code | 0 | 248 code | 0 |
| Low 5 female | 0 | 38 code | 0 | 268 code | 0 |
| 6 code | 0 | 46 code | 0 | 278 code | 0 |
| 7 code | 0 | 47 code | 0 | 289 code | 0 |
| 8 code | 0 | 48 code | 0 | 468 code | 0 |
| 9 code | 0 | 49 code | 0 | 469 code | 0 |
| 12 code | 0 | 68 code | 0 | 478 code | 0 |
| 13 code | 0 | 69 code | 13 | 489 code | 0 |
| 18 code | 0 | 78 code | 0 | 678 code | 0 |
| 23 code | 0 | 89 code | 0 | 689 code | 0 |
| 24 code | 0 | 123 code | 0 | 789 code | 0 |

### Table D8  Vincent Biographical Inventory Item: One of My Children Has a Physical Handicap

| Comparison Data | Frequency (%) |
|---|---|
| Mythical Average Patient Code: | 2 |
| L greater than T-score 70: | 0 |
| F greater than Raw Score 15: | 13 |
| K greater than T-score: | 0 |
| False Normal Code: | 2 |

| Code Type | Frequency (%) | Code Type | Frequency (%) | Code Type | Frequency (%) |
|---|---|---|---|---|---|
| 1 code | 9 | 26 code | 0 | 128 code | 0 |
| 2 code | 0 | 27 code | 7 | 237 code | 0 |
| 3 code | 0 | 28 code | 3 | 238 code | 14 |
| 4 code | 6 | 36 code | 0 | 246 code | 14 |
| 5 code | 0 | 37 code | 9 | 248 code | 0 |
| Low 5 female | 14 | 38 code | 14 | 268 code | 17 |
| 6 code | 0 | 46 code | 12 | 278 code | 4 |
| 7 code | 0 | 47 code | 0 | 289 code | 0 |
| 8 code | 5 | 48 code | 0 | 468 code | 0 |
| 9 code | 0 | 49 code | 0 | 469 code | 0 |
| 12 code | 0 | 68 code | 12 | 478 code | 0 |
| 13 code | 0 | 69 code | 13 | 489 code | 0 |
| 18 code | 0 | 78 code | 3 | 678 code | 11 |
| 23 code | 0 | 89 code | 5 | 689 code | 0 |
| 24 code | 0 | 123 code | 0 | 789 code | 0 |

### Table D9  Vincent Biographical Inventory Item: One of My Children Has an Emotional Problem

| Comparison Data | Frequency (%) |
|---|---|
| Mythical Average Patient Code: | 6 |
| L greater than T-score 70: | 0 |
| F greater than Raw Score 15: | 13 |
| K greater than T-score: | 0 |
| False Normal Code: | 7 |

| Code Type | Frequency (%) | Code Type | Frequency (%) | Code Type | Frequency (%) |
|---|---|---|---|---|---|
| 1 code | 27 | 26 code | 0 | 128 code | 29 |
| 2 code | 0 | 27 code | 21 | 237 code | 8 |
| 3 code | 10 | 28 code | 3 | 238 code | 14 |
| 4 code | 13 | 36 code | 0 | 246 code | 29 |
| 5 code | 0 | 37 code | 9 | 248 code | 10 |
| Low 5 female | 16 | 38 code | 14 | 268 code | 0 |
| 6 code | 0 | 46 code | 18 | 278 code | 8 |
| 7 code | 0 | 47 code | 0 | 289 code | 0 |
| 8 code | 9 | 48 code | 0 | 468 code | 0 |
| 9 code | 24 | 49 code | 14 | 469 code | 0 |
| 12 code | 14 | 68 code | 6 | 478 code | 0 |
| 13 code | 15 | 69 code | 13 | 489 code | 0 |
| 18 code | 29 | 78 code | 3 | 678 code | 22 |
| 23 code | 21 | 89 code | 5 | 689 code | 0 |
| 24 code | 14 | 123 code | 14 | 789 code | 0 |

## Table D10 Vincent Biographical Inventory Item: I'm Having Difficulty Caring for My Children

| Comparison Data | Frequency (%) |
| --- | --- |
| Mythical Average Patient Code: | 10 |
| L greater than T-score 70: | 0 |
| F greater than Raw Score 15: | 0 |
| K greater than T-score: | 0 |
| False Normal Code: | 0 |

| Code Type | Frequency (%) | Code Type | Frequency (%) | Code Type | Frequency (%) |
| --- | --- | --- | --- | --- | --- |
| 1 code | 0 | 26 code | 0 | 128 code | 0 |
| 2 code | 7 | 27 code | 0 | 237 code | 0 |
| 3 code | 10 | 28 code | 3 | 238 code | 0 |
| 4 code | 19 | 36 code | 0 | 246 code | 14 |
| 5 code | 0 | 37 code | 0 | 248 code | 10 |
| Low 5 female | 7 | 38 code | 0 | 268 code | 33 |
| 6 code | 0 | 46 code | 12 | 278 code | 8 |
| 7 code | 24 | 47 code | 14 | 289 code | 0 |
| 8 code | 5 | 48 code | 0 | 468 code | 14 |
| 9 code | 0 | 49 code | 0 | 469 code | 0 |
| 12 code | 0 | 68 code | 12 | 478 code | 0 |
| 13 code | 8 | 69 code | 0 | 489 code | 0 |
| 18 code | 14 | 78 code | 8 | 678 code | 11 |
| 23 code | 14 | 89 code | 5 | 689 code | 0 |
| 24 code | 14 | 123 code | 14 | 789 code | 0 |

## Table D11 Vincent Biographical Inventory Item: I Am Currently Employed

| Comparison Data | Frequency (%) |
| --- | --- |
| Mythical Average Patient Code: | 72 |
| L greater than T-score 70: | 43 |
| F greater than Raw Score 15: | 50 |
| K greater than T-score: | 60 |
| False Normal Code: | 49 |

| Code Type | Frequency (%) | Code Type | Frequency (%) | Code Type | Frequency (%) |
| --- | --- | --- | --- | --- | --- |
| 1 code | 55 | 26 code | 57 | 128 code | 71 |
| 2 code | 73 | 27 code | 64 | 237 code | 67 |
| 3 code | 50 | 28 code | 69 | 238 code | 71 |
| 4 code | 75 | 36 code | 33 | 246 code | 43 |
| 5 code | 100 | 37 code | 73 | 248 code | 60 |
| Low 5 female | 52 | 38 code | 43 | 268 code | 50 |
| 6 code | 56 | 46 code | 59 | 278 code | 76 |
| 7 code | 88 | 47 code | 93 | 289 code | 71 |
| 8 code | 62 | 48 code | 71 | 468 code | 100 |
| 9 code | 76 | 49 code | 71 | 469 code | 64 |
| 12 code | 71 | 68 code | 59 | 478 code | 53 |
| 13 code | 77 | 69 code | 75 | 489 code | 83 |
| 18 code | 29 | 78 code | 68 | 678 code | 100 |
| 23 code | 57 | 89 code | 73 | 689 code | 38 |
| 24 code | 29 | 123 code | 71 | 789 code | 50 |

Table D12  Vincent Biographical Inventory Item:  I Am Unhappy in My Career

| Comparison Data | Frequency (%) |
| --- | --- |
| Mythical Average Patient Code: | 22 |
| L greater than T-score 70: | 14 |
| F greater than Raw Score 15: | 13 |
| K greater than T-score: | 0 |
| False Normal Code: | 2 |

| Code Type | Frequency (%) | Code Type | Frequency (%) | Code Type | Frequency (%) |
| --- | --- | --- | --- | --- | --- |
| 1 code | 9 | 26 code | 0 | 128 code | 29 |
| 2 code | 13 | 27 code | 14 | 237 code | 0 |
| 3 code | 0 | 28 code | 31 | 238 code | 43 |
| 4 code | 25 | 36 code | 0 | 246 code | 14 |
| 5 code | 0 | 37 code | 0 | 248 code | 10 |
| Low 5 female | 9 | 38 code | 0 | 268 code | 17 |
| 6 code | 0 | 46 code | 18 | 278 code | 24 |
| 7 code | 18 | 47 code | 29 | 289 code | 29 |
| 8 code | 14 | 48 code | 21 | 678 code | 29 |
| 9 code | 14 | 49 code | 14 | 469 code | 25 |
| 12 code | 14 | 68 code | 12 | 478 code | 20 |
| 13 code | 8 | 69 code | 13 | 489 code | 17 |
| 18 code | 14 | 78 code | 16 | 678 code | 22 |
| 23 code | 0 | 89 code | 9 | 689 code | 0 |
| 24 code | 0 | 123 code | 0 | 789 code | 17 |

Table D13  Vincent Biographical Inventory Item:  I Am Currently on Disability

| Comparison Data | Frequency (%) |
| --- | --- |
| Mythical Average Patient Code: | 6 |
| L greater than T-score 70: | 0 |
| F greater than Raw Score 15: | 25 |
| K greater than T-score: | 0 |
| False Normal Code: | 4 |

| Code Type | Frequency (%) | Code Type | Frequency (%) | Code Type | Frequency (%) |
| --- | --- | --- | --- | --- | --- |
| 1 code | 9 | 26 code | 0 | 128 code | 14 |
| 2 code | 7 | 27 code | 0 | 237 code | 8 |
| 3 code | 10 | 28 code | 3 | 238 code | 0 |
| 4 code | 13 | 36 code | 0 | 246 code | 14 |
| 5 code | 0 | 37 code | 9 | 248 code | 10 |
| Low 5 female | 2 | 38 code | 0 | 268 code | 17 |
| 6 code | 0 | 46 code | 12 | 278 code | 0 |
| 7 code | 0 | 47 code | 0 | 289 code | 29 |
| 8 code | 10 | 48 code | 7 | 468 code | 14 |
| 9 code | 0 | 49 code | 0 | 469 code | 0 |
| 12 code | 14 | 68 code | 0 | 478 code | 0 |
| 13 code | 0 | 69 code | 0 | 489 code | 17 |
| 18 code | 43 | 78 code | 3 | 678 code | 0 |
| 23 code | 7 | 89 code | 14 | 689 code | 0 |
| 24 code | 14 | 123 code | 0 | 789 code | 0 |

### Table D14  Vincent Biographical Inventory Item: I Have a Work-related Lawsuit Pending

| Comparison Data | Frequency (%) |
|---|---|
| Mythical Average Patient Code: | 6 |
| L greater than T-score 70: | 14 |
| F greater than Raw Score 15: | 13 |
| K greater than T-score: | 0 |
| False Normal Code: | 0 |

| Code Type | Frequency (%) | Code Type | Frequency (%) | Code Type | Frequency (%) |
|---|---|---|---|---|---|
| 1 code | 0 | 26 code | 0 | 128 code | 0 |
| 2 code | 7 | 27 code | 0 | 237 code | 0 |
| 3 code | 0 | 28 code | 3 | 238 code | 0 |
| 4 code | 0 | 36 code | 0 | 246 code | 0 |
| 5 code | 0 | 37 code | 0 | 248 code | 0 |
| Low 5 female | 0 | 38 code | 0 | 268 code | 17 |
| 6 code | 0 | 46 code | 0 | 278 code | 0 |
| 7 code | 0 | 47 code | 0 | 289 code | 14 |
| 8 code | 3 | 48 code | 7 | 468 code | 0 |
| 9 code | 5 | 49 code | 0 | 469 code | 0 |
| 12 code | 0 | 68 code | 0 | 478 code | 0 |
| 13 code | 0 | 69 code | 0 | 489 code | 0 |
| 18 code | 0 | 78 code | 0 | 678 code | 0 |
| 23 code | 0 | 89 code | 5 | 689 code | 0 |
| 24 code | 0 | 123 code | 0 | 789 code | 0 |

### Table D15 Vincent Biographical Inventory Item: I Have Trouble Holding a Job

| Comparison Data | Frequency (%) |
|---|---|
| Mythical Average Patient Code: | 8 |
| L greater than T-score 70: | 0 |
| F greater than Raw Score 15: | 13 |
| K greater than T-score: | 0 |
| False Normal Code: | 0 |

| Code Type | Frequency (%) | Code Type | Frequency (%) | Code Type | Frequency (%) |
|---|---|---|---|---|---|
| 1 code | 0 | 26 code | 0 | 128 code | 14 |
| 2 code | 7 | 27 code | 7 | 237 code | 0 |
| 3 code | 0 | 28 code | 7 | 238 code | 0 |
| 4 code | 13 | 36 code | 0 | 246 code | 0 |
| 5 code | 0 | 37 code | 0 | 248 code | 10 |
| Low 5 female | 7 | 38 code | 0 | 268 code | 0 |
| 6 code | 0 | 46 code | 0 | 278 code | 4 |
| 7 code | 12 | 47 code | 29 | 289 code | 0 |
| 8 code | 3 | 48 code | 29 | 468 code | 14 |
| 9 code | 0 | 49 code | 0 | 469 code | 0 |
| 12 code | 0 | 68 code | 6 | 478 code | 33 |
| 13 code | 0 | 69 code | 0 | 489 code | 0 |
| 18 code | 0 | 78 code | 8 | 678 code | 0 |
| 23 code | 0 | 89 code | 5 | 689 code | 0 |
| 24 code | 0 | 123 code | 0 | 789 code | 17 |

## Table D16 Vincent Biographical Inventory Item: As a Child I Had Few Friends

| Comparison Data | Frequency (%) |
| --- | --- |
| Mythical Average Patient Code: | 34 |
| L greater than T-score 70: | 14 |
| F greater than Raw Score 15: | 13 |
| K greater than T-score: | 0 |
| False Normal Code: | 11 |

| Code Type | Frequency (%) | Code Type | Frequency (%) | Code Type | Frequency (%) |
| --- | --- | --- | --- | --- | --- |
| 1 code | 27 | 26 code | 43 | 128 code | 57 |
| 2 code | 40 | 27 code | 36 | 237 code | 17 |
| 3 code | 0 | 28 code | 55 | 238 code | 43 |
| 4 code | 25 | 36 code | 0 | 246 code | 14 |
| 5 code | 14 | 37 code | 18 | 248 code | 40 |
| Low 5 female | 18 | 38 code | 43 | 268 code | 50 |
| 6 code | 19 | 46 code | 18 | 278 code | 36 |
| 7 code | 29 | 47 code | 7 | 289 code | 57 |
| 8 code | 45 | 48 code | 36 | 468 code | 71 |
| 9 code | 5 | 49 code | 0 | 469 code | 12 |
| 12 code | 0 | 68 code | 53 | 478 code | 33 |
| 13 code | 31 | 69 code | 25 | 489 code | 50 |
| 18 code | 29 | 78 code | 26 | 678 code | 22 |
| 23 code | 43 | 89 code | 32 | 689 code | 25 |
| 24 code | 71 | 123 code | 43 | 789 code | 33 |

## Table D17 Vincent Biographical Inventory Item: As a Child I Had (Have) Frequent Temper Tantrums

| Comparison Data | Frequency (%) |
| --- | --- |
| Mythical Average Patient Code: | 24 |
| L greater than T-score 70: | 14 |
| F greater than Raw Score 15: | 50 |
| K greater than T-score: | 0 |
| False Normal Code: | 7 |

| Code Type | Frequency (%) | Code Type | Frequency (%) | Code Type | Frequency (%) |
| --- | --- | --- | --- | --- | --- |
| 1 code | 9 | 26 code | 14 | 128 code | 0 |
| 2 code | 0 | 27 code | 21 | 237 code | 0 |
| 3 code | 10 | 28 code | 28 | 238 code | 0 |
| 4 code | 38 | 36 code | 0 | 246 code | 29 |
| 5 code | 14 | 37 code | 9 | 248 code | 70 |
| Low 5 female | 18 | 38 code | 0 | 268 code | 33 |
| 6 code | 19 | 46 code | 35 | 278 code | 24 |
| 7 code | 18 | 47 code | 43 | 289 code | 43 |
| 8 code | 29 | 48 code | 50 | 468 code | 57 |
| 9 code | 14 | 49 code | 0 | 469 code | 38 |
| 12 code | 0 | 68 code | 29 | 478 code | 33 |
| 13 code | 8 | 69 code | 25 | 489 code | 33 |
| 18 code | 57 | 78 code | 26 | 678 code | 11 |
| 23 code | 14 | 89 code | 32 | 689 code | 12 |
| 24 code | 43 | 123 code | 0 | 789 code | 0 |

Table D18  Vincent Biographical Inventory Item: As a Child I Had (Have) Frequent Crying Spells and Became Easily Upset

| Comparison Data | Frequency (%) |
| --- | --- |
| Mythical Average Patient Code: | 24 |
| L greater than T-score 70: | 0 |
| F greater than Raw Score 15: | 50 |
| K greater than T-score: | 0 |
| False Normal Code: | 7 |

| Code Type | Frequency (%) | Code Type | Frequency (%) | Code Type | Frequency (%) |
| --- | --- | --- | --- | --- | --- |
| 1 code | 9 | 26 code | 43 | 128 code | 14 |
| 2 code | 20 | 27 code | 21 | 237 code | 17 |
| 3 code | 0 | 28 code | 34 | 238 code | 14 |
| 4 code | 38 | 36 code | 0 | 246 code | 57 |
| 5 code | 14 | 37 code | 9 | 248 code | 60 |
| Low 5 female | 36 | 38 code | 14 | 268 code | 50 |
| 6 code | 19 | 46 code | 41 | 278 code | 28 |
| 7 code | 24 | 47 code | 21 | 289 code | 43 |
| 8 code | 40 | 48 code | 43 | 468 code | 43 |
| 9 code | 14 | 49 code | 29 | 469 code | 25 |
| 12 code | 14 | 68 code | 41 | 478 code | 33 |
| 13 code | 15 | 69 code | 13 | 489 code | 50 |
| 18 code | 71 | 78 code | 34 | 678 code | 22 |
| 23 code | 0 | 89 code | 36 | 689 code | 25 |
| 24 code | 71 | 123 code | 14 | 789 code | 17 |

Table D19  Vincent Biographical Inventory Item: I Was Often Sick As a Child

| Comparison Data | Frequency (%) |
| --- | --- |
| Mythical Average Patient Code: | 28 |
| L greater than T-score 70: | 0 |
| F greater than Raw Score 15: | 0 |
| K greater than T-score: | 10 |
| False Normal Code: | 16 |

| Code Type | Frequency (%) | Code Type | Frequency (%) | Code Type | Frequency (%) |
| --- | --- | --- | --- | --- | --- |
| 1 code | 0 | 26 code | 29 | 128 code | 43 |
| 2 code | 47 | 27 code | 7 | 237 code | 25 |
| 3 code | 10 | 28 code | 28 | 238 code | 43 |
| 4 code | 31 | 36 code | 33 | 246 code | 29 |
| 5 code | 0 | 37 code | 0 | 248 code | 30 |
| Low 5 female | 23 | 38 code | 29 | 268 code | 67 |
| 6 code | 38 | 46 code | 35 | 278 code | 16 |
| 7 code | 12 | 47 code | 21 | 289 code | 29 |
| 8 code | 34 | 48 code | 29 | 468 code | 14 |
| 9 code | 10 | 49 code | 14 | 469 code | 38 |
| 12 code | 14 | 68 code | 29 | 478 code | 47 |
| 13 code | 15 | 69 code | 25 | 489 code | 33 |
| 18 code | 29 | 78 code | 37 | 678 code | 33 |
| 23 code | 7 | 89 code | 36 | 689 code | 38 |
| 24 code | 29 | 123 code | 14 | 789 code | 0 |

## Table D20  Vincent Biographical Inventory Item:
## As a Teenager I Have (Had) Few Friends

| Comparison Data | Frequency (%) |
| --- | --- |
| Mythical Average Patient Code: | 34 |
| L greater than T-score 70: | 0 |
| F greater than Raw Score 15: | 25 |
| K greater than T-score: | 0 |
| False Normal Code: | 9 |

| Code Type | Frequency (%) | Code Type | Frequency (%) | Code Type | Frequency (%) |
| --- | --- | --- | --- | --- | --- |
| 1 code | 27 | 26 code | 43 | 128 code | 29 |
| 2 code | 27 | 27 code | 36 | 237 code | 17 |
| 3 code | 0 | 28 code | 31 | 238 code | 29 |
| 4 code | 13 | 36 code | 0 | 246 code | 0 |
| 5 code | 14 | 37 code | 18 | 248 code | 20 |
| Low 5 female | 14 | 38 code | 0 | 268 code | 33 |
| 6 code | 13 | 46 code | 18 | 278 code | 28 |
| 7 code | 24 | 47 code | 7 | 289 code | 57 |
| 8 code | 33 | 48 code | 21 | 468 code | 29 |
| 9 code | 5 | 49 code | 0 | 469 code | 12 |
| 12 code | 0 | 68 code | 24 | 478 code | 40 |
| 13 code | 31 | 69 code | 0 | 489 code | 33 |
| 18 code | 43 | 78 code | 29 | 678 code | 0 |
| 23 code | 29 | 89 code | 23 | 689 code | 0 |
| 24 code | 43 | 123 code | 14 | 789 code | 33 |

## Table D21  Vincent Biographical Inventory Item:
## As a Teenager I Didn't (Don't) Date at All

| Comparison Data | Frequency (%) |
| --- | --- |
| Mythical Average Patient Code: | 10 |
| L greater than T-score 70: | 0 |
| F greater than Raw Score 15: | 13 |
| K greater than T-score: | 0 |
| False Normal Code: | 4 |

| Code Type | Frequency (%) | Code Type | Frequency (%) | Code Type | Frequency (%) |
| --- | --- | --- | --- | --- | --- |
| 1 code | 27 | 26 code | 14 | 128 code | 14 |
| 2 code | 20 | 27 code | 14 | 237 code | 17 |
| 3 code | 0 | 28 code | 21 | 238 code | 29 |
| 4 code | 19 | 36 code | 0 | 246 code | 0 |
| 5 code | 14 | 37 code | 0 | 248 code | 0 |
| Low 5 female | 9 | 38 code | 0 | 268 code | 17 |
| 6 code | 6 | 46 code | 12 | 278 code | 8 |
| 7 code | 0 | 47 code | 0 | 289 code | 43 |
| 8 code | 22 | 48 code | 14 | 468 code | 29 |
| 9 code | 0 | 49 code | 0 | 469 code | 0 |
| 12 code | 14 | 68 code | 6 | 478 code | 27 |
| 13 code | 8 | 69 code | 0 | 489 code | 17 |
| 18 code | 29 | 78 code | 21 | 678 code | 11 |
| 23 code | 7 | 89 code | 18 | 689 code | 0 |
| 24 code | 0 | 123 code | 14 | 789 code | 17 |

### Table D22  Vincent Biographical Inventory Item: I Was Adopted or Raised Away from My Natural Parents

| Comparison Data | Frequency (%) |
|---|---|
| Mythical Average Patient Code: | 22 |
| L greater than T-score 70: | 0 |
| F greater than Raw Score 15: | 25 |
| K greater than T-score: | 10 |
| False Normal Code: | 18 |

| Code Type | Frequency (%) | Code Type | Frequency (%) | Code Type | Frequency (%) |
|---|---|---|---|---|---|
| 1 code | 9 | 26 code | 14 | 128 code | 14 |
| 2 code | 20 | 27 code | 21 | 237 code | 25 |
| 3 code | 20 | 28 code | 24 | 238 code | 43 |
| 4 code | 19 | 36 code | 17 | 246 code | 29 |
| 5 code | 29 | 37 code | 18 | 248 code | 40 |
| Low 5 female | 34 | 38 code | 43 | 268 code | 17 |
| 6 code | 13 | 46 code | 35 | 278 code | 12 |
| 7 code | 24 | 47 code | 0 | 289 code | 0 |
| 8 code | 19 | 48 code | 29 | 468 code | 43 |
| 9 code | 24 | 49 code | 14 | 469 code | 12 |
| 12 code | 14 | 68 code | 29 | 478 code | 13 |
| 13 code | 8 | 69 code | 0 | 489 code | 0 |
| 18 code | 43 | 78 code | 11 | 678 code | 11 |
| 23 code | 21 | 89 code | 18 | 689 code | 12 |
| 24 code | 14 | 123 code | 0 | 789 code | 0 |

### Table D23  Vincent Biographical Inventory Item: I Was Abused as a Child

| Comparison Data | Frequency (%) |
|---|---|
| Mythical Average Patient Code: | 24 |
| L greater than T-score 70: | 0 |
| F greater than Raw Score 15: | 25 |
| K greater than T-score: | 0 |
| False Normal Code: | 16 |

| Code Type | Frequency (%) | Code Type | Frequency (%) | Code Type | Frequency (%) |
|---|---|---|---|---|---|
| 1 code | 27 | 26 code | 14 | 128 code | 29 |
| 2 code | 20 | 27 code | 7 | 237 code | 50 |
| 3 code | 40 | 28 code | 10 | 238 code | 43 |
| 4 code | 19 | 36 code | 17 | 246 code | 14 |
| 5 code | 0 | 37 code | 9 | 248 code | 20 |
| Low 5 female | 34 | 38 code | 29 | 268 code | 17 |
| 6 code | 31 | 46 code | 35 | 278 code | 12 |
| 7 code | 29 | 47 code | 21 | 289 code | 29 |
| 8 code | 24 | 48 code | 36 | 468 code | 29 |
| 9 code | 14 | 49 code | 14 | 469 code | 12 |
| 12 code | 14 | 68 code | 29 | 478 code | 27 |
| 13 code | 23 | 69 code | 0 | 489 code | 17 |
| 18 code | 29 | 78 code | 18 | 678 code | 33 |
| 23 code | 57 | 89 code | 27 | 689 code | 38 |
| 24 code | 57 | 123 code | 29 | 789 code | 17 |

## Table D24  Vincent Biographical Inventory Item:
## I Have (Had) a Learning Problem in School

| Comparison Data | Frequency (%) |
|---|---|
| Mythical Average Patient Code: | 12 |
| L greater than T-score 70: | 0 |
| F greater than Raw Score 15: | 25 |
| K greater than T-score: | 0 |
| False Normal Code: | 4 |

| Code Type | Frequency (%) | Code Type | Frequency (%) | Code Type | Frequency (%) |
|---|---|---|---|---|---|
| 1 code | 9 | 26 code | 0 | 128 code | 29 |
| 2 code | 7 | 27 code | 14 | 237 code | 17 |
| 3 code | 10 | 28 code | 14 | 238 code | 0 |
| 4 code | 6 | 36 code | 17 | 246 code | 0 |
| 5 code | 0 | 37 code | 9 | 248 code | 10 |
| Low 5 female | 0 | 38 code | 0 | 268 code | 33 |
| 6 code | 13 | 46 code | 12 | 278 code | 20 |
| 7 code | 18 | 47 code | 7 | 289 code | 29 |
| 8 code | 21 | 48 code | 21 | 468 code | 29 |
| 9 code | 14 | 49 code | 0 | 469 code | 0 |
| 12 code | 0 | 68 code | 41 | 478 code | 7 |
| 13 code | 15 | 69 code | 13 | 489 code | 33 |
| 18 code | 43 | 78 code | 16 | 678 code | 0 |
| 23 code | 7 | 89 code | 27 | 689 code | 12 |
| 24 code | 24 | 123 code | 14 | 789 code | 17 |

## Table D25  Vincent Biographical Inventory Item:
## I Have Been Diagnosed as Being Hyperactive

| Comparison Data | Frequency (%) |
|---|---|
| Mythical Average Patient Code: | 6 |
| L greater than T-score 70: | 0 |
| F greater than Raw Score 15: | 0 |
| K greater than T-score: | 0 |
| False Normal Code: | 2 |

| Code Type | Frequency (%) | Code Type | Frequency (%) | Code Type | Frequency (%) |
|---|---|---|---|---|---|
| 1 code | 0 | 26 code | 0 | 128 code | 0 |
| 2 code | 7 | 27 code | 0 | 237 code | 0 |
| 3 code | 0 | 28 code | 3 | 238 code | 0 |
| 4 code | 0 | 36 code | 17 | 246 code | 0 |
| 5 code | 14 | 37 code | 0 | 248 code | 20 |
| Low 5 female | 0 | 38 code | 0 | 268 code | 0 |
| 6 code | 6 | 46 code | 24 | 278 code | 0 |
| 7 code | 6 | 47 code | 0 | 289 code | 29 |
| 8 code | 5 | 48 code | 7 | 468 code | 0 |
| 9 code | 5 | 49 code | 0 | 469 code | 38 |
| 12 code | 0 | 68 code | 0 | 478 code | 0 |
| 13 code | 0 | 69 code | 0 | 489 code | 0 |
| 18 code | 0 | 78 code | 0 | 678 code | 0 |
| 23 code | 7 | 89 code | 5 | 689 code | 0 |
| 24 code | 0 | 123 code | 0 | 789 code | 0 |

### Table D26  Vincent Biographical Inventory Item:
### I Have (Had) Frequent Problems with Teachers in School

| Comparison Data | Frequency (%) |
|---|---|
| Mythical Average Patient Code: | 14 |
| L greater than T-score 70: | 0 |
| F greater than Raw Score 15: | 25 |
| K greater than T-score: | 0 |
| False Normal Code: | 0 |

| Code Type | Frequency (%) | Code Type | Frequency (%) | Code Type | Frequency (%) |
|---|---|---|---|---|---|
| 1 code | 0 | 26 code | 0 | 128 code | 12 |
| 2 code | 13 | 27 code | 7 | 237 code | 0 |
| 3 code | 10 | 28 code | 17 | 238 code | 0 |
| 4 code | 13 | 36 code | 0 | 246 code | 14 |
| 5 code | 0 | 37 code | 0 | 248 code | 30 |
| Low 5 female | 5 | 38 code | 0 | 268 code | 17 |
| 6 code | 6 | 46 code | 24 | 278 code | 4 |
| 7 code | 0 | 47 code | 0 | 289 code | 14 |
| 8 code | 7 | 48 code | 36 | 468 code | 29 |
| 9 code | 24 | 49 code | 14 | 469 code | 25 |
| 12 code | 0 | 68 code | 12 | 478 code | 13 |
| 13 code | 8 | 69 code | 0 | 489 code | 50 |
| 18 code | 14 | 78 code | 0 | 678 code | 11 |
| 23 code | 0 | 89 code | 18 | 689 code | 0 |
| 24 code | 14 | 123 code | 14 | 789 code | 33 |

### Table D27  Vincent Biographical Inventory Item:
### I Have (Had) Frequent Fights at School

| Comparison Data | Frequency (%) |
|---|---|
| Mythical Average Patient Code: | 6 |
| L greater than T-score 70: | 0 |
| F greater than Raw Score 15: | 25 |
| K greater than T-score: | 0 |
| False Normal Code: | 0 |

| Code Type | Frequency (%) | Code Type | Frequency (%) | Code Type | Frequency (%) |
|---|---|---|---|---|---|
| 1 code | 0 | 26 code | 0 | 128 code | 14 |
| 2 code | 0 | 27 code | 0 | 237 code | 0 |
| 3 code | 0 | 28 code | 10 | 238 code | 0 |
| 4 code | 6 | 36 code | 0 | 246 code | 0 |
| 5 code | 0 | 37 code | 0 | 248 code | 10 |
| Low 5 female | 0 | 38 code | 0 | 268 code | 0 |
| 6 code | 0 | 46 code | 12 | 278 code | 4 |
| 7 code | 6 | 47 code | 0 | 289 code | 14 |
| 8 code | 7 | 48 code | 14 | 468 code | 29 |
| 9 code | 10 | 49 code | 14 | 469 code | 12 |
| 12 code | 0 | 68 code | 0 | 478 code | 0 |
| 13 code | 0 | 69 code | 0 | 489 code | 17 |
| 18 code | 14 | 78 code | 5 | 678 code | 0 |
| 23 code | 0 | 89 code | 5 | 689 code | 0 |
| 24 code | 0 | 123 code | 0 | 789 code | 17 |

### Table D28  Vincent Biographical Inventory Item: I Have (Had) Difficulty Making Friends at School

| Comparison Data | Frequency (%) |
|---|---|
| Mythical Average Patient Code: | 8 |
| L greater than T-score 70: | 0 |
| F greater than Raw Score 15: | 13 |
| K greater than T-score: | 0 |
| False Normal Code: | 0 |

| Code Type | Frequency (%) | Code Type | Frequency (%) | Code Type | Frequency (%) |
|---|---|---|---|---|---|
| 1 code | 18 | 26 code | 14 | 128 code | 14 |
| 2 code | 20 | 27 code | 21 | 237 code | 17 |
| 3 code | 0 | 28 code | 21 | 238 code | 14 |
| 4 code | 13 | 36 code | 0 | 246 code | 0 |
| 5 code | 14 | 37 code | 0 | 248 code | 10 |
| Low 5 female | 2 | 38 code | 14 | 268 code | 33 |
| 6 code | 0 | 46 code | 6 | 278 code | 4 |
| 7 code | 6 | 47 code | 0 | 289 code | 29 |
| 8 code | 12 | 48 code | 14 | 468 code | 0 |
| 9 code | 0 | 49 code | 0 | 469 code | 12 |
| 12 code | 0 | 68 code | 18 | 478 code | 20 |
| 13 code | 15 | 69 code | 0 | 489 code | 33 |
| 18 code | 14 | 78 code | 5 | 678 code | 11 |
| 23 code | 0 | 89 code | 9 | 689 code | 12 |
| 24 code | 14 | 123 code | 0 | 789 code | 0 |

### Table D29  Vincent Biographical Inventory Item: I Failed a Grade in School

| Comparison Data | Frequency (%) |
|---|---|
| Mythical Average Patient Code: | 8 |
| L greater than T-score 70: | 0 |
| F greater than Raw Score 15: | 25 |
| K greater than T-score: | 0 |
| False Normal Code: | 4 |

| Code Type | Frequency (%) | Code Type | Frequency (%) | Code Type | Frequency (%) |
|---|---|---|---|---|---|
| 1 code | 9 | 26 code | 14 | 128 code | 14 |
| 2 code | 20 | 27 code | 14 | 237 code | 25 |
| 3 code | 10 | 28 code | 24 | 238 code | 14 |
| 4 code | 31 | 36 code | 0 | 246 code | 29 |
| 5 code | 0 | 37 code | 18 | 248 code | 30 |
| Low 5 female | 7 | 38 code | 14 | 268 code | 33 |
| 6 code | 19 | 46 code | 24 | 278 code | 20 |
| 7 code | 18 | 47 code | 7 | 289 code | 0 |
| 8 code | 16 | 48 code | 43 | 468 code | 43 |
| 9 code | 33 | 49 code | 14 | 469 code | 0 |
| 12 code | 0 | 68 code | 29 | 478 code | 13 |
| 13 code | 8 | 69 code | 21 | 489 code | 17 |
| 18 code | 14 | 78 code | 5 | 678 code | 44 |
| 23 code | 21 | 89 code | 14 | 689 code | 12 |
| 24 code | 14 | 123 code | 0 | 789 code | 0 |

### Table D30  Vincent Biographical Inventory Item:
### One (or Both) of My Parents Is (Are) Dead

| Comparison Data | Frequency (%) |
|---|---|
| Mythical Average Patient Code: | 48 |
| L greater than T-score 70: | 43 |
| F greater than Raw Score 15: | 38 |
| K greater than T-score: | 30 |
| False Normal Code: | 60 |

| Code Type | Frequency (%) | Code Type | Frequency (%) | Code Type | Frequency (%) |
|---|---|---|---|---|---|
| 1 code | 64 | 26 code | 43 | 128 code | 71 |
| 2 code | 47 | 27 code | 43 | 237 code | 67 |
| 3 code | 50 | 28 code | 41 | 238 code | 43 |
| 4 code | 25 | 36 code | 33 | 246 code | 43 |
| 5 code | 29 | 37 code | 45 | 248 code | 40 |
| Low 5 female | 61 | 38 code | 57 | 268 code | 50 |
| 6 code | 56 | 46 code | 29 | 278 code | 44 |
| 7 code | 53 | 47 code | 43 | 289 code | 43 |
| 8 code | 41 | 48 code | 29 | 468 code | 43 |
| 9 code | 38 | 49 code | 29 | 469 code | 50 |
| 12 code | 71 | 68 code | 47 | 478 code | 33 |
| 13 code | 54 | 69 code | 63 | 489 code | 17 |
| 18 code | 57 | 78 code | 32 | 678 code | 33 |
| 23 code | 64 | 89 code | 32 | 689 code | 38 |
| 24 code | 43 | 123 code | 14 | 789 code | 0 |

### Table D31  Vincent Biographical Inventory Item:
### One of My Close Family Members Has a Drinking Problem

| Comparison Data | Frequency (%) |
|---|---|
| Mythical Average Patient Code: | 40 |
| L greater than T-score 70: | 29 |
| F greater than Raw Score 15: | 63 |
| K greater than T-score: | 20 |
| False Normal Code: | 29 |

| Code Type | Frequency (%) | Code Type | Frequency (%) | Code Type | Frequency (%) |
|---|---|---|---|---|---|
| 1 code | 27 | 26 code | 29 | 128 code | 57 |
| 2 code | 53 | 27 code | 36 | 237 code | 67 |
| 3 code | 60 | 28 code | 45 | 238 code | 29 |
| 4 code | 63 | 36 code | 17 | 246 code | 29 |
| 5 code | 29 | 37 code | 45 | 248 code | 40 |
| Low 5 female | 48 | 38 code | 43 | 268 code | 50 |
| 6 code | 31 | 46 code | 41 | 278 code | 32 |
| 7 code | 41 | 47 code | 71 | 289 code | 43 |
| 8 code | 48 | 48 code | 43 | 468 code | 43 |
| 9 code | 48 | 49 code | 57 | 469 code | 25 |
| 12 code | 29 | 68 code | 53 | 478 code | 47 |
| 13 code | 31 | 69 code | 38 | 489 code | 83 |
| 18 code | 43 | 78 code | 55 | 678 code | 44 |
| 23 code | 64 | 89 code | 68 | 689 code | 38 |
| 24 code | 43 | 123 code | 29 | 789 code | 67 |

Table D32  Vincent Biographical Inventory Item:  One of My Close
Family Members Has (Had) a Drug Problem

| Comparison Data | Frequency (%) |
| --- | --- |
| Mythical Average Patient Code: | 10 |
| L greater than T-score 70: | 0 |
| F greater than Raw Score 15: | 38 |
| K greater than T-score: | 10 |
| False Normal Code: | 2 |

| Code Type | Frequency (%) | Code Type | Frequency (%) | Code Type | Frequency (%) |
| --- | --- | --- | --- | --- | --- |
| 1 code | 27 | 26 code | 0 | 128 code | 43 |
| 2 code | 7 | 27 code | 7 | 237 code | 25 |
| 3 code | 0 | 28 code | 14 | 238 code | 0 |
| 4 code | 25 | 36 code | 0 | 246 code | 14 |
| 5 code | 0 | 37 code | 9 | 248 code | 20 |
| Low 5 female | 18 | 38 code | 0 | 268 code | 0 |
| 6 code | 6 | 46 code | 24 | 278 code | 4 |
| 7 code | 18 | 47 code | 14 | 289 code | 0 |
| 8 code | 21 | 48 code | 21 | 468 code | 14 |
| 9 code | 19 | 49 code | 29 | 469 code | 0 |
| 12 code | 0 | 68 code | 6 | 478 code | 20 |
| 13 code | 0 | 69 code | 13 | 489 code | 67 |
| 18 code | 43 | 78 code | 13 | 678 code | 0 |
| 23 code | 14 | 89 code | 23 | 689 code | 0 |
| 24 code | 14 | 123 code | 0 | 789 code | 33 |

Table D33  Vincent Biographical Inventory Item:  One of My Close Family
Members Has (Had) a Nervous Breakdown

| Comparison Data | Frequency (%) |
| --- | --- |
| Mythical Average Patient Code: | 32 |
| L greater than T-score 70: | 0 |
| F greater than Raw Score 15: | 50 |
| K greater than T-score: | 20 |
| False Normal Code: | 16 |

| Code Type | Frequency (%) | Code Type | Frequency (%) | Code Type | Frequency (%) |
| --- | --- | --- | --- | --- | --- |
| 1 code | 45 | 26 code | 29 | 128 code | 86 |
| 2 code | 33 | 27 code | 21 | 237 code | 42 |
| 3 code | 30 | 28 code | 48 | 238 code | 29 |
| 4 code | 31 | 36 code | 33 | 246 code | 29 |
| 5 code | 14 | 37 code | 36 | 248 code | 40 |
| Low 5 female | 30 | 38 code | 57 | 268 code | 0 |
| 6 code | 56 | 46 code | 41 | 278 code | 32 |
| 7 code | 24 | 47 code | 29 | 289 code | 14 |
| 8 code | 29 | 48 code | 43 | 468 code | 43 |
| 9 code | 29 | 49 code | 14 | 469 code | 25 |
| 12 code | 43 | 68 code | 47 | 478 code | 40 |
| 13 code | 38 | 69 code | 13 | 489 code | 67 |
| 18 code | 43 | 78 code | 24 | 678 code | 11 |
| 23 code | 36 | 89 code | 36 | 689 code | 64 |
| 24 code | 0 | 123 code | 29 | 789 code | 33 |

#### Table D34 Vincent Biographical Inventory Item: I Have Been Arrested

| Comparison Data | Frequency (%) |
|---|---|
| Mythical Average Patient Code: | 30 |
| L greater than T-score 70: | 14 |
| F greater than Raw Score 15: | 50 |
| K greater than T-score: | 30 |
| False Normal Code: | 11 |

| Code Type | Frequency (%) | Code Type | Frequency (%) | Code Type | Frequency (%) |
|---|---|---|---|---|---|
| 1 code | 18 | 26 code | 14 | 128 code | 0 |
| 2 code | 33 | 27 code | 29 | 237 code | 17 |
| 3 code | 10 | 28 code | 24 | 238 code | 0 |
| 4 code | 50 | 36 code | 0 | 246 code | 43 |
| 5 code | 14 | 37 code | 18 | 248 code | 30 |
| Low 5 female | 7 | 38 code | 0 | 268 code | 50 |
| 6 code | 38 | 46 code | 47 | 278 code | 24 |
| 7 code | 35 | 47 code | 36 | 289 code | 57 |
| 8 code | 33 | 48 code | 71 | 468 code | 43 |
| 9 code | 19 | 49 code | 43 | 469 code | 25 |
| 12 code | 14 | 68 code | 47 | 478 code | 60 |
| 13 code | 0 | 69 code | 13 | 489 code | 50 |
| 18 code | 57 | 78 code | 27 | 678 code | 0 |
| 23 code | 21 | 89 code | 32 | 689 code | 38 |
| 24 code | 29 | 123 code | 0 | 789 code | 50 |

#### Table D35 Vincent Biographical Inventory Item: I Have (Had) a Drinking Problem

| Comparison Data | Frequency (%) |
|---|---|
| Mythical Average Patient Code: | 16 |
| L greater than T-score 70: | 14 |
| F greater than Raw Score 15: | 50 |
| K greater than T-score: | 0 |
| False Normal Code: | 11 |

| Code Type | Frequency (%) | Code Type | Frequency (%) | Code Type | Frequency (%) |
|---|---|---|---|---|---|
| 1 code | 0 | 26 code | 14 | 128 code | 14 |
| 2 code | 20 | 27 code | 29 | 237 code | 17 |
| 3 code | 10 | 28 code | 17 | 238 code | 14 |
| 4 code | 31 | 36 code | 0 | 246 code | 0 |
| 5 code | 14 | 37 code | 18 | 248 code | 30 |
| Low 5 female | 14 | 38 code | 14 | 268 code | 17 |
| 6 code | 13 | 46 code | 29 | 278 code | 20 |
| 7 code | 24 | 47 code | 29 | 289 code | 29 |
| 8 code | 26 | 48 code | 57 | 468 code | 14 |
| 9 code | 19 | 49 code | 14 | 469 code | 25 |
| 12 code | 14 | 68 code | 18 | 478 code | 20 |
| 13 code | 0 | 69 code | 13 | 489 code | 33 |
| 18 code | 14 | 78 code | 18 | 678 code | 11 |
| 23 code | 14 | 89 code | 32 | 689 code | 12 |
| 24 code | 0 | 123 code | 0 | 789 code | 33 |

### Table D36  Vincent Biographical Inventory Item: I Have (Had) a Drug Problem

| Comparison Data | Frequency (%) |
|---|---|
| Mythical Average Patient Code: | 28 |
| L greater than T-score 70: | 14 |
| F greater than Raw Score 15: | 50 |
| K greater than T-score: | 0 |
| False Normal Code: | 11 |

| Code Type | Frequency (%) | Code Type | Frequency (%) | Code Type | Frequency (%) |
|---|---|---|---|---|---|
| 1 code | 0 | 26 code | 0 | 128 code | 43 |
| 2 code | 27 | 27 code | 7 | 237 code | 8 |
| 3 code | 0 | 28 code | 24 | 238 code | 0 |
| 4 code | 38 | 36 code | 0 | 246 code | 43 |
| 5 code | 29 | 37 code | 9 | 248 code | 50 |
| Low 5 female | 9 | 38 code | 0 | 268 code | 17 |
| 6 code | 25 | 46 code | 53 | 278 code | 12 |
| 7 code | 18 | 47 code | 14 | 289 code | 29 |
| 8 code | 25 | 48 code | 43 | 468 code | 29 |
| 9 code | 24 | 49 code | 29 | 469 code | 12 |
| 12 code | 0 | 68 code | 24 | 478 code | 7 |
| 13 code | 0 | 69 code | 25 | 489 code | 17 |
| 18 code | 71 | 78 code | 26 | 678 code | 22 |
| 23 code | 14 | 89 code | 18 | 689 code | 38 |
| 24 code | 29 | 123 code | 0 | 789 code | 67 |

### Table D37  Vincent Biographical Inventory Item: I Have (Had) a Problem with Gambling

| Comparison Data | Frequency (%) |
|---|---|
| Mythical Average Patient Code: | 2 |
| L greater than T-score 70: | 0 |
| F greater than Raw Score 15: | 0 |
| K greater than T-score: | 0 |
| False Normal Code: | 2 |

| Code Type | Frequency (%) | Code Type | Frequency (%) | Code Type | Frequency (%) |
|---|---|---|---|---|---|
| 1 code | 0 | 26 code | 0 | 128 code | 0 |
| 2 code | 0 | 27 code | 0 | 237 code | 0 |
| 3 code | 0 | 28 code | 0 | 238 code | 0 |
| 4 code | 0 | 36 code | 0 | 246 code | 0 |
| 5 code | 0 | 37 code | 0 | 248 code | 0 |
| Low 5 female | 0 | 38 code | 0 | 268 code | 0 |
| 6 code | 0 | 46 code | 0 | 278 code | 0 |
| 7 code | 0 | 47 code | 7 | 289 code | 14 |
| 8 code | 5 | 48 code | 0 | 468 code | 0 |
| 9 code | 0 | 49 code | 0 | 469 code | 0 |
| 12 code | 0 | 68 code | 0 | 478 code | 0 |
| 13 code | 0 | 69 code | 0 | 489 code | 0 |
| 18 code | 14 | 78 code | 8 | 678 code | 0 |
| 23 code | 0 | 89 code | 9 | 689 code | 0 |
| 24 code | 0 | 123 code | 0 | 789 code | 33 |

**Table D38  Vincent Biographical Inventory Item: I Have a Chronic Illness, a Major Handicap, or Other Health Problem**

| Comparison Data | Frequency (%) |
|---|---|
| Mythical Average Patient Code: | 40 |
| L greater than T-score 70: | 43 |
| F greater than Raw Score 15: | 13 |
| K greater than T-score: | 60 |
| False Normal Code: | 31 |

| Code Type | Frequency (%) | Code Type | Frequency (%) | Code Type | Frequency (%) |
|---|---|---|---|---|---|
| 1 code | 82 | 26 code | 43 | 128 code | 71 |
| 2 code | 40 | 27 code | 14 | 237 code | 25 |
| 3 code | 90 | 28 code | 38 | 238 code | 43 |
| 4 code | 31 | 36 code | 33 | 246 code | 71 |
| 5 code | 0 | 37 code | 18 | 248 code | 60 |
| Low 5 female | 50 | 38 code | 57 | 268 code | 33 |
| 6 code | 44 | 46 code | 53 | 278 code | 48 |
| 7 code | 24 | 47 code | 21 | 289 code | 57 |
| 8 code | 34 | 48 code | 57 | 468 code | 57 |
| 9 code | 19 | 49 code | 29 | 469 code | 50 |
| 12 code | 86 | 68 code | 53 | 478 code | 33 |
| 13 code | 62 | 69 code | 25 | 489 code | 17 |
| 18 code | 86 | 78 code | 29 | 678 code | 11 |
| 23 code | 64 | 89 code | 32 | 689 code | 50 |
| 24 code | 57 | 123 code | 71 | 789 code | 17 |

**Table D39  Vincent Biographical Inventory Item: I Am Currently on Medication**

| Comparison Data | Frequency (%) |
|---|---|
| Mythical Average Patient Code: | 12 |
| L greater than T-score 70: | 14 |
| F greater than Raw Score 15: | 0 |
| K greater than T-score: | 30 |
| False Normal Code: | 11 |

| Code Type | Frequency (%) | Code Type | Frequency (%) | Code Type | Frequency (%) |
|---|---|---|---|---|---|
| 1 code | 18 | 26 code | 0 | 128 code | 0 |
| 2 code | 7 | 27 code | 21 | 237 code | 17 |
| 3 code | 0 | 28 code | 7 | 238 code | 29 |
| 4 code | 13 | 36 code | 0 | 246 code | 29 |
| 5 code | 0 | 37 code | 18 | 248 code | 10 |
| Low 5 female | 9 | 38 code | 38 | 268 code | 17 |
| 6 code | 6 | 46 code | 24 | 278 code | 12 |
| 7 code | 12 | 47 code | 7 | 289 code | 14 |
| 8 code | 7 | 48 code | 7 | 468 code | 29 |
| 9 code | 5 | 49 code | 14 | 469 code | 25 |
| 12 code | 0 | 68 code | 12 | 478 code | 7 |
| 13 code | 15 | 69 code | 13 | 489 code | 0 |
| 18 code | 0 | 78 code | 11 | 678 code | 0 |
| 23 code | 14 | 89 code | 9 | 689 code | 0 |
| 24 code | 14 | 123 code | 14 | 789 code | 17 |

### Table D40  Vincent Biographical Inventory Item: I Have Been in Psychotherapy as an Outpatient

| Comparison Data | Frequency (%) |
|---|---|
| Mythical Average Patient Code: | 14 |
| L greater than T-score 70: | 14 |
| F greater than Raw Score 15: | 13 |
| K greater than T-score: | 20 |
| False Normal Code: | 24 |

| Code Type | Frequency (%) | Code Type | Frequency (%) | Code Type | Frequency (%) |
|---|---|---|---|---|---|
| 1 code | 9 | 26 code | 57 | 128 code | 0 |
| 2 code | 20 | 27 code | 21 | 237 code | 42 |
| 3 code | 10 | 28 code | 34 | 238 code | 29 |
| 4 code | 38 | 36 code | 0 | 246 code | 14 |
| 5 code | 0 | 37 code | 27 | 248 code | 30 |
| Low 5 female | 9 | 38 code | 43 | 268 code | 17 |
| 6 code | 19 | 46 code | 24 | 278 code | 28 |
| 7 code | 6 | 47 code | 29 | 289 code | 14 |
| 8 code | 22 | 48 code | 36 | 468 code | 29 |
| 9 code | 14 | 49 code | 0 | 469 code | 38 |
| 12 code | 14 | 68 code | 0 | 478 code | 13 |
| 13 code | 8 | 69 code | 38 | 489 code | 0 |
| 18 code | 14 | 78 code | 13 | 678 code | 11 |
| 23 code | 29 | 89 code | 9 | 689 code | 0 |
| 24 code | 0 | 123 code | 29 | 789 code | 50 |

### Table D41  Vincent Biographical Inventory Item: I Have Had a Nervous Breakdown or Psychiatric Hospitalization

| Comparison Data | Frequency (%) |
|---|---|
| Mythical Average Patient Code: | 28 |
| L greater than T-score 70: | 43 |
| F greater than Raw Score 15: | 38 |
| K greater than T-score: | 20 |
| False Normal Code: | 29 |

| Code Type | Frequency (%) | Code Type | Frequency (%) | Code Type | Frequency (%) |
|---|---|---|---|---|---|
| 1 code | 18 | 26 code | 0 | 128 code | 57 |
| 2 code | 27 | 27 code | 36 | 237 code | 8 |
| 3 code | 30 | 28 code | 38 | 238 code | 14 |
| 4 code | 19 | 36 code | 0 | 246 code | 29 |
| 5 code | 0 | 37 code | 9 | 248 code | 40 |
| Low 5 female | 25 | 38 code | 29 | 268 code | 50 |
| 6 code | 25 | 46 code | 35 | 278 code | 44 |
| 7 code | 47 | 47 code | 36 | 289 code | 57 |
| 8 code | 31 | 48 code | 14 | 468 code | 29 |
| 9 code | 19 | 49 code | 14 | 469 code | 25 |
| 12 code | 14 | 68 code | 29 | 478 code | 33 |
| 13 code | 23 | 69 code | 13 | 489 code | 17 |
| 18 code | 57 | 78 code | 24 | 678 code | 11 |
| 23 code | 14 | 89 code | 27 | 689 code | 25 |
| 24 code | 43 | 123 code | 43 | 789 code | 17 |

# References

APA Task Force on Nomenclature and Statistics. *Diagnostic and statistical manual of mental disorders-III (DSM-III).* Washington, DC: American Psychiatric Association, 1980.

Butcher, J.N. & Owen. P.L. Objective personality inventories: recent research and some contemporary issues. In B. B. Wolman (Ed.), *Clinical diagnosis of mental disorders.* New York: Plenum Press, 1978.

Caldwell, A.B. Recent developments in automated interpretation of the MMPI; cited in Marks, P.A., Seeman, W. & Haller, D.L., *The actuarial use of the MMPI with adolescents and adults.* Baltimore, MD: Williams & Wilkins, 1974.

Committee on Nomenclature and Statistics. *Diagnostic and statistical manual of mental disorders-II* (DSM-II). Washington, DC: American Psychiatric Association, 1967.

Dahlstrom, W.G., Welsh, G.S., & Dahlstrom, L.E. *A MMPI handbook, Vol. 1.* Minneapolis, MD: University of Minnesota Press, 1972.

Dean, E.F. A lengthened Mini: the Midi-Mult. *Journal of Clinical Psychology,* 1972, *28,* 68–71.

Drake, L.E., & Oetting, E.R. *An MMPI codebook for counselors.* Minneapolis, MN: University of Minnesota, 1959.

Duckworth, J.C. *MMPI interpretation manual for counselors and clinicians.* Muncie, IN: Accelerated Development, Inc., 1979.

Faschingbauer, T.R. A short written form of the group MMPI (doctoral dissertation, University of North Carolina, 1973). *Dissertation Abstracts International,* 1973, *34,* 409B.

Ferguson, R.G. A useful adjunct to the MMPI scoring and analysis. *Journal of Clinical Psychology,* 1946, *2,* 248–253; cited in Stevens, M.R., & Reilly, R.R., MMPI short forms: a literature review. *Journal of Personality Assessment,* 1980, *44,* 368–376.

Finney, J.C. Programmed interpretation of the MMPI and CPI. *Archives of General Psychiatry,* 1966, *15,* 75–81.

Fowler, R.D. Automated interpretation of personality test data. In J.N. Butcher (Ed.), *MMPI: Research developments and clinical applications.* New York: McGraw-Hill, 1969.

Gilberstadt, H., & Duker, J. *A handbook for clinical and actuarial MMPI interpretation.* Philadelphia, PA: W.B. Saunders Co., 1965.

Gold, S.N. Relation between level of ego development and adjustment patterns in adolescents. *Journal of Personality Assessment,* 1980, *44,* 630–638.

Graham, J.R. *The MMPI: A practical guide.* New York: Oxford University Press, 1977.

Griffin, P.T., & Danahy, S. Short form MMPI's in medical consultation: accuracy of the Hs-Hy dyad compared to the standard form. *Journal of Clinical Psychology*, 1982, *38*, 134–136.

Hauser, S.T. Loevinger's model and measurement of ego development: a critical review. *Psychological Bulletin*, 1976. *83*, 928–955.

Holmes, T.H., & Rahe, R.H. The Social Readjustment Rating Scale. *Journal of Psychosomatic Research*. 1976, *11*, 213–218.

Kincannon, J.C. Prediction of the standard MMPI scale scores from 71 items: the Mini-Mult. *Journal of Consulting and Clinical Psychology*, 1968, *32*, 319–325.

King, G.D., & Kelley, C.K. Behavioral correlates for spike 4, spike 9, and 49–94 MMPI profiles in students at a university mental health center. *Journal of Clinical Psychology*, 1977, *33*, 718–724.

Lachar, D. Accuracy and generalizability of an automated MMPI interpretive system. *Journal of Consulting and Clinical Psychology*, 1974, *42*, 267–273(a).

Lachar, D. *The MMPI: Clinical assessment and automated interpretation*. Los Angeles, CA: Western Psychological Services, 1974(b).

Lachar D., & Alexander, R.S. Validity of self-report: replicated correlates of the Wiggins MMPI content scale. *Journal of Consulting Psychology*, 1978, *46*, 1349–1356.

Lachar, D.,Klinge, V., & Grissell, J.L. Relative accuracy of automated MMPI narratives generated from adult norm and adolescent norm profiles. *Journal of Consulting and Clinical Psychology*, 1976, *44*, pp. 20–24.

Leavitt, F., & Garron, D.C. Rorschach and pain characteristics of patients with low back pain and "conversion V" MMPI profiles. *Journal of Personality Assessment*, 1982, *46*, pp. 18–25.

Loevinger, J., & Wessler, R. *Measuring ego development, (Vol. 1)*. San Francisco, CA: Jossey-Bass, 1970.

Loevinger, J., Wessler, R., & Redmore, C. *Measuring ego development, (Vol. 2)*. San Francisco, CA: Jossey-Bass, 1970.

Marks, P.A., Seeman, W., & Haller, D.L. *The actuarial use of the MMPI with adolescents and adults*. Baltimore, MD: Williams & Wilkins Co., 1974.

Maslow, A.H. *Motivation and personality* (2nd. ed.). New York: Harper & Row, 1970.

Meehl, P.E. *Clinical versus statistical prediction*. Minneapolis, MN: University of Minnesota Press, 1954.

Moreland, K.L. A comparison of methods of scoring the MMPI-168. *Journal of Consulting and Clinical Psychology*, 1982, *50*, 451.

Newmark, C.S., Conger, A.J., & Faschinghauer, T.R. The interpretive validity and effective test length functioning of an abbreviated MMPI relative to the standard MMPI. *Journal of Clinical Psychology*, 1976, *32*, 27–32.

Newmark, C.S., & Faschingbauer, T.S. Bibliography of short forms of the MMPI. *Journal of Personality Assessment*, 1978, *40*, 10–12.

Newmark, C.S., & Finch, A.J. Comparing the diagnostic validity of an abbreviated and standard MMPI. *Journal of Personality Assessment*, 1976, *40*, 10–12.

Newmark, C.S., Newmark, L., & Cook, L. The MMPI-168 with psychiatric patients. *Journal of Clinical Psychology*, 1975, *31*, 61–64.

Newmark, C.S., & Thibodeau, J.R. Interpretive accuracy and empirical validity of the abbreviated forms of the MMPI with hospitalized adolescents. In C.S. Newmark (Ed.), *MMPI clinical and research trends*. New York: Praeger, 1979.

Newmark, C.S., Zifl, D.R., Finch, A.J., Jr., & Kendall, P.C. Comparing the empirical validity of the standard form with two abbreviated MMPI's. *Journal of Consulting and Clinical Psychology*, 1978, *46*, 53–61.

Overall, J.E. Phenomenological classification of depressive disorders. *Journal of Clinical Psychology*, 1980, *36*, 372–277.

Overall, J.E. & Gomez-Mont, F. The MMPI-168 for psychiatric screening. *Educational and Psychological Measurement*, 1974, *34*, 315–319.

Overall, J.E., Higgins, W., & DeSchweinitz, A. Comparison of differential diagnostic discrimination for abbreviated and standard MMPI. *Journal of Clinical Psychology*, 1976, *32*, 239–245.

Pearson, J.S., & Swenson, W.M. *A users guide to the Mayo Clinic automated MMPI program.* New York: The Psychological Corporation, 1967.

*Physicians Desk Reference.* Oradel, NJ: Medical Economics Co., 1982.

Rusk, R., Hyerstay, B.J., Calsyn, D.A., & Freman, C.W. Comparison of the utility of two abbreviated forms of the MMPI for psychiatric screening of the elderly. *Journal of Clinical Psychology*, 1979, *35*, 104–107.

Schwartz, M.S., Osborne, D., & Krupp, N.E. Moderating effects of age and sex on the association of diagnoses and 13-31 MMPI profiles. *Journal of Clinical Psychology*, 1972, *28*, 502–505.

Spera, J., & Robertson, M. A 104 item MMPI: the Maxi-Mult. Paper presented at the meeting of the American Psychological Association, New Orleans, 1974.

Svanum, S., Lantz, J.B., Laver, J.B., Wampler, R.S., & Madura, J.A. Correspondence of the MMPI and the MMPI–168 with intestinal bypass surgery patients. *Journal of Clinical Psychology*, 1981, *37*, 137–139.

Swenson, W.M., Pearson, J.S., & Osborne, D. *An MMPI source book.* Minneapolis, MN: University of Minnesota Press, 1973.

Vincent, K.R. Validity of the MMPI-168 on private clinic subpopulations. *Journal of Clinical Psychology*, 1978, *34*, 61–63.

Vincent, K.R. Semi-automated full battery. *Journal of Clinical Psychology*, 1980, *36*, 437–446(a).

Vincent, K.R. *Semi-automated full battery.* Houston, TX: Psychometric Press, 1980(b).

Vincent, K.R. *MMPI semi-automated interpretative statements.* Houston, TX: Psychometric Press, 1980(c).

Vincent, K.R. *Vincent Biographical Inventory.* Richland, WA: Psychological Software Specialists, 1982.

Vincent, K.R., Castillo, I.M., Hauser, R.I., Stuart, H.J., Zapata, J.A., Cohn, C.K., & O'Shanick, G.J. MMPI code types and DSM-III diagnosis. *Journal of Clinical Psychology*, 1984, *39*, 829–842.

Vincent, L.R., & Vincent, K.R. Ego development and psychopathology. *Psychological Reports*, 1979, *44*, 408–410.

Ward, L.C., Wright, H.W., & Taulbee, E.S. An improvement in the statistical validity of the MMPI-168 through modified scoring. *Journal of Consulting and Clinical Psychology*, 1979, *47*, 618–619.

Wechsler, D. *WAIS manual.* New York: The Psychological Corp., 1955.

Zukerman, M., Sola, S., Masterson, J., & Angelone, J. MMPI patterns in drug abusers, before and after treatment in therapeutic communities. *Journal of Consulting and Clinical Psychology*, 1975, *43*, 286–296.